EXTREME
BRAIN
WORKOUT

EXTREME
BRAIN
WORKOUT

500 FUN AND CHALLENGING PUZZLES
TO BOOST YOUR BRAIN POWER

Marcel Danesi, Ph.D.

EXTREME BRAIN WORKOUT

ISBN-13: 978-0-373-89243-3

© 2011 by Marcel Danesi

Library of Congress Cataloging-in-Publication Data

Danesi, Marcel, 1946-
Extreme brain workout : 500 Fun and Challenging Puzzles to Boost Your Brain Power / Marcel Danesi.
p. cm.
ISBN 978-0-373-89243-3 (trade pbk.)
1. Puzzles. I. Title.
GV1493.D333 2011
793.73--dc22
2010032861

www.eHarlequin.com

Designed and typeset by Liney Li / 2 Eggs On A Roll

Printed in U.S.A.

Contents

Introduction

We do not stop playing because we get old, we get old because we stop playing.

GEORGE BERNARD SHAW (1856–1950)

DO YOU LIKE PUZZLES? If so, you're in luck, because research shows they are very good for your brain. If not, maybe this book will help you become accustomed to them and even like them by the end. It is both a compilation of puzzles and a training manual on how to solve them. It is also designed to help activate particular parts of the brain.

I recently searched the internet for relevant psychology, neuroscience, aging and education websites to get a sense of the kind of findings related to puzzles. I found a vast number of such sites. I then narrowed my search by looking up sources that I considered to be scientifically reliable. As it turns out, much of the research is still very encouraging. For example, a study published in *Brain and Cognition* in 2001 showed that older people performed significantly poorer on the Towers of Hanoi puzzle than younger people. However, subsequent studies have shown that if elderly people do such puzzles routinely, their skills not only improve, but they often become superior to those of younger people.

PUZZLES IN HUMAN LIFE

Since the dawn of civilization, human beings have been fascinated by puzzles of all kinds. There seems to exist a "puzzle instinct" in our species that has no parallel in any other species. Puzzles have been discovered by archaeologists across the world and across time. Throughout history, puzzles have also captivated the fancy of many famous figures. The

Biblical Kings Solomon and Hiram organized riddle contests. Edgar Allan Poe, Lewis Carroll, Benjamin Franklin and many others devoted countless hours to the making of mind teasers. The widespread popularity of puzzle magazines, "brain-challenging" sections in newspapers, TV quiz shows, game tournaments and of course millions of puzzle websites bears testimony to the power that the puzzle instinct has over us. Millions of people the world over simply enjoy solving puzzles for their own sake.

Like an instinct, puzzle-solving involves a large element of commonsense thinking. But it is also true that without a basic understanding of how such thinking unfolds, and what techniques can be employed to enhance, practice and sustain it, the chances are that the ability to solve puzzles with facility will not emerge in many people. Without some form of systematic training and practice in puzzle-solving, frustration, disinterest and fear will probably ensue. Success at solving puzzles requires that several basic principles and "lines of attack" be grasped firmly and enduringly from the very beginning.

This book is designed to teach you precisely that. But this book by itself will not guarantee 100 percent success. It will, however, put you in a better mental position to attack puzzles of any kind more efficiently and intelligently. The kinds of techniques you will be learning and practicing systematically in this book will help you see why certain puzzles are best approached in particular ways.

If you are already an accomplished puzzle-solver, you can use this book as a collection to solve during your leisure hours. You will find plenty here to keep you occupied and entertained. No advanced knowledge is needed to solve any of the puzzles in this book.

PUZZLES AND THE BRAIN

Research makes it obvious that doing puzzles diminishes the ravaging effects on mental skills brought about by the process of aging. I became interested in the relation between puzzles, games and intelligence after working with brain-damaged children in Italy in the mid-1980s. Here's what I did. If a child was assessed as having a weak visual memory, impairing how she or he spelled words or read them, I would prepare appropriate puzzle material, such as jumbled letters that the child was asked to unscramble to construct words. If the word were *tiger* I would give the child the jumbled form *gerti* and a picture of a tiger. What surprised me was how quickly the children improved in their writing and reading skills. However, I had no real explanation for the improvement. And I still don't, even after publishing my findings and engaging in various theoretical debates with other researchers. We know so little about the connection between brain activities and learning processes that the outcomes I was able to produce may indicate nothing more than a "co-occurrence," or coincidence, between an input and a brain activity, not a "correlation," or relationship, between the two. Nevertheless, it is my cautious opinion that puzzles are indeed beneficial to brain activity and I will attempt to explain here why I believe this is so.

Consider a simple riddle such as "What is yours yet others use more than you do?" This riddle stumps many people because it seems to defy common logic. The solver has to think outside the box, as the expression goes, in order to solve it. The answer is "Your name." Once the answer is reached, memory for it remains much more permanent because it is unexpected. The psychologists Sternberg and Davidson argued, as far back as 1982, that solving puzzles entails the ability to compare hidden information in a puzzle with information already in memory, and, more importantly, the ability to combine these two to form novel information and ideas. The thinking involved in solving puzzles can thus be characterized as a blend of logic, imagination, inference and memory. It is this blend, I would claim, that leads to a kind of "clairvoyance" that typically provokes an *Aha!* effect.

There is little doubt in my mind that puzzles are beneficial. I saw this with my own eyes within my own family. I once suggested to an ailing relative, who suffered from a serious brain-degenerative disease, to engage in crosswords and sudoku. He had never done puzzles in his life. His doctor immediately saw a significant slowing down of the degeneration. The relative eventually died of the disease, but I am convinced that his newfound passion for puzzles delayed his eventual loss of consciousness.

DESIGN OF THIS BOOK

In many ways, I have designed this book to complement and supplement my previous book, *Total Brain Workout* (Harlequin, 2009). Those who worked their way through that book will see a few of the same puzzle genres, but also many new and challenging types of puzzles.

The book is divided into three main parts. The first one consists of four chapters containing puzzles designed to activate the verbal part of the brain. The second part consists of five chapters organized to activate the logic centers. Many of these concepts derive from a university course I teach on puzzles—a course which has given me the unique opportunity to investigate, research and discuss the benefits of specific puzzle forms. The third part consists of one chapter that gives you practice doing so-called "IQ tests."

Each puzzle genre is explained fully at the beginning of the set and a model puzzle is explained in detail. The puzzles in a particular set are organized in order of difficulty, thus giving you a chance to build your skills gradually as you go along. This book also features sidebars, peppered through each chapter, containing brain facts for your own information and edification. The answer section at the back of the book goes through all the solutions step-by-step. But you should not read these until you have attempted to solve the puzzles on your own first, no matter how frustrated you might be with any particular puzzle. If you get the answer using a different line of attack than the one suggested in the book, you should still study the given solution simply to get a different perspective on the puzzle-solving process itself. You might even get another legitimate answer. This too will enhance your puzzle-solving skills. Incidentally, these skills are not correlated with quickness of thought. A slow thinker can solve a puzzle just as successfully as a fast one can.

As you can see, this is a self-contained brain exercise manual utilizing research on puzzles to activate the brain effectively. You will likely spend many hours being both entertained and frustrated. So be it. My hope is that it will have been worth the while.

—Marcel Danesi
University of Toronto

PART I

Puzzles Activating the Verbal Part of the Brain

LANGUAGE AREAS OF THE BRAIN

⌘ Language is controlled by the left hemisphere of the brain.

⌘ The left hemisphere controls the major speech systems, such as pronunciation and grammar, the literal meaning of words and verbal memory.

⌘ Broca's Area, which is located in the left hemisphere, is responsible for the muscle movements of the throat and the mouth used in speaking. It is where words are produced.

⌘ Wernicke's Area, also located in the left hemisphere, controls the comprehension of words and phrases.

⌘ A "supplementary area," discovered by Canadian neurologist Wilder Penfield in the 1950s, is involved in several functions previously thought to be restricted to Broca's and Wernicke's areas.

⌘ The right hemisphere also plays a part in language. It controls intonation and accentuation and, more important, metaphorical and emotional meaning along with the intent of words and phrases.

I
WORD PUZZLES

Truthful words are not beautiful; beautiful words are not truthful.
Good words are not persuasive; persuasive words are not good.

LAO-TZU (6TH CENTURY BCE)

NO OTHER FACULTY DISTINGUISHES HUMAN BEINGS from other species the way language does. We use it to encode knowledge, to pass it on to subsequent generations, to think, to communicate, to entertain ourselves, and so on. The very survival of human civilization depends on the preservation of words and their meanings, because without them we would have to start anew, literally rebuilding knowledge with new words.

Many of the brain centers that are involved in the production and decipherment of words are located in the left hemisphere. Alone, however, they do not produce the whole richness of language, or even the subtle nuances built into simple words. The right hemisphere has actually been shown to play a significant role in how we determine subtle and figurative meanings. The left hemisphere will interpret *cat* as the common four-legged mammal we know so well; but it takes the collaboration of the right hemisphere for the brain to recognize the figurative meaning of the same word in a sentence such as *He's a real cool cat.*

Research on the positive effects of word games on the brain is extensive. Let me cite just one typical example—a study by E. J. Meinze and his associates examining the correlation between aging and word games such as crosswords published in *The Psychology of Aging* in 2000. The study found solid evidence to suggest that a high level of experience with crossword puzzles in older subjects partially decreases the negative effects of age on memory. In other words, doing crossword puzzles delays brain decline. So it is appropriate to start off the brain exercises in this book with five sets of word puzzles, including a specific type of crossword puzzle called *frameworks*. The other types are anagrams, word ladders, hidden words and word squares. Psychologists use similar games for assessing intelligence and memory skills. And not only do these puzzles have beneficial brain effects, but they are also fun to do.

ANAGRAM FUN

The most classic of all word puzzles is, undoubtedly, the anagram. This is a word, phrase or sentence made by rearranging the letters of another word, phrase or sentence. Anagrams go right back to the dawn of recorded history, when they were perceived as harboring secret or prophetic messages. There is only one rule in doing anagrams—every letter must be used with exactly the same number of occurrences as in the original word or phrase.

The writer John Dryden aptly characterized anagrams as the "torturing of one poor word ten thousand ways," and indeed many words produce multiple anagrams. So to keep the solutions here within reasonable limits, you are told what specific anagram is the expected one with hints and clues. For example, rearranging the letters in the word *pots* produces five legitimate words: *stop, opts, post, tops* and *spot*. If the required anagram is *stop* you will be given a clue such as: *to cease*.

If you get stuck, here's a tip. Simply try out each letter in combination with the others. For example, if given the word *care*, start by considering *c* in combination with the other letters. Does any combination produce a word? It does not seem to. Go on to *a*. This can be combined with the other letters to produce *acre*. Go on to *r* and it becomes quickly obvious that it can be combined with the other letters to produce *race*. No words or phrases can be produced with the final *e*.

These ten exercises consist of four anagrams each, thus giving you plenty of work in this brain-building area. Some of these are classics and can be found in various collections and places, such as anagram websites.

1. Let's start off very simply with *word-to-word anagrams.* These are solved by rearranging the letters of a given word to produce a new word. For instance, the letters in the word *evil* can be rearranged to produce *veil* or *live.* As this example shows, there might be more than one solution. But you are required to find one and only one, as specified by the given clue.

(a) end (Clue: starts with *d*)
(b) arm (Clue: starts with *r*)
(c) came (Clue: starts with *m*)
(d) mane (Clue: is given to you at birth)

2. Now try your hand at making word anagrams from slightly longer words. This exercise is still fairly easy.

(a) teach (Clue: starts with *c*)
(b) trial (Clue: just rearrange two adjacent letters)
(c) sister (Clue: starts with *r*)
(d) carte (Clue: respond)

3. Here's one last set of anagrams of this type.

(a) peat (Clue: starts with *t*)
(b) spate (Clue: can be used as an adhesive)
(c) stain (Clue: a smooth glossy fabric)
(d) bedroom (Clue: results from having nothing to do)

4. Let's turn the difficulty level up a notch. Can you rearrange the letters in each word to produce the indicated phrase? For example, by rearranging the letters of *astronomer* you get *moon starer* or *no more star.*

(a) theater (Clue: two-word phrase indicating amount to be paid)
(b) bather (Clue: two word-phrase indicating "what she has to pay")
(c) doggish (Clue: two-word phrase describing what a pet might do; the phrase consists of the pet + a verb)
(d) eventful (Clue: two-word phrase describing a small opening)

5. Now try your hand at the reverse type of puzzle. Can you make a single word from the given phrase? For example, from *evil's agent* you can make *evangelist*. Eliminating punctuation is permitted.

(a) a bet (Clue: part of rhythm)
(b) to bore (Clue: restart)
(c) the rat (Clue: starts with *th*)
(d) ripe sin (Clue: arouse)

6. Here's more of the same. This time the difficulty notch has been turned up quite a bit, except for the very first one. You might have to eliminate punctuation and turn uppercase letters into lowercase ones, or vice versa.

(a) She'll fish. (Clue: examples are oysters and shrimps)
(b) the cute pair (Clue: starts with *th*)
(c) But lose more. (Clue: causing difficulties)
(d) Rot, like me! (Clue: a measurement)

7. Now try your hand at celebrity anagrams. You are given a phrase or sentence that tells you something about the person. By rearranging the letters you will get his or her name. For example, by rearranging the letters of *Old West action,* you will get the name *Clint Eastwood,* who was the original actor in the so-called spaghetti Westerns. These anagrams are well-known ones among puzzle aficionados, by the way.

(a) radium came (Clue: a female scientist)
(b) occasional nude income (Clue: three-word name of an iconic female pop singer)
(c) Seen alive? Sorry, pal! (Clue: full name of an iconic male rock and roll singer)
(d) I end lives. (Clue: has played an adventure hero)

8. Can you make a new phrase or sentence from the given phrase or sentence? For example, by rearranging the letters in *the golden days* you will get the sentence *They gladden so!*

(a) *La mode* (as they say in French) (Clue: someone who poses)
(b) Hi, heart! (Clue: part of the body)
(c) The fine game of nil (Clue: expression with a philosophical meaning)
(d) No city dust here (Clue: a place away from the city)

9. Now we will mix things up a bit, increasing the difficulty level. Can you make either a new word or a new phrase from the given phrase or sentence? You will not be told whether a word or phrase is the required anagram. Put your thinking cap on!

(a) Cry editor (Clue: a listing)
(b) Cook, catch her! (Clue: This is a well-known "insect" anagram)
(c) Love lab (Clue: worthy of affection)
(d) Evil voices rant on (Clue: unpleasant exchange)

10. Here's more of the same. Can you make either a new word or a new phrase from the given phrase or sentence? Again, you will not be told whether a word or phrase is the required anagram.

(a) Elvis, listen! (Clue: tacit beings)
(b) Secret ID (Clue: careful and circumspect)
(c) Claim us (Clue: melodious)
(d) More nasty notes (Clue: piece of building material used in a building where religious laws are observed)

WORD LADDERS

A word ladder is a puzzle in which you are given two words, with steps or links in between them, as in a ladder. For example, there are three steps between *LOVE* and *HATE*.

LOVE

_____

_____

_____

HATE

You are supposed to change just one letter on each step as you go from the top word to the bottom word. Each step must be a common English word. Proper names are not allowed. And you cannot change the order of the letters.

LOVE

cove

cave

have

HATE

Here's one possibility. First, change the *L* in *LOVE* to *c* to produce the word *cove*. Then, change the *o* in *cove* to *a* to produce the word *cave*. Then change the *c* in *cave* to *h* to get *have*. Finally, by changing the *v* in *have* to *t* you will get the word *HATE*.

The inventor of this puzzle was the great children's author and mathematician Lewis Carroll, who called it a *doublet*. He likely took the name for his puzzle from the witches' incantation in *Macbeth*: "Double, double, toil and trouble." It was Dimitri Borgmann in his classic puzzle collection, *Language on Vacation* (1965), who renamed the puzzle a word ladder. This type of puzzle will give the verbal part of your brain considerable exercise.

11. Let's start off nice and easy with a one-step word ladder. The intent in the first few puzzles is to familiarize you with the solution process involved by using increasing numbers of steps.

MAD

_____

BED

12. Let's continue at this level.

NONE

_____

LOVE

13. Try solving a two-step puzzle this time.

EASE

_____

_____

PEST

14. Here's a three-step puzzle, making it a tad more difficult to solve.

SPOON

_____

_____

_____

SCOOP

15. The next four-step puzzle will take some effort to solve.

DUST

_____

_____

_____

_____

HOME

16. Now try your hand at a five-step puzzle.

WHITE

_____

_____

_____

_____

_____

FLAKE

17. In 1879, Carroll began publishing his doublet puzzles in *Vanity Fair*, which offered prizes for solutions. They became popular, but predictable, so he added a rule to make the puzzles more difficult. In the new version, you go from one step to the next by introducing a new letter (as you have been doing) or by rearranging the letters of the word (as in anagrams).

For example here's how to go from *HATE* to *VEIL* in three steps using the new anagram rule: *HATE—have* (changing *t* to *v*)—*hive* (changing *a* to *i*)—*live* (changing *h* to *l*)—*VEIL* (rearranging the letters of *live*).

For this puzzle you will be told which step is an anagram step involving the rearrangement of letters.

SCARE

_____

_____

_____

NOTES *(rearrangement)*

18. Here's one more in this genre. This time you will not be told which step or steps involve letter rearrangement, or even if there is such rearrangement. This is a challenging four-step puzzle.

TOPS

_____

_____

_____

_____

FATE

19. Other versions of this puzzle have been devised over the years. One of these is to add a letter to a previous word. A simple example would be to change *BAD* to *BEARD* in one step: *BAD—bard* (adding *r*)—*BEARD* (adding *e*). Try your hand at the following four-step additive doublet, as it is called. It looks more challenging than it really is.

I

‾‾‾‾‾‾‾‾‾‾‾‾‾‾‾‾‾‾‾‾‾‾‾

‾‾‾‾‾‾‾‾‾‾‾‾‾‾‾‾‾‾‾‾‾‾‾

‾‾‾‾‾‾‾‾‾‾‾‾‾‾‾‾‾‾‾‾‾‾‾

‾‾‾‾‾‾‾‾‾‾‾‾‾‾‾‾‾‾‾‾‾‾‾

STRING

20. The counterpart to the additive doublet is the subtractive doublet. In this case you have to take away a letter from a previous word. An example would be to change *BEAST* to *BE* in two steps, subtracting a letter at each step: *BEAST—best* (subtracting *a*)—*bet* (subtracting *s*)—*BE* (subtracting *t*). Try your hand at the following three-step subtractive doublet.

STONED

‾‾‾‾‾‾‾‾‾‾‾‾‾‾‾‾‾‾‾‾‾‾‾

‾‾‾‾‾‾‾‾‾‾‾‾‾‾‾‾‾‾‾‾‾‾‾

‾‾‾‾‾‾‾‾‾‾‾‾‾‾‾‾‾‾‾‾‾‾‾

ON

SAME-FIRST-LETTER FRAMEWORKS

The framework puzzle is a very popular derivative of the crossword. The difference is that there are no "black squares" as in the crossword grid. You are given just the squares in which to put the appropriate letters. In this specific version, you are given a number of clues. Each answer starts with the same letter, as indicated. Then you are supposed to insert the words into the framework logically.

Let's go through one model puzzle together. This one is a five-word puzzle. All the words start with *p*. First answer the clues. The answers to the clues are given in parenthesis.

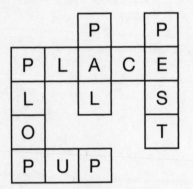

CLUES

1. used to address someone informally *(pal)*
2. someone who is always a nuisance *(pest)*
3. a very young dog *(pup)*
4. to drop something quickly and heavily *(plop)*
5. an area, spot or position *(place)*

The clues produce two three-letter words *(pal, pup)*, two four-letter words *(plop, pest)* and one five-letter word *(place)*. Now, the only way to insert them into the framework is shown below. You can try other ways, but they will not work. All words must cross correctly.

As you can see, what makes this puzzle interesting and challenging is that it consists of two parts—guessing clues and then placing words in a grid logically. As a tip, if you get stuck on the clues, you might have to go back and forth between the clues and the grid to get to the solution, inserting those words of a certain length that correspond to a row or column length in the grid. For example, if there is only a six-cell row in the grid and you get only one six-letter word from the clues, then you should insert it in the framework right away.

21. Let's start simply with a three-word framework. The words all start with *r*.

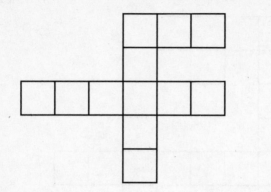

CLUES

1. to stand firmly against
2. the color of blood
3. period of rule

22. Now try this four-word framework. The words all start with *w*. The puzzle is still fairly simple.

CLUES

1. awe, amazement
2. period comprising Saturday and Sunday
3. to stay in one place
4. H_2O

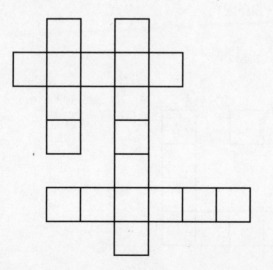

23. The words in this five-word framework all start with *a*.

CLUES

1. the years you have lived
2. quick, lively musical tempo
3. once a year
4. not here
5. every one

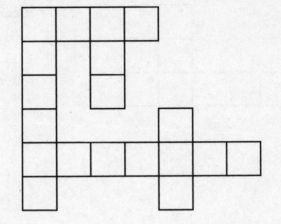

24. The words in this six-word framework all start with *b*.

CLUES

1. to lay a wager
2. lacking originality
3. cake and bread maker
4. sport played by Hank Aaron and Mickey Mantle
5. intense in color
6. curved

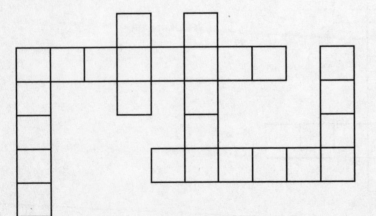

25. The words in this seven-word framework all start with *c*.

CLUES

1. another name for ketchup
2. sharp of mind
3. to stop
4. feline
5. dog-like
6. to give up something
7. to gather together

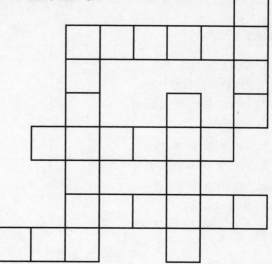

26. The words in this eight-word framework all start with *d*.

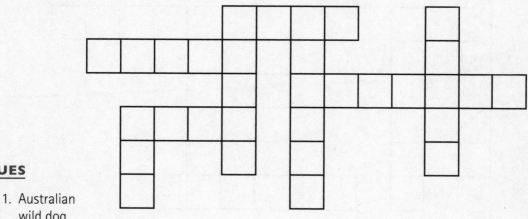

CLUES

1. Australian wild dog
2. to swindle someone
3. European artistic movement
4. Disney character
5. to be excessively fond of
6. decorative sticker
7. a complete failure, fiasco
8. punctuation mark

27. The words in this nine-word framework also all start with *d*.

CLUES

1. illegal drug
2. loud persistent noise
3. corruption, debauchery
4. boring
5. easily led or managed
6. pronunciation or accent mark
7. drawn conclusion
8. to give a speech
9. persistent false belief

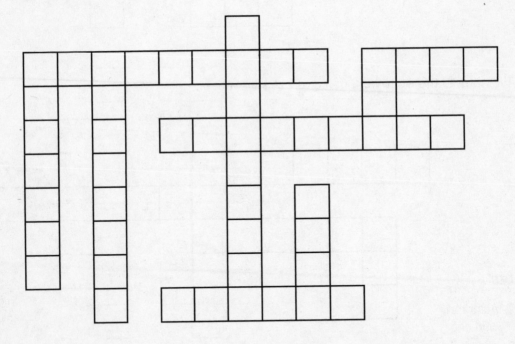

28. The words in this ten-word framework all start with *s*.

CLUES

1. irony or sarcasm that exposes or denounces
2. impudent
3. sexual male
4. biological subdivision
5. apparently true, but actually false
6. different from what it claims to be
7. male or female
8. consequently
9. board game
10. messily written

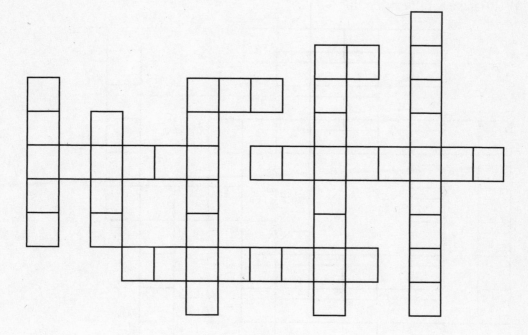

29. The words in this eleven-word framework all start with *t*.

CLUES

1. to move slowly
2. brass instrument
3. showing great resolve
4. child
5. this evening
6. number of digits in the decimal system
7. type of bag with handles
8. aggressive, sullen
9. musical speed
10. figure of speech
11. to tangle or ruffle hair or fur

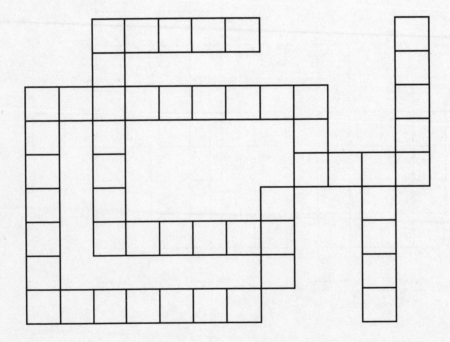

30. The words in this twelve-word framework all start with *v*.

CLUES

1. twining plant
2. the age of a wine, high quality wine
3. full name of the cello
4. soft, lustrous fabric
5. by word of mouth, or "___ voce"
6. used in making plastics
7. in truth
8. with the voice
9. lively, vigorous spirit
10. blood vessel
11. to subject someone to scrutiny
12. offered in fulfillment of a vow

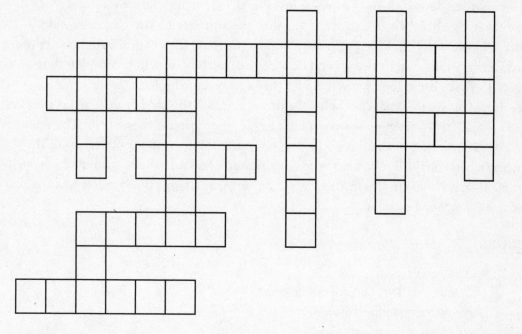

HIDDEN WORDS

Here's another derivative of the crossword puzzle concept. You have to use clues to solve these three-by-three word squares. Note that the number of the clue corresponds to the number in the first cell. Moreover, note that in the first (upper) grid you have to insert the words horizontally and in the second (lower grid) vertically. When completed, the shaded diagonal will spell a hidden word. Let's go through one example together.

Here you are told that the theme is animals and that the hidden word refers to a Western movie character. Note that all answers to the clues are three-letter words. The answers are given in parentheses. In the top grid insert *cat* in the top row horizontally, *dog* in the second row, and *cow* in the third row. Insert the last three answers into the bottom grid vertically: *bat* in the left-hand column, *boa* in the middle column, and *toy* in the last column. As you can see the hidden word is *cowboy*.

CLUES

1. a small feline (cat)
2. a Labrador or Dalmatian, for example (dog)
3. grass-eating quadruped (cow)
4. nocturnal flying mammal (bat)
5. large snake (boa)
6. miniature human-made version of an animal, such as a dog (toy)

¹C	A	T
²D	O	G
³C	O	W

⁴B	⁵B	⁶T
A	O	O
T	A	Y

There really is no way to organize these puzzles in order of increasing difficulty. You either know the clues or you don't, so the difficulty level will vary according to your knowledge.

31. The clues in this puzzle are connected with writing and computers, and the hidden word refers to something people wrote on long before the age of computers.

CLUES

1. a key on a computer with various functions
2. type of letter used at the beginning of a sentence (in abbreviated form)
3. metal tip on the end of a pen, common in the precomputer age
4. room where a group of computers are used for educational or training purposes (in abbreviated form)
5. computer key referring to an erasing function
6. computer key pressed together with another key to change its function

Hidden Word:

_____

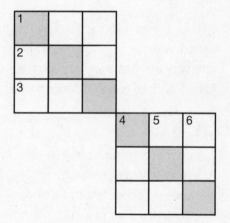

32. The clues are connected with being a boy, and the hidden word is often used to describe a young boy.

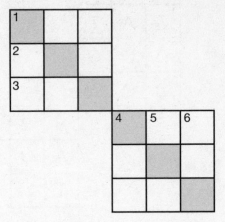

CLUES

1. word used to refer to a boy
2. a young child (male or female)
3. a very young child
4. first name of a boy character in a famous Mark Twain story
5. what a boy will become as he ages
6. a common boy name or an informal way of referring to an ordinary man

Hidden Word:

_____

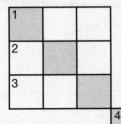

33. To even things out, the clues in this puzzle are connected with being a female, and the hidden word refers to the first name of an actress who became famous as Fred Astaire's dance partner.

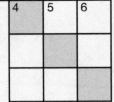

CLUES

1. informal term for a girl
2. a relative (male or female)
3. opposite or counterpart of *women*
4. usually referring to a man, but now used to refer to anyone of either sex, especially as part of a group
5. woman who is responsible for a group of people; a "___ mother"
6. the feminine equivalent to *his*

Hidden Word:

_____

34. The clues in this puzzle are connected with religion, and the hidden word refers to the highest point reached, for example, during meditation.

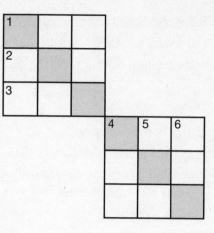

CLUES

1. a major school of Buddhism
2. a wooden bench used for kneeling in a church or synagogue
3. number of Commandments given to Moses
4. in some people's versions (as for example in Dante's *Divine Comedy*), hell consists of this substance
5. abbreviation of *sainte* used as a title for women saints
6. expression of contempt

Hidden Word:

_____

35. The clues in this puzzle are connected with the house, and the hidden word refers to a space in the kitchen.

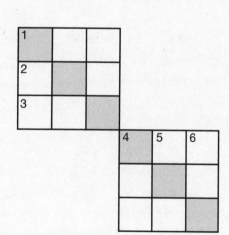

CLUES

1. container, usually of metal, used for cooking
2. cooking pot, usually with a handle, for use on a stove
3. sealed metal container for food or drink
4. lidded container, or "___ can"
5. to cook something in fat
6. a type of window

Hidden Word:

_____

36. The clues in this puzzle are connected with the farm, and the hidden word refers to the mood people generally are in when they go to the countryside to relax.

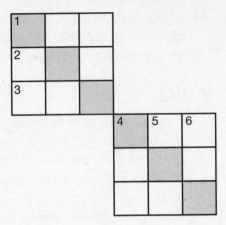

CLUES

1. hog or pig enclosure
2. general animal enclosure
3. a peasant commune in czarist Russia; also the name of a space station
4. female sheep
5. insect found commonly on the farm; favorite food of aardvarks
6. female deer

Hidden Word:

_____

37. The clues in this puzzle are connected with music, and the hidden word is the surname of a famous American composer.

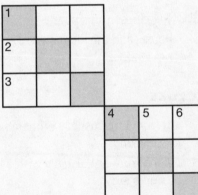

CLUES

1. unit of musical tempo
2. what musicians do for fun or to try out new songs
3. also known as an English horn: "___ anglais"
4. shortened Italian word used commonly in musical notation and meaning "well"; for example, "___ marcato" (well marked)
5. number of songs a band performs on a single occasion
6. number of beats ___ bar, that is, in each bar

Hidden Word:

_____

38. The clues in this puzzle are connected with scientific ideas. The hidden word refers to a type of machine (found, for example, in a car).

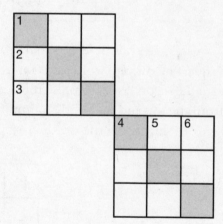

CLUES

1. unit of energy
2. colored liquid used for writing
3. the power to which a fixed number must be raised to equal a given number (abbreviated form)
4. movement or doctrine, scientific or otherwise
5. point at which something, such as a project, is complete
6. a flying insect

Hidden Word:

---

39. The clues in this puzzle are connected with quantity or measurement, and the hidden word also refers to a quantitative concept.

CLUES

1. a large number of something
2. not very many
3. abbreviation of a trigonometric measure (the ratio of the side adjacent to an acute angle in a right-angled triangle to the hypotenuse)
4. abbreviation of another trigonometric measure (the ratio of the side opposite a given angle in a right-angled triangle to the hypotenuse)
5. the usual base for computing logarithms
6. imperial unit of weight

Hidden Word:

---

40. The clues in this puzzle are all definitions of verbs, and the hidden word is also a verb.

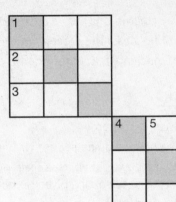

CLUES

1. to strike or beat something with a sharp blow
2. to perceive with the eyes
3. to transport passengers to a specific destination
4. to be able to
5. to move rapidly on foot
6. in the expression "____ the line" it means to play by the rules

Hidden Word:

_____

WORD SQUARES

Word squares are grids of letters that cross horizontally and vertically. For example, in the word square below, the word *plot* is inserted in the top row and left-most column; *love* is inserted in the second row from the top and the second column from the left; *oven* in the third row from the top and the third column from the left; and *tent* in the bottom row and in the right-most column. All the words cross perfectly in a square arrangement.

P	L	O	T
L	O	V	E
O	V	E	N
T	E	N	T

You are given clues that correspond to the rows and columns. Three clues means that there are three rows and columns and that the answers are three-letter words; four clues means that there are four rows and columns and that the answers are four-letter words; and so on. All you have to do is insert the answers accordingly to complete the square. Take, for example, the word square below. The answers to the clues are given in parentheses. So we put the answer to the first clue in the first row and left-most column, the answer to the second clue in the second row and middle column, and the answer to the third clue in the third row and right-most column.

CLUES

1. plaything (toy)
2. a mineral (ore)
3. an affirmative answer (yes)

T	O	Y
O	R	E
Y	E	S

BRAIN FACT #4

There exists interesting research which shows that listening to classical music, especially the music of Mozart, can have beneficial effects on memory and intelligence. This makes a lot of sense to me. I always have such music on as I work. And throughout the years I have no doubt that it has helped me become a better thinker and manipulator of information. Although this is anecdotal, there is no reason to believe that others would not garner the same benefits from it. So, as you solve the puzzles in this book, let me recommend putting on the music of Mozart at the same time. It certainly can't hurt.

That's all there is to it. As a tip, if you get stuck on the clues, you might have to go back and forth between them and the grid to get to the solution. Insert the words you have found in the appropriate rows and columns and work from there back to the clues. In the last five puzzles, however, the clues will not be in order, making them much more challenging.

41. As always, let's start easy with a simple three-by-three word square.

CLUES

1. single, the first number (not zero)
2. neither ____
3. time period

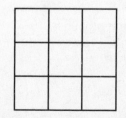

42. Let's continue at this fairly easy level of difficulty.

CLUES

1. pinnacle
2. used to row a boat
3. snoop

43. You might find a four-by-four version just a bit more difficult.

CLUES

1. painful
2. unlocked
3. go through a book reflectively
   (what you do with a book)
4. objectives

44. Here's another four-by-four word square.

CLUES

1. a martial art
2. part of the eye
3. adroit
4. common name of a grass that has
   edible seeds; used in the expression
   "to sow one's wild _____"

45. Here's yet another four-by-four word square.

CLUES

1. as of, since; used in the expression, "_____ now on"
2. uncommon
3. spoken
4. thaw

46. Let's turn up the difficulty level a bit. The four clues in the remaining puzzles are not numbered. Thus, you will have to figure out how the answers fit into the word square on your own. Good luck!

CLUES *in no particular order*

the world's largest continent
musical tempo
effortlessness
squad

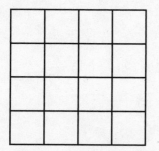

47. Here's another word square of the same challenging type.

CLUES *in no particular order*

a gemstone
shine brightly
acronym of an international organization founded in 1949
short text set to music

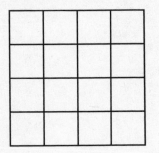

BRAIN FACT #5

As harsh as it may sound, comparing the brain to a machine is a useful way to understand the importance of keeping it in good working condition, just as you would keep your car, for instance. Research has shown that the more you use a particular part of the brain, the more blood is pumped into it by the heart. Like fuel for an engine, this makes the brain "work better," at least in that part. Thus doing puzzles is similar to filling up the tank with fuel so that the machine can do its work.

48. Now try your hand at this one.

CLUES *in no particular order*

a woodwind instrument
retain
type of popular music, especially associated with Elvis Presley
to approach

49. Here's your last four-by-four puzzle.

CLUES *in no particular order*

design style popular in the 1930s based on geometrical designs and bold colors
person with an excessively high opinion of himself or herself
gentlemen who do not behave as they should toward women
expression used at the end of many prayers

50. Let's turn the difficulty level up to maximum, with a final five-by-five word square. Again, the clues are in no particular order and they are hard. This is, of course, good for your brain, if not so good for your patience!

CLUES *in no particular order*

marine
a Native American people, formerly inhabiting a valley in Missouri
rub out
skirmish
poison

2
VERBAL KNOW-HOW PUZZLES

The words of the world want to make sentences.

GASTON BACHELARD (1884–1962)

I N THIS CHAPTER YOU WILL AGAIN FIND PUZZLES that activate the verbal centers of the brain. These puzzles require knowledge, or more accurately know-how, of how words are combined and what they mean. They are designed to activate verbal recall, which is an intrinsic part of memory. Over the last number of years various studies have shown that puzzles such as the ones here stimulate the development of more cells than considered normal for those who are of a certain age, which seems to improve memory and enhance general intelligence.

A research group headed by Karlene Ball at the University of Alabama in 2006, for instance, found that intensive puzzle training among older adults led to a marked increase in intellectual performance. Even those with Alzheimer's were helped significantly. As I have already mentioned, I am not sure why this is so or how to explain the relevant research. One theory—called the theory of cognitive reserve—suggests that doing puzzles early in life enhances the brain's ability to produce and maintain extra neurons and that, later in life, this compensates in cases of brain decline that accompany normal aging.

The five sets of puzzles include rebuses, hidden sayings, wheel of fortune, cryptography and think-of-a-word conundrums. Have fun as you exercise your verbal memory!

A rebus is a representation of words, phrases or sentences in the form of pictures, letters and symbols. It is a kind of mixed-alphabet puzzle, and it will activate both the visual and verbal centers in the brain.

Let's go through one puzzle together. Can you decode the following secret message?

BRIDGE
DUCK

We see the word *bridge*, a line and the word *duck*. What could this possibly mean? Let's start with *duck*. Note that *duck* is under the word *bridge*, as if it were a digit under the line in a fraction. The word *duck* can also be used as a verb, meaning to lower your head quickly so as not to be seen. So the answer is the phrase *Duck under the bridge!*

As you can see, some rebuses rely on the physical layout or relative positions of certain symbols or words on the page. Another common rebus technique is to combine pictures and letters. The pictures are to be sounded out. So, for example:

$$\text{(eye)} + \text{LAND} = eye + land = island$$

Rebus puzzles became popular in the 1600s—so much so that the English writer Ben Jonson trenchantly ridiculed them in his play *The Alchemist*. The puzzles here are straightforward and most are well-known. You will be given hints in the first few puzzles to help you get started.

51. This is a fairly easy one to figure out. It is a rebus of a common four-word phrase. As a hint, note that the numeral one is in the word. What's that word? Put them together and what do you get?

MILLIO$_1$N

52. Here's another similar one. In this case you will be searching for a two-word phrase. You might have to eliminate spaces and adjust the spelling to reflect pronunciation. Thus, the 4 is written *four*. But note that this is a homonym (same-sounding word) of *for*, which could be what you are looking for.

STAN4CE

53. Here's one more of this type. This time you are looking for a two-word phrase.

LANGU4AGE

54. This one is a little different, but similar to the model puzzle above. Look at the layout and the position of the words. The puzzle conceals a six-word phrase.

SITTING
_____
WORLD

55. Here's a puzzle that is very similar to the previous one. You are looking for a four-word expression.

_____

READ
_____

56. From now on, no more hints. This rebus hides a well-known three-word saying.

HISTORY
HISTORY
HISTORY
HISTORY

57. This rebus hides a two-word expression.

X QQQQ ME

58. This rebus also hides a two-word phrase.

TRAVEL
_____
CCCCC

59. What message does the following rebus conceal?

PRESSURE
_____
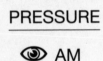 AM

60. This is a tricky one. Good luck!

GO

GO   ME   GO

GO

PHRASE SEARCHES

Finding words hidden in letter arrays is a classic type of puzzle. Now called a word search puzzle, it is actually a kind of cipher. It appeared in its modern form in 1968 in the March 1 issue of *The Selenby Digest* in Norman, Oklahoma. The puzzle caught on quickly, as teachers in the local schools started asking for reprints of the word searches for their classes.

The ten puzzles here are similar to the classic word search genre, but rather than hide words, they hide phrases, such as a saying, a proverb, a quotation and the like. Hence, they can be called *phrase searches*. The phrase can appear from left to right or up and down, but always starting from the top.

Below is an example of both. The first is a quotation by the great Anglo-Irish writer Oscar Wilde (1854–1900) from his work *Chameleon*. The quotation is "Ambition is the last refuge of the failure." As you can see, it starts at the top row and is read in a downward fashion in the rows.

The second is the well-known opening line—"To be or not to be"—from Hamlet's famous soliloquy in the Shakespearean play. As you can see, it starts at the top and is read in a vertical fashion (from left to right) in the columns of the grid.

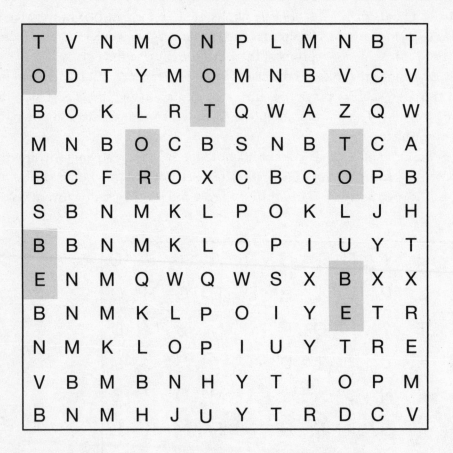

For the first eight puzzles you are given three clues. Use them to help you envision the words of the phrase. To make the puzzles more manageable, all words will lie wholly within a vertical or horizontal line. They will not break or run on within the grid.

61. This first puzzle contains a famous proverb.

```
T  O  C  A  D  S  V  B  N  M  M  O
P  O  I  U  Y  T  R  E  V  B  N  N
E  V  E  R  Y  T  H  I  N  G  B  M
B  G  R  T  G  M  K  I  E  V  R  T
E  T  H  E  R  E  T  Y  U  I  O  P
N  M  K  L  P  O  I  U  Y  T  R  F
N  I  S  M  A  N  B  M  L  O  P  D
M  K  O  P  L  M  K  J  H  G  T  R
S  E  A  S  O  N  P  B  N  M  O  P
N  M  K  L  P  O  R  D  S  E  S  A
N  M  K  L  O  P  N  M  K  I  O  L
M  N  B  V  C  F  R  G  T  H  U  P
```

Proverb:

_____

CLUES

1. The proverb can be read horizontally from left to right, starting at the very top.
2. There are six words in the proverb.
3. One of the words is *season*.

62. This puzzle contains a famous saying attributed to William of Occam (1285–1349), the English monk to whom we owe the expression *Occam's Razor.*

I	T	A	I	S	C	V	A	I	N	D	S
Q	E	W	S	D	C	V	B	N	H	J	M
K	T	O	G	D	O	M	L	P	O	T	R
S	B	N	M	K	L	P	Y	T	R	D	S
W	I	T	H	N	M	O	R	E	M	K	L
Q	S	C	E	D	V	R	F	B	T	G	H
M	K	O	P	Y	T	I	K	L	F	G	M
W	H	A	T	V	C	A	N	N	B	E	M
B	G	T	Y	H	N	M	J	U	K	I	L
D	O	N	E	N	W	I	T	H	M	N	B
V	B	N	M	J	K	L	L	P	O	M	N
N	M	L	E	S	S	B	N	M	K	L	P

Saying:

_____

CLUES

1. Again, the saying can be read horizontally from left to right, starting at the very top.
2. There are thirteen words in the saying.
3. Two of the words are *vain* and *done*. No word has more than four letters in it.

63. The following puzzle conceals another Oscar Wilde saying, taken from his 1882 lecture *House Decoration.*

```
B S V V D V V R T Y P
A N A M E B T N M A R T
D B N M A N H L P T R W
N B G M L B A T F V C B
N N R M N B N V B A Y T
A M E B W N M K L L O A
R K A B O N N N M L V C
T L T G R H O H J K L M
N O G O S O D C A D S L
M P B N E M A L O P M A
I W N B M N R M K L N V
S S C A D S T C A D S T
```

Saying:

_____

CLUES

1. The saying can be read vertically, starting in the left-most column.
2. There are twelve words in it.
3. The saying is about art.

64. The next puzzle contains a famous line from Charles Dickens's 1844 novel *Martin Chuzzlewit*. It has become a kind of maxim.

```
N  C  Q  S  V  H  G  T  R  C  N  R
M  H  A  B  L  O  J  G  F  A  E  T
K  A  Z  E  Y  M  U  B  V  D  X  Y
L  R  X  G  L  E  S  N  B  S  T  H
O  I  S  I  V  T  T  M  N  C  G  Y
P  T  W  N  L  A  I  K  M  A  J  U
R  Y  E  S  V  N  C  L  B  D  H  O
T  B  D  E  L  D  E  P  E  S  N  P
G  N  C  A  V  P  B  O  G  V  M  D
H  M  V  T  L  Q  N  I  I  V  L  O
Y  K  F  V  V  W  M  U  N  L  P  O
R  I  R  V  L  S  K  Y  S  L  U  R
```

Line:

_____

CLUES

1. The line can be read vertically, but it does not start in the left-most column.
2. There are nine words in it.
3. One of the words, a verb, is used twice.

65. The puzzle below conceals two lines from a poem by the great American poet Emily Dickinson (1830–1886).

```
P A R T I N G V I S V V
V V C A D S B N M M L P
V A L L M W E N K N O W
B V L M D V L M D S O M
B N M K O P I U Y T G F
O F R H E A V E N Q W S
Q A Z X C D E R G B N W
P A N D B A L L M W E Q
X C V B N M K L O P R T
N E E D B O F N J I O P
Q A Z X D E R F V B G F
N H Y U M H E L L N O P
```

Lines:

_____

CLUES

1. The lines can be read horizontally, starting at the very top.
2. There are thirteen words in all.
3. The poem is about parting.

66. The next puzzle contains a famous saying about New York, said by New Yorkers themselves.

```
Q  N  V  W  P  H  A  P  P  T  W  F
W  E  L  I  L  G  L  L  L  H  Q  I
S  W  V  L  M  F  G  A  M  E  S  N
D  R  L  L  N  R  R  C  N  Y  D  I
C  V  V  G  B  W  E  E  B  D  P  S
V  Y  V  B  V  Z  A  G  V  F  L  H
F  O  D  E  H  P  T  W  D  P  M  J
R  R  W  N  G  L  M  W  B  L  N  I
T  K  S  M  F  M  Q  H  N  M  B  T
G  V  C  L  R  N  W  E  M  N  V  I
B  V  V  K  W  B  S  N  K  B  B  L
N  I  B  P  Z  V  X  V  I  V  N  D
```

Saying:

_____

CLUES

1. The saying can be read vertically.
2. There are eleven words in it.
3. The saying contains the name of the city.

67. The following phrase search contains a famous quotation by British author Rose Tremain (b. 1943), from the December 24, 1989, issue of the *Sunday Correspondent*.

```
A  W  C  V  L  B  N  N  M  P  Q  A
C  V  W  S  I  Q  Z  O  S  R  O  P
P  H  I  Z  F  I  A  T  C  E  H  A
D  S  C  A  E  V  L  B  N  H  M  P
Q  W  S  D  F  H  B  A  W  E  Q  R
Q  A  Z  X  D  E  R  V  B  A  M  P
W  T  Y  I  O  N  M  B  N  R  M  O
C  V  B  N  M  P  R  D  Q  S  C  V
B  N  M  N  I  M  P  R  F  A  S  C
G  H  K  L  S  P  Q  E  W  L  X  C
B  N  M  K  L  P  O  S  V  B  C  X
Z  S  Q  W  R  T  H  S  H  V  V  I
```

Quotation:

_____

CLUES

1. The saying can be read vertically.
2. There are six words in it.
3. The single verb in the quotation is the verb *is*.

68. The following puzzle conceals something Thomas Jefferson (1743–1826) wrote in a letter on October 20, 1820.

```
N  M  B  V  L  V  N  V  W  V  V  V
C  M  O  S  I  M  E  M  I  F  X  M
V  N  I  E  B  N  V  N  T  N  W  N
T  B  S  A  E  B  E  B  H  M  A  B
H  V  T  C  R  V  R  V  O  B  V  V
E  C  E  O  T  C  B  C  U  V  E  C
O  X  R  F  Y  X  Q  X  T  C  C  X
W  Z  O  B  S  Z  A  Z  B  X  A  Z
S  A  U  N  I  A  C  A  A  S  D  A
C  F  S  M  S  F  D  F  N  D  S  F
V  D  R  T  I  D  V  D  M  F  V  D
G  B  V  Y  V  B  L  B  V  R  B  B
```

Quotation:

_____

CLUES

1. The quotation can be read vertically.
2. There are ten words in the quotation.
3. The word *wave* ends the quotation.

69. The next puzzle conceals a line from the 1991 novel *Wise Children* by British author Angela Carter (1940–1992). For this and the next puzzle, you are not given any clues at all.

A	S	Q	W	X	Z	C	V	F	R	T	H
M	P	V	L	V	L	V	L	G	B	V	I
N	M	C	O	M	E	D	Y	B	N	K	I
M	P	V	L	V	L	V	L	G	B	V	I
C	V	W	C	I	S	D	A	C	S	B	N
A	S	Q	W	X	Z	C	V	F	R	T	H
V	T	R	A	G	E	D	Y	L	P	N	N
B	N	T	H	A	T	V	C	B	N	R	T
M	P	V	L	V	L	V	L	G	B	V	I
H	A	P	P	E	N	S	K	T	O	P	M
B	N	M	O	T	H	E	R	B	N	M	P
B	P	E	O	P	L	E	V	L	V	L	E

Line:

_____

70. This last phrase search contains something that the great American comedian Woody Allen (b. 1935) said in his 1975 movie *Love and Death*. In this case you will have to add commas. Again, you are not given any clues.

```
M A N S C O N S I S T S
B N M C F G H K L P W O
O F V T W O L P A R T S
H I S B M I N D N A N D
R H I S B B O D Y N M O
Q W A S Z X V B H Y T R
V H O N L Y O T H E D T
Q W A S Z X V B H Y T R
B O D Y N H A S B B R T
L Q M N K L P Y T R W Q
M O R E M I F U N M N L
Q W A S Z X V B H Y T R
```

Line:

_____

WHEEL OF FORTUNE (SORT OF)

Wheel of Fortune is an American television game show created by the late Merv Griffin and hosted by Pat Sajak and Vanna White. Three contestants (occasionally three pairs of contestants) compete against each other to solve a word puzzle for cash and prizes. The show first aired in 1975 on daytime network television. The current version has been syndicated in prime time since September 19, 1983. It is the longest-running syndicated game show in American television history and the second-longest in either network or syndication (behind the current CBS version of *The Price Is Right,* which began airing in 1972). Clearly, people love word puzzles of this type.

The game is simple. Contestants ask for consonants after spinning a wheel, which indicates how much money (or whatever else is on the wheel) they get for the consonant. They can also buy vowels if they have enough money to do so. This continues until one of the contestants can figure out what the hidden phrase is. The puzzle format in this section is derived from the game show concept, but is, obviously, going to be a little different.

You are given only a few consonants and told what the puzzle is about. Unlike the game show, you are also given three clues for each of the puzzles. In the model puzzle below you are supposed to figure out the name of a famous sports celebrity from the past.

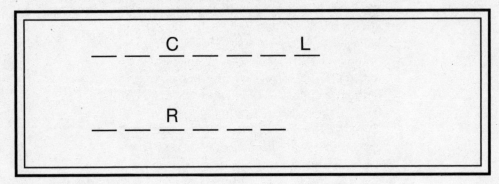

Sports Celebrity

CLUES

1. There are two *A*'s in the name.
2. There is one *N*.
3. The sport involved is basketball.

These clues and a little trial and error will produce the answer: *Michael Jordan*. Have fun!

71. The hidden phrase of this first simple puzzle is a thing (which can also be an idea). You are given five consonants.

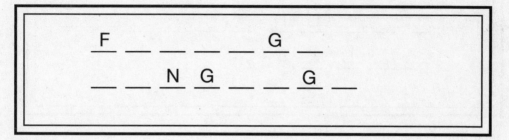

F _ _ _ _ G _

_ _ N G _ _ G _

Thing

CLUES

1. All five vowels (with repetitions) are found in the phrase.
2. There are two *N*'s in it.
3. It is something commonly studied in high school or college.

72. This next puzzle contains the name of a U.S. president. You are given four consonants.

_ H _ _ _ R _

_ _ S _ _ L _

President

CLUES

1. There is no *A, I* or *U* in the name.
2. He was a vice president when the incumbent president was assassinated, thereupon assuming the presidency.
3. He was the twenty-sixth president.

73. The puzzle below contains the title of a famous rock song. Again, you are given four consonants.

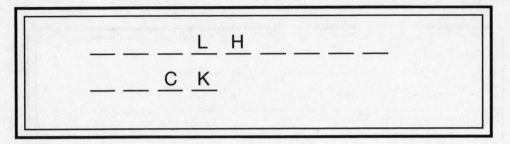

Song Title

CLUES

1. The title contains all five vowels.
2. The song was a top-of-the-charts hit in 1957.
3. It was also the title of the movie that featured the song.

74. The next puzzle contains the name of a famous scientist. As before, you are given four consonants.

Scientist

CLUES

1. There are no *O*'s or *U*'s in the name.
2. He won a Nobel Prize in 1921.
3. His theory changed how we think about the nature of time and space.

75. The puzzle below contains the name of a place. As in previous puzzles, you are given four consonants.

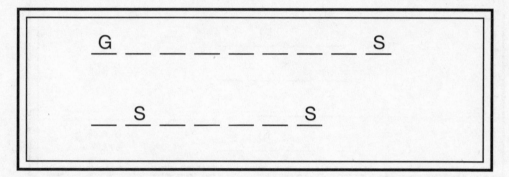

Place

CLUES

1. Incredibly, there are no *E*'s in the name.
2. The place is an archipelago located near Ecuador.
3. The place is famous for its rare species, including giant tortoises, which attracted Charles Darwin to visit it.

76. Can you figure out the name of the movie title contained in this next puzzle, with only the three consonants provided?

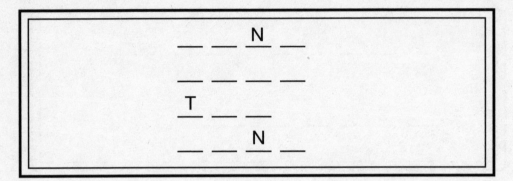

Movie Title

CLUES

1. There are no *A*'s or *U*'s in the title.
2. It won the Oscar for best picture in 1939.
3. It was produced by David O. Selznick, famous for his movie adaptations of popular novels.

77. The topic of this puzzle is household utensils. You are given three consonants.

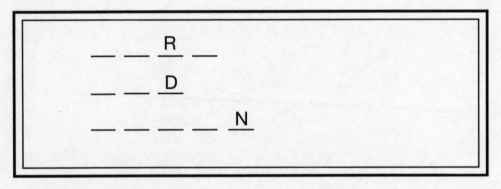

Household Utensils

1. Only the vowels *A* and *O* are found in the phrase.
2. The utensils go together.
3. They are put on the dinner table.

78. This puzzle hides the title of a famous American TV sitcom. You are given only two clues.

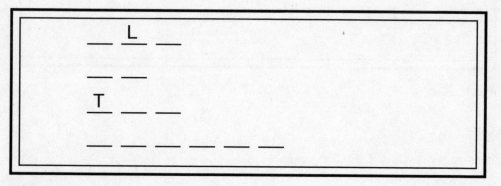

TV Sitcom

CLUES

1. There are no *O*'s or *U*'s in the title.
2. It debuted on CBS in 1971.
3. It costarred Rob Reiner.

79. This next puzzle contains the name of a famous movie star from the past. No consonants are provided.

— — — — — —

— — — — — — —

Movie Star

CLUES

1. There are no *O*'s or *U*'s in the name.
2. She was Swedish.
3. She starred in the 1945 movie *Spellbound*.

80. The topic of this last puzzle is a book title. Again, you are not given any consonants.

— — —

— —

— — — — —

— — — —

CLUES

1. It was a runaway bestseller in the early 2000s.
2. It was turned into a blockbuster movie.
3. The title refers to a famous Italian artist and scientist.

CRYPTOGRAPHY PUZZLES

Secret writing is as old as civilization. The sacred Jewish writers, for instance, concealed their messages by substituting one letter of the Hebrew alphabet with another—the last letter in place of the first, the second last in place of the second, and so on. The code was called *atbash,* now called a substitution cipher or a Caesar cipher, because Julius Caesar used a similar technique. As an example of how a secret code of this type works, can you figure out what English word the following sequence of letters encodes?

J   M P W F   Z P V

The phrase it encodes is *I love you.* Each letter in the phrase is replaced with the one coming after it in the normal alphabetic sequence. So the *I* is replaced by the letter after it, which is *J,* the *L* by *M,* and so on.

J   M P W F   Z P V

I   L O V E   Y O U

A second type of substitution cipher, called a Polybius cipher, involves replacing the letters of the message with numbers. It is called Polybius because it is attributed to the Greek historian Polybius (c. 200–118 BCE). One simple system would be to replace each letter of the alphabet with digits in numerical order: A = 1, B = 2 and so on. The encoded message below conceals the title of a Shakespearean play using this very pattern. Note that the apostrophe is to be preserved in the appropriate spot.

1   13 9 4 19 21 13 13 5 18

A   M I D S U M M E R

14 9 7 8 20 ' 19   4 18 5 1 13

N I G H T ' S   D R E A M

As you can see, the title is *A Midsummer Night's Dream.*

That's all there is to cryptography puzzles. The puzzles here are all substitution ciphers. The first four are Caesar ciphers, the next four are Polybius ciphers, and the last two are a combination of the two. You are told what the message is about—it could be a name, a phrase, a title or a quotation. You are given three clues to help you out.

As a tip, start by considering which words are more likely to occur in certain positions in sentences and titles (for example, sentences frequently start with *the*). Also look for linguistic patterns. This will give you a hint as to what a word might be: for instance, single letters stand for either *I* or *a,* and three-letter sequences usually stand for high-frequency words such as *the, are* and *you,* for instance. One more thing before you start. As you know, the alphabet ends at *Z,* but the substitution pattern can go beyond it. For instance, if a letter such as *Y* occurs in the hidden message and you discover that the substitution pattern is to replace it with, say, the fourth letter after it in the alphabetic sequence, then you simply continue counting after *Z.* The sequence in question would be: *Z* (first letter after *Y*), *A* (second letter after *Y,* starting from the beginning of the alphabet), *B* (third letter after it), *C* (fourth letter after it). Thus, *C* is the substitute for *Y.*

81. Edgar Allan Poe introduced cryptography as part of a detective story plot. He used it for the first time in an 1843 story, whose title has been encoded below. Can you figure the title out?

V J G   I Q N F   D W I

_ _ _   _ _ _ _   _ _ _

CLUES

1. The vowels in the title are *E, O* and *U.*
2. One of the words in the title is a synonym for *insect.*
3. Another word refers to a precious metal.

82. The following Caesar cipher hides a common figurative English expression.

P M Z M R K   L M K L

– – – – –   – – – –

S J J   X L I   L S K

– – –   – – –   – – –

CLUES

1. The saying has the vowels, *E, I* and *O.*
2. Two of the words end in *G.*
3. A synonym for the entire expression could be *luxurious lifestyle.*

83. The following Caesar cipher hides a common saying.

R D D H M F   H R

– – – – – –   – –

A D K H D U H M F

– – – – – – – – –

CLUES

1. The expression contains only two vowels, *E* and *I.*
2. The expression is a rhyming one.
3. One of the words in it refers to one of the senses.

84. The following Caesar cipher encodes a famous quotation by President John F. Kennedy. Note that there is an em dash (—) in the cipher. There is a twist to this puzzle, as you will read in the clues.

D V N   Q R W   Z K D W

_ _ _   _ _ _   _ _ _ _

B R X U   C R X Q W U B   C D Q

_ _ _ _   _ _ _ _ _ _ _   _ _ _

G R   I R U   B R X — D V N

_ _   _ _ _   _ _ _ — _ _ _

Z K D W   B R X   C D Q   G R

_ _ _ _   _ _ _   _ _ _   _ _

I R U   B R X U   C R X Q W U B.

_ _ _   _ _ _ _   _ _ _ _ _ _ _.

CLUES

1. The quotation comes from JFK's inaugural address on January 20, 1961.
2. It actually starts off with "My fellow Americans" (which is not included in the cipher).
3. This cipher also contains a small twist. One of the consonants in the quotation has not been substituted; it is preserved in all the locations in which it occurs. This little twist increases the difficulty level considerably.

85. Below is your first, and easiest, Polybius cipher. It conceals the name of a famous activist and writer.

7   5 18 13 1 9 14 5   7 18 5 5 18

— — — — — — — —   — — — — —

CLUES

1. There are three vowels in the name, *A, E* and *I.*
2. The writer as a well-known Australian feminist.
3. Her most important work is *The Female Eunuch* of 1970.

86. This next Polybius cipher conceals a common expression.

40 16 10   8 2 50   2 12 40 10 36

— — —   — — —   — — — — —

40 30 26 30 36 36 30 46

— — — — — — — —

CLUES

1. The expression refers to a time period.
2. There are three vowels in the expression, *A, E* and *O.*
3. In this case, only a certain type of digit is used. This increases the difficulty level somewhat. But it's not that hard to figure out, actually. Just look at the type of digits used carefully. For example, are the digits odd or even?

V
E
R
B
A
L

K
N
O
W
•
H
O
W

P
U
Z
Z
L
E
S

87. The Polybius cipher below conceals a quotation by the American writer Maya Angelou, taken from the 1989 book *Conversations with Maya Angelou*.

23 17 11 9   23 29 43 9 37   39 15 9

_ _ _ _   _ _ _ _ _   _ _ _

23 17 43 9 35   29 11   17 39.

_ _ _ _ _   _ _   _ _.

CLUES

1. The quotation is a philosophical one about life.
2. There is no *A* or *U* in the quotation.
3. As in the previous puzzle, only a certain type of digit is used (even or odd).

88. The following Polybius cipher hides the title of a classic American book.

31 11 4   2 5 33 4 21 31 10 27 4 29

_ _ _   _ _ _ _ _ _ _ _ _ _

8 7   11 10 3 15 17 4 1 4 27 27 39

_ _   _ _ _ _ _ _ _ _ _ _ _

7 6 21 21

_ _ _ _

CLUES

1. The book was published in 1884.
2. It was written by a famous American writer and humorist.
3. A certain type of digit (even or odd) is used with a certain set of letters (either the vowels or the consonants), and a second type of digit is used with the other set of letters.

89. This puzzle is a "mixed" one consisting of both letter and digit substitutes. It conceals a quotation by the Swiss writer Hermann Hesse (1877–1962).

3 1 O H 4 P F 4 H

_ _ _ _ _ _ _ _ _

O 5 U 3 E D 2 E 1 5 U 2

_ _ _ _ _ _ _ _ _ _ _

3 V 3 U U 4 1 O 4 T 1 N

_ _ _ _ _ _ _ _ _ _ _ _

CLUES

1. The quotation is from his novel *Demian*.
2. Note that the digits replace all the vowels. So, when you see a vowel in the cipher it replaces a consonant, not another vowel.
3. The saying is about one of the arts. Note: The quotation in the puzzle is missing the phrase *I think* of the original.

BRAIN FACT #9

In the late nineteenth century, scientists observed that damage to particular parts of the brain caused the same pattern of language disabilities in people. Damage to the left frontal lobe in Broca's area destroyed the ability to speak. Damage to the left temporal lobe in Wernicke's area caused difficulty understanding language. Thus, early on, scientists became aware of the role of language centers in controlling mental tasks, activities and faculties.

90. This last cryptogram is also a mixed one. It conceals a well-known proverb.

16 Q   16 C 9 8   18 K 16 6 Q W 16

— —   — — — —   — — — — — — —

16 6 K 11 8 K 11 5   K 15   16 Q

— — — — — — — —   — —   — —

15 6 Q Q 16   18 K 16 6 Q W 16

— — — — —   — — — — — — —

C K 10 K 11 5.

— — — — — —.

CLUES

1. It is an eighteenth century English proverb.
2. It equates communication with shooting.
3. One word, a preposition, is repeated twice. Look for a substitution pattern that is similar to the one used for puzzle 89, but obviously not exactly the same.

THINK-OF-A-WORD PUZZLES

This last set of puzzles will really test your verbal know-how. The genre is actually quite uncomplicated, but getting the answer is challenging. You are first asked to think of a word made up of a specific number of letters, then told to remove one of the letters to produce a second word, and finally to add a letter to produce a third word. Here's an example:

Think of a four-letter word meaning "not moving quickly," remove the first letter to get a word meaning the opposite of "high," then add one letter at the front to produce a word that describes the way water moves.

The first word is *slow*. Removing the first letter produces *low*. Adding the letter *f* at the front produces *flow*.

91. Think of a four-letter word referring to a catching device, remove the first letter and you will get a word referring to a popular contemporary music style, then add a letter after the first one to produce a word meaning "harvest" or "gather."

92. Think of a five-letter word referring to an edible juicy berry, remove the second letter and you will get a word meaning "to stare wide-mouthed," then remove the last letter and you will get a word that is part of the expression "generation ___."

93. Think of a five-letter word referring to a list of candidates in an election, remove the first letter to get a word meaning "tardy," then add a letter at the front and you will get a word referring to a kind of dish.

94. Think of a two-letter verb referring to existence, add a letter at the end to get a word that refers to something you do when you play poker, then add a letter just before the last one to produce a basic musical term.

95. Think of a three-letter word referring to a color, add a letter just before the last one and you will get a word referring to something you do with books, then add a letter at the front to get a word referring to something you eat.

96. Think of a five-letter word referring to a dimensional concept, remove the final letter and you will get a kind of diagram or list, then add a letter at the end to get something you will find in nature.

97. Think of a five-letter word meaning "fault," remove the first letter and you will get a word referring to someone who is either disabled or weak, then add a letter at the front to produce a word that is connected with fire.

98. To increase the difficulty level, you will not be told where the letters are to be removed or added. So, think of a three-letter word meaning "perceive," add another letter and you will get a word referring to something that gives life, then add one more letter and you will get a word referring to an equine concept.

99. Think of a five-letter word referring to a common household object, remove a letter from it and you will get a word referring to something on your body, then remove one more letter and you will get a word referring to something you need to survive.

100. Think of a five-letter word meaning "precipitous," remove one letter and you will get a word meaning "to leak," then remove one more letter and you will get a verb referring to one of the senses.

3
TRIVIA PUZZLES

The human tendency to regard little things as important
has produced very many great things.

G. C. LICHTENBERG (1742–99)

N THE EARLY 1980s, a game called *Trivial Pursuit* came onto the market to revive the board-game industry. Developed by two Canadians, the game produced sales of over $777 million in 1984 alone. Obviously, trivia is not seen as trivial by millions of people.

The puzzles in this chapter will test your knowledge of celebrities, composers, movies and cities, but not as in the board game, through questions and answers. It will do so with puzzles of various kinds, including word searches, cryptograms and jumbled words.

The puzzles are designed to engage both the memory and verbal parts of the brain in a holistic fashion. I searched relevant websites to get a sense of the kind of research being conducted on the relation between knowledge-based puzzles and general brain functioning. The claims made are perhaps a bit too self-serving, as the more scientific studies indicate. But, cumulatively, they are telling us something that is music to my ears—puzzles are good for brain functioning. The scientific reason for this is, seemingly, the fact that the brain is a life-long learning organ that continues to function through diverse and rich sensory, emotional and intellectual experiences.

There's one more interesting and relevant fact to know before trying your hand at the puzzles. Research conducted on rats has shown enhanced neuronal growth in young and aging rats raised in complex environments—that is, rats projected into situations involving puzzle-solving activities. If the same results apply to humans, then the implications are obvious, aren't they?

CELEBRITY NAMES

In this first set of trivia puzzles, you have to find the name of a celebrity by means of clues that relate to features in how his or her name is spelled, what it may mean (in some cases), and what things he or she may have done in the world of show business.

Let's do a model puzzle together.

Late British-born American entertainer.

CLUES

1. There are three letters in his first name and four in his last.
2. His first name is also a word that means "to move up and down."
3. His last name is also a word referring to a wish or desire.
4. He costarred with Bing Crosby in comedy films and often performed for soldiers overseas.

The answer is *Bob Hope*. That's all there is to it. Have fun!

101. Late versatile American motion-picture actor.

CLUES

1. There are four letters in his first name and six in his last.
2. His roles ranged from amiable young men to grumpy old ones.
3. If you took away one letter from his last name, you would get a word referring to a fruit.
4. He won the Academy Award for Best Actor for *Save the Tiger* (1973) and also directed the film *Kotch* (1971).

102. Late American music legend.

CLUES

1. There are five letters in his first name and seven in his last.
2. Rock and roll was his primary claim to fame.
3. Among his first great hits was *Heartbreak Hotel* (1956).
4. After serving in the U.S. Army he appeared in many musical films.

103. American talk show superstar.

CLUES

1. There are five letters in her first name and seven in her last.
2. By modifying her first name a little, you will get a word referring to a staged musical genre.
3. Her motion-picture roles include *The Color Purple* (1985).
4. She also produced and costarred in the television miniseries *The Women of Brewster Place* (1989).

104. American actress, daughter of a famous movie actor. For this and the next four puzzles you are given just three clues.

CLUES

1. There are eight letters in her first name and five in her last.
2. Her last name is also a French word meaning "happy" or "nice."
3. She won the Oscar for Best Supporting Actress for the 1999 movie *Girl, Interrupted*.

105. Late Hollywood icon.

CLUES

1. There are seven letters in her first name and six in her last.
2. She is noted for her sexy roles in movies such as *All About Eve* (1950) and *The Seven-Year Itch* (1955).
3. She married the great baseball player Joe DiMaggio in 1954.

106. American actor born in Syracuse, New York.

CLUES

1. There are three letters in his first name and six in his last.
2. His last name is also a word meaning "to sail about."
3. *Top Gun* (1986) is among the films in which he has starred.

107. American motion-picture actor born in Shawnee, Oklahoma.

CLUES

1. There are four letters in his first name and four in his last.
2. Take away one letter from his last name and you will get a word referring to a large hole in the ground.
3. He costarred in the movie *Seven* (1995).

108. Pop culture celebrity who comes from a rich and famous family.

CLUES

1. There are five letters in her first name and six in her last.
2. Her first name is also the name of a city.
3. Her last name refers to a hotel chain and, of course, the family into which she was born.

109. Famous Italian actress. For this and the next puzzle you are given only two clues.

CLUES

1. Her first name is also a word that originally meant "wisdom."
2. She often starred opposite Marcello Mastroianni in movies such as *Marriage, Italian Style* (1964).

110. African-American motion-picture star.

CLUES

1. His surname can be separated into two words meaning someone who has been liberated.
2. He starred in the movie *Seven* (1995).

COMPOSER CRYPTOGRAMS

Remember cryptography from the previous chapter? Well, here is a version of the Polybius genre. If you have forgotten how to solve this particular kind of puzzle, go back and review it.

As in a typical Polybius cipher, a specific number will correspond to a specific letter. But in this case that correspondence is carried over to all the puzzles. For example, if you establish that *H* is replaced by 1 in the first puzzle, then you can go ahead and substitute *H* for each occurrence of the digit 1 in the remaining puzzles. All cryptograms conceal the names of famous composers. For instance, in the first one, you are given these clues: 3 = *D* and 13 = *H*. Insert these substitutes for those numbers in all the remaining puzzles right away. Look at the clues in the other puzzles (if there are any) and do the same thing right away. You may have to go back and forth among puzzles. Note that the numbers substituting the letters are below the slot where the letters are supposed to be. Also, unlike the puzzles in the previous chapter, there really is no pattern here in assigning numbers to letters, just consistency.

Incidentally, it may seem that I have given you too few clues. That may well be, but there are still enough for you to complete all the puzzles, together with a little bit of trial and error and background knowledge. I will, however, tell you that the letters *Q* and *X* do not occur.

111. One of the greatest composers of classical music of all time.

```
_   _   D   _   _   _        _   _   _ .
1   2   3   4   5   6        7   8   9

_   _   _   _   H   _   _   _   _
10  11  11  12  13  14  7   11  9
```

112. Another of the greatest composers of classical music of all time.

_ _ _ _ _ _ _   _ _ _ _ _ _ _
4 14 1 15 6 8 9 6   8 16 8 3 11 2 17

_ _ _ _ _ _
16 14 18 8 19 12

113. Yet another of the greatest composers of all time.

_ _ _ _ _ _   _ _ _ _ _ _ _ _ _
20 14 13 8 9 9   17 11 10 8 17 12 5 8 9

_ _ _ _
10 8 21 13

114. Another great composer, known especially for his ballets.

_ _ _ _ _   _ _ _ _ _
22 11 12 11 19   5 1 5 21 13

_ _ _ _ _ K _ _ _ _ _
12 21 13 8 5 23 14 7 17 23 24

72

115. American composer who wrote the music for musicals and motion pictures.

— — — — — —   — — — —
20 11 19 14 16 11   23 11 19 9

116. American composer and songwriter known for his motion picture and television scores.

— — — — Y   — — — — — — —
13 11 9 19 24   16 8 9 21 5 9 5

117. Composer, singer, dancer and actress known generally by her first name only.

— — — — — — —   — — — — — —
16 8 3 14 9 9 8   1 14 2 5 17 11

— — — — — — —
21 5 21 21 14 9 11

118. Great American composer who fused jazz with classical style.

— — — — — —   — — — — — — — —
6 11 14 19 6 11   6 11 19 17 13 4 5 9

119. Popular American country- and pop-music composer and singer.

— — — — — —   — — — — — —
4 5 1 1 5 11   9 11 1 17 14 9

120. British composer of theatrical music.

— — — — — —   — — — — —

8 9 3 19 11 4   1 1 14 24 3

— — — — — —

4 11 10 10 11 19

MOVIE TRIVIA MAZES

Remember the phrase searches in the previous chapter? Here's a variant of that puzzle, which can be called simply a trivia maze. In this case the puzzle could contain the name of a Hollywood director, the name of a movie, and so on. The name starts somewhere on one side and exits at another, just like in a maze. The letters go straight, up, down and of course turn logically. Below are two examples of how the names of two directors have been embedded in the maze of letters.

```
    F  R  A  N  D  C  A  S
    J  B  J  U  T  P  R  S
 →  J  O  H  N  S  Q  E  M
    A  L  D  H  S  C  D  C
    V  X  F  U  M  M  G  H
    A  V  B  S  R  T  B  A
    J  U  Y  T  O  P  M  P
    E  B  O  O  M  I  S  E
    C  D  A  N  A  M  E  A
             ↓
```

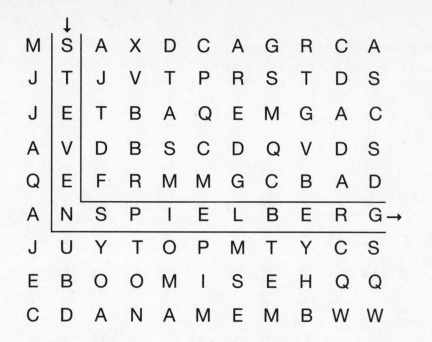

As you can see, the names are *John Huston* and *Steven Spielberg*. Note that you will have to find the entry point to the maze and then follow the letters through to one of the other sides, which is the exit point. The names can go in any direction except diagonally, including left-right, right-left, up-down and down-up. Also, note that the maze structure will vary in size and that there is no space between words.

Here's a tip. The name will start at one of the edge letters on one of the four sides. Once you locate the first name, it is easy to go through the rest of the maze.

BRAIN FACT #12

Scientists have found evidence that the brains of men and women differ in some ways. The corpus callosum—the thick band of nerve fibers connecting the cerebral hemispheres—is larger in women. The studies have found that men generally use only their left cerebral hemisphere for processing language, but women use both. This confirms something that my students and I also discovered. We gave 100 adult men and women puzzles of all kinds to solve and found that women did significantly better. This does not mean that men are necessarily worse off in puzzle-solving. Most of these differences likely have a cultural genesis, since each culture conditions the sexes to develop in specific ways according to gender roles. And fulfilling these roles might very well change brain structure.

121. American filmmaker who won an Academy Award for *The Godfather, Part II* (1974). Two of the words in the name (consisting of three words) can be read in a horizontal fashion.

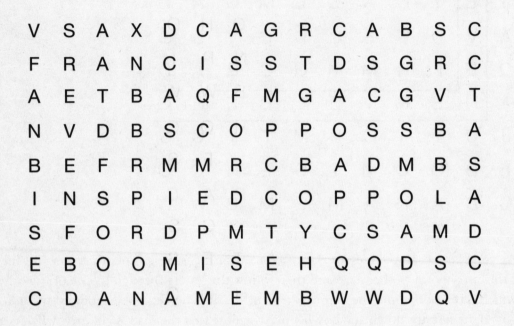

```
V  S  A  X  D  C  A  G  R  C  A  B  S  C
F  R  A  N  C  I  S  S  T  D  S  G  R  C
A  E  T  B  A  Q  F  M  G  A  C  G  V  T
N  V  D  B  S  C  O  P  P  O  S  S  B  A
B  E  F  R  M  M  R  C  B  A  D  M  B  S
I  N  S  P  I  E  D  C  O  P  P  O  L  A
S  F  O  R  D  P  M  T  Y  C  S  A  M  D
E  B  O  O  M  I  S  E  H  Q  Q  D  S  C
C  D  A  N  A  M  E  M  B  W  W  D  Q  V
```

122. American actor, producer, director and writer, born in Kenosha, Wisconsin, who is best known for directing and starring in the ground-breaking motion picture *Citizen Kane* (1941).

```
G V D S O B E H Q H O
A N S P R N L B N R I
O D I S S M Q Q B W W
E B O O O K S E H Q Q
F T J R N W E L L E S
J E T S O Q E M P A C
R U Y M O P M T Y C S
K S A N N W E L T E S
Z E F R M I S E H Q Q
```

123. Two-word phrase that is sometimes used to characterize Hollywood. Keep in mind that the words can be read in any direction (left-right, right-to-left, up-down, down-up). One of the two words is read in a bottom-up direction.

```
A  V  D  B  S  C  D  Q  V  D  S
A  N  S  P  I  E  L  B  E  R  G
C  D  A  N  A  M  E  M  B  W  W
E  B  O  O  M  L  L  T  O  W  N
J  T  J  V  T  P  E  S  T  D  S
J  E  T  B  A  Q  S  M  G  A  C
J  U  Y  T  O  P  N  T  Y  C  S
M  S  A  X  D  C  I  G  R  C  A
Q  E  F  R  M  M  T  C  B  A  D
```

124. These are presented annually for outstanding achievements in filmmaking. Winners receive a gold-plated statue commonly called an Oscar.

```
J  T  O  V  T  P  S  S  T  D  S  S
J  E  J  S  O  P  D  D  G  A  C  D  M
A  V  D  B  S  C  R  F  Z  D  B  C  D
Q  E  F  R  W  M  A  A  B  A  D  B  N
A  N  S  P  I  E  W  W  S  Z  G  J  K
J  C  K  A  D  N  A  A  Y  C  S  L  B
A  C  A  D  E  M  Y  E  H  Q  Q  M  D
D  D  A  N  A  M  E  M  B  W  M  S  C
W  S  B  X  D  Z  A  G  R  C  A  C  T
```

125. Cecil B. DeMille's religious blockbuster of 1923, remade in 1956.

```
T H E X D C A G R C C S O P H
H T T V T P R S T D S C H A D
R T E B A Q E M G A C H W L S
A V N C O M M A N D M E N T S
Q E F R M M G C B A D A W Y T
A N S P I E L B E R G D I D Y
J U Y T O P M T Y C S S C I U
E B O O M I S E H Q Q A K A O
D D A N A M E M B W A R I O M
```

126. British director best known for his suspense films, such as *Psycho* (1960). Recall that the letters can be read in any direction (except diagonally).

```
C S T P I E L P R C A
J T A V T P R S T D S
J F S Y T D E R F L A
A V M B S H D Q V D S
Q P L R M I E B F L A
A T O P L T L V R R S
J E Y T O C M T Y C S
E V O O M H S E H Q Q
D D A N A C E M B W S
F R M M G O F R M M G
Q Q A K A C Q Q A K A
S O P H I K C H A D W
```

127. Italian filmmaker whose works, such as *La Dolce Vita* (1960) and *Amarcord* (1973), mingle social satire with elements of fantasy.

```
N V A W F L A G R L J
J T J V T P R V T D V
F E D E R I C O G A L
A V D B V L D F V D V
Q G F R L L G E B A D
A N V P I G L L G R F
J U Y T O P L L Y L V
G B O O L L S I H Q F
L D A N A C F N B L L
M M G O F P N I N O P
```

128. American actress and performer best remembered for her role as Dorothy in *The Wizard of Oz* (1939).

```
C  S  A  U  J  T  O  J  J  C  A
J  U  D  Y  T  P  R  S  T  D  S
A  E  T  G  A  Q  E  M  C  A  C
S  V  D  A  S  C  D  Q  T  D  J
M  E  F  R  M  C  D  C  A  A  D
A  N  S  L  I  R  L  B  S  R  G
J  I  E  A  O  P  M  T  M  C  S
E  B  O  N  M  T  S  E  H  Q  J
C  D  A  D  A  M  E  J  B  J  W
```

129. Famous 1977 Steven Spielberg movie.

```
C S A M C D Q M J C G I
L P J V T P R S Y D S P
O E T B A Q E S D A C Q
S R D B S V D Q F D S C
E E N C O U N T E R S C
A N S P I E L R Y R O R
J U Y T O Y L E H T F P
E B O O S I S T H Q Q L
C D D C M C D H C W K A
D A S C D D F I P O N N
B O N M T S M R D R S S
N M T S E D R D K I N D
```

130. British stage and motion-picture actress, known for her portrayals of strong-willed and independent women.

```
V V V A X D C A V R C
J M A J V T P R M T D
J C N Y B A Q E M G A
A V E D B M C D Q V D
V D S F R M M G C B A
A G S M P I E L K E J
J M A R E D G R A V E
E Q B O O M I M E H Q
V W D A N A M E S B V
```

BRAIN FACT #13

The Mayo Clinic's website lists ten steps that anyone can follow in order to keep the brain fit. The first, and most crucial, one is to "Exercise Your Mind." The website recommends crossword puzzles and reading to keep the brain active. However, my own view is that all kinds of puzzles will do the trick. All puzzle-based activities can keep the mind invigorated because they involve a huge dose of imagination, memory, strategy-formulation, pattern recognition and associative thinking—all skills that are perfect for getting your brain going.

This next type of puzzle will test both your knowledge of cities and sharpen your verbal eye. Ignoring spaces, punctuation and so on, the letters making up the city's name is hidden in the given sentence. For example, what city is hidden in the following sentence?

Even I celebrate Carnival when I am in that city.

The city is Venice, as you can see.

E*ven I ce*lebrate Carnival when I am in that city.
ven + I + ce = Venice

Note that you will have to join up the letters, add the appropriate capital letter, and make other necessary changes. That's all there is to it. Get ready to hone your word skills.

131. If par is a criterion, then this French city is above par for beauty, history and importance, alongside many other great cities of the world.

132. As a capital city and hub of secret government information, it is not unusual to find much "laundering" there of the information that is made public, as if washing tons of bad information out of government documents, so to speak, could ever keep the truth from coming out in the end.

133. Francis, my brother, does not like Parmesan; Francis could eat any other cheese, however, especially in his favorite delicatessen in the West Coast city, by the bay, where he lives.

> ## BRAIN FACT #14
>
> Intriguing research indicates that language-based puzzles are the equivalent of anti-aging drugs. They are the perfect, and safe, antidotes to such age-related conditions as Alzheimer's and dementia. They also seem to help in the recovery of mental functions after strokes and various head injuries. Perhaps the reason for this is that they stimulate damaged areas of the brain and activate the recovery of their functions, at least to some degree.

134. If you are new, have no fear; you will still be welcomed by the students of the friendly and distinguished Ivy League university located in this city.

135. After both wars, awful things happened to many cities, including this Eastern European capital city.

136. No matter how you interpret or I analyze our current situation, we cannot travel to this Southern Hemisphere city, which is the administrative capital of the country.

137. If you're often mad, rid yourself of all your frustrations by visiting this beautiful Spanish city.

138. If you feel a little tired from jet lag, first take a bath, ensuring that you will feel better; and then go out to see the historical delights of this great ancient city.

139. In a beautiful garden, verdant in the summer but snow-covered in the winter, I met the love of my life in this west central U.S. city.

140. In this West German city, women wore beautiful bonnets on Sunday strolls in the eighteenth century.

POP CULTURE JUMBLES

Jumbles are words whose letters have been scrambled. For example, the letters of the word *believe* can be scrambled to produce the jumble *ebilvee*. So in this last trivia puzzle exercise you are given a statement about a pop culture celebrity, event or the like that contains the name of that celebrity, event, etc. in a scrambled form. Here's an example:

drfe asairet was an American actor and dancer noted for his partnership with Ginger Rogers in several musical films.

Unscrambling, we get *Fred Astaire*. You will have to adjust the case of the jumbles accordingly to uppercase if need be.

141. In 1958 over 100 million Americans bought the *lhua oohp* for play and for exercise.

142. *teh labir whtic pjrecot,* a 1999 horror movie filmed in real time, became a pop culture phenomenon.

143. The American sitcom *lal ni het yfailm,* which debuted in 1971 on CBS, was created by Norman Lear.

144. Incredibly, the *tpe ckor* became one of the top ten crazes in 1975, according to *Time Magazine.* The fad was conceived by California ad executive Gary Dahl.

145. The *dseel,* introduced in 1957, was a colossal failure, becoming part of pop culture lore. Today, in fact, it has become a highly collectible item among enthusiasts.

146. *rismte de* was an American sitcom that debuted in 1961 on CBS. Its star was a talking horse.

147. *rafnk sniarta* became famous for his mellifluous voice, rising to stardom already in the 1940s. Among his best-loved hit songs is "Chicago."

148. The 1990 science fiction blockbuster movie *sujrcasi apkr* was based on a novel by Michael Crichton.

149. In 1938 a radio docudrama, directed and narrated by Orson Welles, created panic in parts of the United States. The program was based on the novel *eht raw fo het dowrls.*

150. These inexpensive fiction magazines, which were first published in 1896, were called *pplu ciftnio* because they were printed on cheap paper.

> ## BRAIN FACT #15
>
> There are two main forms of memory that are activated by solving language-based trivia puzzles. They are called semantic and episodic memory by psychologists. The former refers to the recall of words. How many times have you forgotten or cannot drum up the right word, or *le mot juste* as the French term it? That forgetfulness is a gap in semantic memory. Episodic memory refers to recollection of past incidents. Forgetting what happened at your wedding, for example, is a symptom of episodic memory loss.

4
VERBAL LOGIC PUZZLES

Language is using us to talk. We think we're using the language,
but language is doing the thinking, we're its slavish agents.

HARRY MATHEWS (B. 1930)

IT IS INTERESTING AND relevant to note that the word *logic* comes from the Greek word *logos,* where it meant both "reasoning" and "word." The Greeks were aware of the relation between logic and language, and they coined the perfect term for it. So in a sense the term *verbal logic* is an oxymoron. If it is verbal, it is logical. It can be deceptive and conceal the truth, of course, but we will be duped by the deception only if it is logical. In this chapter you will be confronted with puzzles testing your verbal logic in a holistic fashion.

In the previous chapters I have been harping on a singular point, namely that puzzle-solving is good for the brain and especially for the aging brain. A large part of this comes from my own anecdotal experiences. So it is always encouraging to find scientific studies corroborating my experiences. For example, a 2003 study in *The New England Journal of Medicine* showed that keeping one's brain active may protect against future memory loss. The study adds to the scientific evidence that suggests mentally challenging activities may offer protection against Alzheimer's disease and dementia. And this is why Alzheimer's groups endorse puzzles of all kinds. The study indicated that any mentally challenging activity might spur the brain to establish new connections or even to grow new brain cells. This extra brainpower may help compensate for brain cells lost to the aging process.

LETTER LOGIC

This first set of ten puzzles will put your verbal logic skills to work and give the language centers of your brain some good exercise. You are asked to change a letter in each pair of words to make new ones (proper names and archaic words are excluded). Put the letter in the middle parentheses. The letters (read downward) will then form a word. So, the letter chosen must both make a pair of new words and fit in the middle as part of a third word, as well.

Let's do one puzzle together.

ANT   (__) CAP

TOP   (__) CAT

MAKE (__) PAT

Start with the top pair. Ask yourself, Which letter can I use to make two new words from *ant* and *cap*? That letter is *r*. Replacing the *n* of *ant* with *r* produces *art* and replacing the *p* of *cap* with the same letter produces *car*. Put this letter in the middle.

ART   (R) CAR *(New words)*

TOP   (__) CAT

MAKE (__) PAT

Now, consider the middle pair. By replacing the *p* in *top* and the *c* in *cat* with *e*, we will produce *toe* and *eat*. Put this letter in the middle.

ART   (R) CAR

TOE   (E) EAT *(New words)*

MAKE (__) PAT

Finally, if we change the *k* in *make* and the *t* in *pat* to *d*, we get *made* and *pad*. The middle word is, therefore, *red*.

ART   (R) CAR

TOE   (E) EAT

MADE (D) PAD *(New words)*

151. Let's start off nice and easy with a three-pair puzzle.

GLUE   (__)   AUNT

TRIP   (__)   POD

BALL   (__)   CHAP

152. Here's another three-pair puzzle.

BUDGE   (__)   FADE

TRICK   (__)   HINT

TREAT   (__)   FLINT

153. Here's one more three-pair puzzle.

SPA   (__)   WHO

PLAY   (__)   TEN

MOCK   (__)   TRYST

154. Now, let's turn up the difficulty level a bit, with a four-pair puzzle.

BEAT   (__)   GRAFT

OTHER   (__)   FLOCK

LAND   (__)   MOAN

LOVE   (__)   CRY

155. Here's another four-pair puzzle.

SPOON   (__)   GROW

TRY   (__)   CHIP

LIKE   (__)   NERVE

BAND   (__)   WHAT

156. Here's the last of the four-pair versions.

CHAR   (__)   MIST

FLAIL   (__)   SPATE

HOE   (__)   TRAMP

WALL   (__)   SWEAT

157. The next puzzle is a five-pair version.

STEER   (__)   MALTED

VEST   (__)   END

CLAN   (__)   ACE

SKY   (__)   FLY

MAJOR   (__)   HELL

158. Here's another five-pair version.

BREW   (__)   SOAK

RUMOR   (__)   WREN

QUICK   (__)   ROVE

WEAK   (__)   BLUE

SAFE   (__)   STORK

159. Here's one more five-pair puzzle.

CLOUD   (__)   OUR

CHAIN   (__)   SCAM

ONION   (__)   TRICK

FUME   (__)   LORRY

BEG   (__)   DULY

160. For the last puzzle in this genre, try your hand at a six-pair version.

TOE   (__) COULD

LIVELY (__) EVER

SPEAK (__) FOR

TWEET (__) ENSURE

TEA   (__) GAL

FEIGN (__) ENGAGE

BRAIN FACT #16

I once had a student who simply hated doing puzzles of any kind. She was a language major who took one of my courses. In that course I used crosswords, acrostics and other language-based puzzles as exercise material. She refused to do them, at least so she said. Secretly, it would emerge she did them outside the classroom. At the end of the course she came up to me and thanked me. "For what?" I asked. "For the puzzles. I actually understood them and was able to practice the course material and unlock my fear of problems." Need I say more?

ACROSTICS

Puzzles in which you form hidden words from the letters of other words laid out in a certain way are called acrostics (from the Greek words *akron*, meaning "head" and *stikhos*, meaning "row, line of verse"). It is believed that acrostics became popular in the nineteenth century, after Queen Victoria made ingenious acrostics of her own.

Doing acrostics is fairly easy, fun and quite beneficial cognitively. Let's look at a completed puzzle together. You are given eight clues corresponding to the numbers in the rows of the puzzle layout. Each answer is inserted in the appropriate row. The hidden word appears in the highlighted column. That word is *maternal*. Notice as well that the clues also refer in some way (directly or indirectly) to the word.

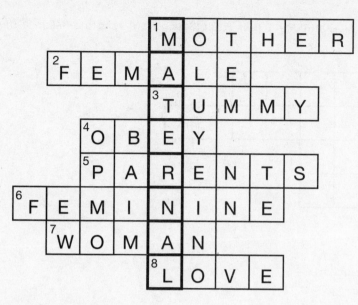

CLUES

1. The opposite of father
2. The opposite of male
3. Word used by children to refer to the stomach (especially the stomach of a pregnant mother)
4. What children should do when their mother gives them good advice
5. Your mother is one of your two ____
6. As a woman, your mother is said to have these qualities
7. The opposite of man
8. One can always count on a mother feeling this for her children

All the acrostics in this section will be of the same type. Part crossword, part word search, this genre of puzzle will give your verbal logic a good workout.

161. Let's start off with an acrostic containing a four-letter hidden word, referring to a measure.

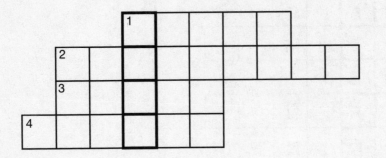

CLUES

1. Plentiful, more than enough
2. Boundary enclosing an area
3. Area of open land
4. Figure made up of four equal sides meeting at right angles

162. Now try your hand at this acrostic, containing a five-letter word referring to a common habitation structure.

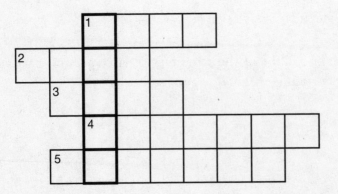

CLUES

1. It's where the heart is, as the saying goes
2. You go through it to enter a building or room
3. Electrical safety device
4. You can put books on them
5. One normally sleeps there

163. This next acrostic contains a six-letter word referring to an activity that we should all probably engage in.

CLUES

1. Winter sport
2. Regular international sports event that originated in ancient Greece
3. Sport whose season ends with the Super Bowl
4. Water sport involving boats and crew members
5. Sport played by Martina Navratilova and John McEnroe
6. Some would say that Pelé was the greatest player of this sport

164. Here's another acrostic containing a six-letter word which, this time, refers to a color.

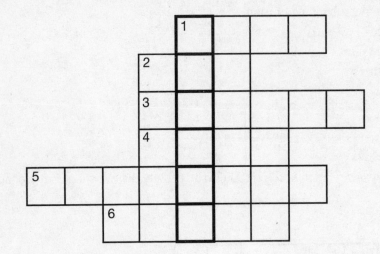

CLUES

1. Part of an egg
2. The color of embarrassment
3. Word sometimes used to describe golden or pale blond hair
4. Color of the sky
5. Yellow flower also called Narcissus
6. Orange-brown or yellowish-brown color

165. Now try your hand at this acrostic containing a seven-letter hidden word referring to a musician.

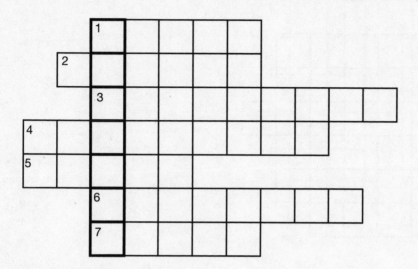

CLUES

1. Instrument with a keyboard
2. Stringed instrument
3. Portable instrument with bellows operated by the player
4. The one who leads an orchestra
5. Type of dance music, derived from jazz, popular in the 1930s and 1940s
6. Major classical work for orchestra
7. Passionate dance music, originating in Argentina

166. Here's an acrostic containing a seven-letter word referring to an animal.

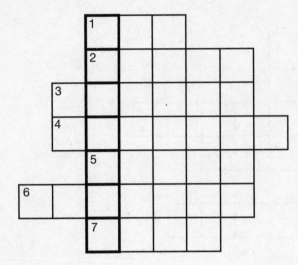

CLUES

1. Common household pet
2. Scavenger resembling a dog, known especially for its laughing cry
3. Category of mammals that includes lions and tigers
4. Longhaired cat named after the former name of Iran
5. Large member of the cat family
6. Shorthaired cat originating and named after Thailand's onetime name
7. What most breeds of cat have

167. Now try your hand at an acrostic containing an eight-letter word referring to human anatomy.

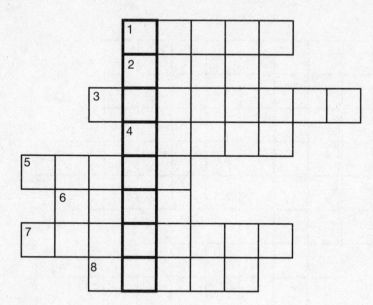

CLUES

1. It is between the neck and the abdomen
2. You need them to walk
3. Lower jaw
4. Blood runs through them
5. The thinking organ
6. It joins the shoulders to the head
7. Fleshy lower parts of the ears
8. You need them to masticate food

168. This hidden eight-letter word refers to an academic subject studied usually in upper high school or early college.

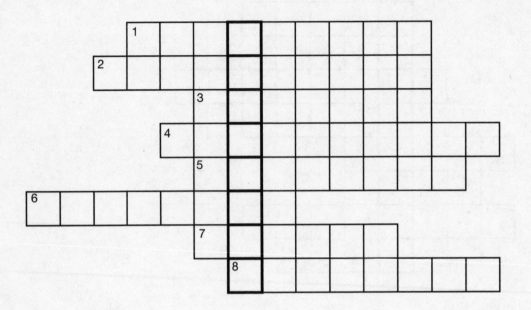

CLUES

1. Work out, compute
2. Ancient Greek mathematician famous for his theorem about triangles that every student has to master
3. It has often been called arithmetic with symbols
4. Ancient Greek mathematician and scientist who is said to have shouted "Eureka" while running naked in the streets
5. The opposite of add
6. Three-sided figure
7. Famous Greek mathematician who wrote *The Elements*
8. In mathematics, an ordered set, as for example, 2, 4, 6, 8, 10, ...

169. This hidden nine-letter word refers to a science.

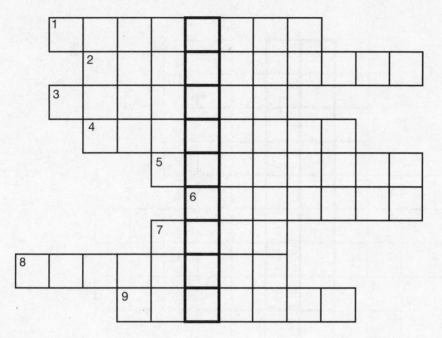

CLUES

1. Smallest particle making up a compound
2. Application of science for practical reasons
3. Part of an atom containing almost all of the mass
4. Relating to chemistry
5. Great scientist known especially for his theory of relativity
6. What physics is
7. Smallest unit of an element
8. Basic unit of electricity
9. The science of matter and energy

170. Finally, try your hand at this acrostic hiding a ten-letter word referring to an academic discipline.

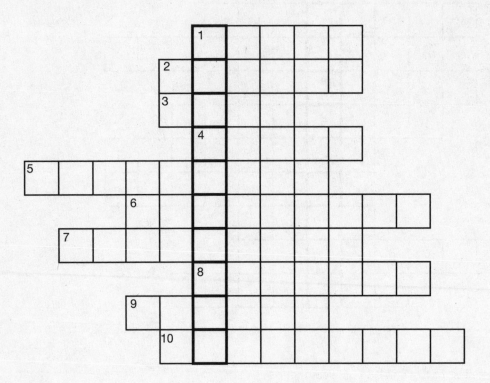

CLUES

1. Greek philosopher, follower of Socrates, who wrote *The Republic*
2. Hypothesis about something
3. What philosophers and psychologists study
4. Study of the principles of reasoning
5. Greek philosopher, pupil of Plato, who profoundly influenced Western thought
6. Philosopher famous for having said *Cogito ergo sum* ("I think; therefore, I am")
7. Thinking logically and on the basis of arguments
8. A contradictory statement that may nonetheless be true
9. Principles of human conduct
10. Spiritual apprehension of inaccessible knowledge or wisdom

I have mentioned the dreaded A word already several times. What is Alzheimer's? It's is a brain disease that causes increasing loss of memory and other mental abilities. It is the most common cause of severe memory loss in older adults. The disease attacks very few people before age 60, but it becomes increasingly common thereafter. In the past, older adults suffering from severe memory loss were often labeled senile, but they were probably suffering from what doctors now recognize as Alzheimer's. The disease is named after Alois Alzheimer, a German psychiatrist, who first described the effect of the disease on brain cells in 1907.

CHANGE-A-LETTER

Do you remember the Think-of-a-Word puzzles in chapter 2? Here's another version of that kind of activity. Let's do a model puzzle together. Change one letter in a four-letter word that means "tardy" to get a word that means "speed or pace." Notice that you are not told what letter to change. The four-letter word is *late* (which means tardy). Changing the first letter of this word to *r* produces *rate* (which means speed or pace). That's all there is to it.

This type of puzzle is trickier than it looks and, as you will soon discover, it will really get your brain cells working.

171. Change one letter in a three-letter word that refers to an organ to get a word that means "to consume food."

172. Change one letter in a four-letter word that means "skin eruption" to get a word that means "rush or hurry about."

173. Change one letter in a five-letter word that refers to the moisture exuded through the skin to get a word that means both "to vow" and "to use bad language."

174. Change one letter in a five-letter word that means "dirt free" to get a word that means "transparent."

175. Change one letter in a six-letter word that means "easy" to get a word that refers to an indentation on the cheek or chin.

176. Change one letter in a six-letter word that refers to a container of liquids to get a word that means "combat."

177. Change one letter in a six-letter word that means "to sell by going from place to place" to get a word that means "to interfere."

178. Change one letter in a six-letter word that means "to confirm" to get a word that means "in truth."

179. Change one letter in a seven-letter word referring to a crustacean to get a word that means "gangster."

180. Change one letter in a seven-letter word meaning "inclination" to get a word that means "significance."

BRAIN FACT #18

I have been discussing memory and puzzles throughout this part of the book. Actually scientists know very little about the extraordinarily complicated processes of remembering. Memory involves processing information in different circuits. These enable the brain to combine information stored by both the senses and by experience. Scientists are just beginning to understand the brain's simplest circuits. Forming abstract ideas and studying difficult subjects must require circuits of astonishing complexity.

PALINDROME SEARCH

A palindrome is a word, phrase, verse or sentence that can be read the same backward and forward. Examples of word palindromes are *wow* and *noon*. An example of a sentence palindrome is *A man, a plan, a canal, Panama!* Note that in the latter case you will have to ignore or add spaces as well as adjust the punctuation and other orthographic elements.

For the present purposes, you will be asked to spot the single palindromic word in a given array of letters. For example, the palindrome *noon* is hidden in the array below as shown. The palindromes can be read either vertically (up-down, down-up, as this one) or horizontally (left-right, right-left). Note also that there are other words in the array, none of which are palindromes, just to make matters more complicated for you.

```
F  R  I  E  N  D  L  Y
J  U  S  T  I  F  Y  S
M  O  O  N  S  H  O  T
B  L  O  O  M  I  N  G
F  L  O  O  R  S  A  T
S  O  O  N  T  H  A  N
H  O  U  S  I  N  G  P
P  R  I  M  A  R  Y  E
L  O  V  E  A  N  D  A
```

That's all there really is to it. You will be given only one clue and the word could be in its singular or plural form. So if you think this is going to be easy, think again!

181. The palindrome in this first puzzle is a polite female title, which is fast becoming archaic.

```
I   C   J   E   C   T   S   Y
N   O   O   K   T   U   E   S
F   M   I   N   L   O   V   E
A   M   A   D   A   M   D   C
T   O   M   O   R   R   O   W
U   N   B   E   A   T   E   N
A   T   T   I   T   U   D   E
T   B   O   O   M   I   N   G
E   N   L   I   S   T   E   D
```

182. The palindrome in this puzzle refers to something carried out.

```
L   O   V   E   A   N   D   Y
M   F   O   R   E   V   E   E
I   C   R   E   A   T   E   S
T   W   O   H   E   A   D   T
A   X   I   O   M   S   G   E
T   E   N   D   E   R   R   R
E   T   R   E   A   T   E   D
E   B   O   O   M   P   A   A
C   D   A   N   A   M   T   Y
```

183. The palindrome in this puzzle is a word meaning flat and horizontal.

```
R  E  V  E  R  S  A  L
O  N  U  S  R  P  R  A
M  O  S  T  E  E  R  S
A  B  R  O  V  C  I  T
N  A  A  O  I  L  V  I
C  I  C  N  V  A  A  N
E  L  E  V  E  L  I  G
S  E  N  S  U  A  L  Q
C  A  R  N  A  L  E  A
```

184. The palindrome this time refers to a principle or established belief.

```
D  E  C  I  S  I  O  N
R  O  M  A  N  T  L  C
M  U  S  I  C  I  A  N
S  C  H  O  L  A  R  C
R  E  M  O  T  E  L  Y
A  V  B  N  E  T  B  A
J  H  H  A  N  S  S  S
N  J  O  K  E  R  S  E
H  E  A  R  T  M  E  A
```

185. The palindrome in this puzzle refers to mythical stories of heroes and their achievements.

```
S  I  N  G  I  N  G  S
A  M  A  T  O  R  Y  M
G  L  A  D  N  E  S  S
A  W  E  S  O  M  E  H
S  V  B  N  R  T  B  A
A  W  K  W  A  R  D  P
A  P  P  R  O  A  C  H
R  E  T  U  R  N  E  D
```

186. The palindrome in this puzzle refers to the sound made, for example, by a horn.

```
H  E  A  R  T  S  L  Y
A  A  M  E  R  P  R  S
P  G  A  N  O  O  E  M
P  E  T  O  O  T  D  C
L  R  E  V  P  M  A  D
N  N  U  A  E  T  R  Y
E  E  R  T  R  S  A  Y
S  O  B  V  U  O  U  S
S  S  A  N  L  T  Y  A
```

187. The palindrome in this puzzle describes music played by single musicians.

```
M   M   I   S   S   I   O   N
A   P   R   O   F   M   E   R
T   H   L   I   P   E   M
E   L   D   O   S   E   D   C
R   O   O   S   T   L   G   H
N   V   B   N   R   I   B   A
A   U   T   H   O   R   M   P
L   O   V   L   N   G   L   Y
C   A   R   E   S   S   E   S
```

188. The palindrome in this puzzle refers to a short, high-pitched sound like that of a baby bird.

```
S   O   P   H   I   S   T   Y
J   B   R   N   T   P   R   E
A   E   O   N   S   Q   E   A
P   I   M   L   S   C   A   R
E   E   I   O   M   M   D   N
P   V   S   O   R   T   B   I
P   E   E   P   E   T   M   N
E   C   L   E   A   R   L   G
R   D   A   N   E   S   A   T
```

189. The palindrome in this puzzle refers to a ring or loop on an animal collar or harness, which is used for attaching a leash to it.

H R I V E C P S
I E B I X O R S
G V E M T R E M
M O T O R R D C
R L T T E E G H
A V E O M C B A
T E R R E T M P
E R O O M I · S E
D G A N A M E A

190. The palindrome in this puzzle refers to a type of physical exercise. The word can also be written in hyphenated form.

```
F P O W E R L Y
M U S T E R R S
V L I K I N G M
A L I K E C D C
L U S C L O U S
A P E A C H Y A
I M P O R T M P
E X P O R T S E
T O U C H I N G
```

REVERSALS

For your last puzzle set in the area of language, try your hand at reversals. These are puzzles in which you write the answer to the first clue in the blank. Then you write the answer backward in the second blank, and the result will match the second clue. Below is a model puzzle: *loop* is the answer to the first clue and its reversal, *pool*, matches the second clue.

circular shape curving   *(loop)*   *(pool)*   small body of still water
back over itself

That's all there really is to it. Like the previous type of puzzle, this looks easier than it really is, especially since you will not be told how many letters are involved.

191. a type of barrier ＿＿＿＿＿ ＿＿＿＿＿ angry, resentful

192. discontinue ＿＿＿＿＿ ＿＿＿＿＿ types of containers

193. small bread rolls ＿＿＿＿＿ ＿＿＿＿＿ ignore someone rudely

194. instrument ＿＿＿＿＿ ＿＿＿＿＿ booty

195. long-tailed rodents ＿＿＿＿＿ ＿＿＿＿＿ celestial body

196. "catching" contrivance ＿＿＿＿＿ ＿＿＿＿＿ portion, piece

197. smack, whack ＿＿＿＿＿ ＿＿＿＿＿ buddies

198. streetcar, cable car ＿＿＿＿＿ ＿＿＿＿＿ small commercial center, market

199. God's foe ＿＿＿＿＿ ＿＿＿＿＿ existed

200. tense, anxious ＿＿＿＿＿ ＿＿＿＿＿ after-meal sweets

BRAIN FACT #20

Memory involves changes at the synapses—the structures where impulses pass from one neuron to another. These may be controlled by glycoproteins or other large molecules. Extensive research will be required to verify this general explanation of memory. However, if the research is in any way correct, the puzzles you have been doing in this chapter and, indeed, in the whole first part of this book, are "synapse friendly."

PART II

Puzzles Activating the Logic Centers of the Brain

NONVERBAL AREAS OF THE BRAIN

⌘ Logic is a left-hemisphere-based ability, especially if the type of logic involved is of a deductive, reasoning nature.

⌘ Logical processes of other kinds, such as inferencing and figuring out how things are connected, are located in right-hemispheric areas, but many of these involve the coordination of both hemispheres.

⌘ Visual thinking is an "interhemispheric" function; that is, it is based primarily in right-hemispheric areas but requires the cooperation of various left-hemispheric areas in order to operate.

⌘ The puzzles in the visual logic chapter (7) are designed to activate right-hemispheric functions. On the other hand, the sudoku and logic puzzle chapters (5, 6 and 8) are intended mainly to activate left-hemispheric functions. Overall, the puzzles in this part of the book are designed to activate the various logic centers of the brain.

5
DETECTIVE LOGIC

*Every man at the bottom of his heart
believes that he is a born detective.*

JOHN BUCHAN (1875–1940)

D O YOU LIKE MYSTERY and detective stories? Are you addicted to *CSI* television programs? If so, you will really like this chapter, which is based on logical thinking processes that are just like those used by fictional detectives. Developing the ability to think logically is a prerequisite for solving crime puzzles, and many of life's other problems for that matter. The great English puzzlist Henry E. Dudeney (1847–1930) went so far as to claim, "The history of puzzles entails nothing short of the actual story of the beginnings and development of exact thinking in man."

The logic used in solving detective-style puzzles is based on various reasoning processes. The primary one is deduction, by which a specific conclusion is inferred from one or more premises. In valid deductive reasoning, the conclusion must be true if all the premises are true. Thus, if it is agreed that all human beings have one head and two arms, and that Mary is a human being, then it can logically be concluded that Mary has one head and two arms (under normal circumstances).

By solving deduction puzzles, one is engaging in a kind of mental detective work, drawing inferences from the available evidence, and reaching the only possible conclusion from the given facts. And this is good for many parts of the brain, but especially those logic-controlling areas in the left hemisphere.

WHODUNIT?

This type of puzzle is actually a deduction logic problem in disguise. This genre was first proposed by Henry Dudeney. We have given it a *whodunit* twist here to make it a little more interesting for you. Let's go through one together.

Inspector Moreau knows that one of three suspects who live in the same household murdered a neighbor, although she doesn't have any sense of why he or she did so. The suspects are the father, the mother and a twenty-year-old daughter, who go by their nicknames—Boo, Jee and Spoo—but not necessarily in that order. Jee is not the mother and Boo is not the daughter. Jee is older than Boo. The inspector figured out that it had to be the daughter who killed the neighbor. What's the killer's nickname?

Here's how to determine who the daughter is and, thus, who the killer is. You are told that Jee is older than Boo. Thus, it is obvious that Jee cannot be the daughter who, logically, is the youngest of the three since she cannot be older than her mother or father. You are also told that Jee is not the mother. By the process of elimination, Jee is the father—since this is the only possibility left for Jee (since Jee is not the daughter, as deduced, or the mother, as told). At this point make a summary chart of the ongoing deductions, just like a real inspector might.

Father	Mother	Daughter
Jee	_____	_____

You are also told that Boo is not the daughter. So if she is not the daughter and, of course, not the father (who is Jee, as just deduced), then Boo has to be the mother, by the process of elimination.

Father	Mother	Daughter
Jee	Boo	_____

This leaves Spoo as the daughter.

Father	Mother	Daughter
Jee	Boo	Spoo

Therefore Spoo is our killer. Easy, no? Well, maybe not so easy when you get to the more complicated puzzles.

As a general hint, you might want to set up a cell chart to solve the more complicated puzzles. For the model puzzle, put the family relations—father, mother, daughter—on one axis and the names of the persons—Boo, Jee, Spoo—on the other.

	Father	Mother	Daughter
Boo			
Jee			
Spoo			

Indicate that Jee cannot be the daughter, because she is older than someone else, by putting an ✗ in the appropriate cell.

	Father	Mother	Daughter
Boo			
Jee			X
Spoo			

Similarly, indicate that Jee is not the mother by placing an ✗ in the appropriate cell.

	Father	Mother	Daughter
Boo			
Jee		x	x
Spoo			

Now, just looking at the chart shows that there is only one cell left for Jee, and that is under the *Father* column. Mark this with an ● and, at the same time, eliminate the *Father* category for Boo and Spoo by placing ✕'s in the appropriate cells.

	Father	Mother	Daughter
Boo	X		
Jee	●	X	X
Spoo	X		

We know that Boo is not the daughter. Mark that fact accordingly in the chart with an ✕.

	Father	Mother	Daughter
Boo	X		X
Jee	●	X	X
Spoo	X		

Now, as you can see from the chart, Boo is the mother, Mark this with an ●, eliminating this possibility for Spoo at the same time with an ✕.

	Father	Mother	Daughter
Boo	X	●	X
Jee	●	X	X
Spoo	X	X	

The chart now shows that Spoo is the daughter.

	Father	Mother	Daughter
Boo	X	•	X
Jee	•	X	X
Spoo	X	X	•

All the cases are from the case files of Inspector Moreau, by the way.

201. Mr. G, Ms. B and Ms. R were the code names given by Inspector Moreau to three suspects in a recent murder. Here's what the Inspector recorded in her notebook. One wore a green shirt, one a brown one, and one a red one. But none of the colors of the shirts matched the letter of the code names; that is, Mr. G did not wear the green shirt, Ms. B did not wear the brown shirt, and Ms. R did not wear the red one. The Inspector also wrote down that Ms. B did not know the suspect who wore the red shirt, although she knew the other one. After considering the evidence very closely, Inspector Moreau figured out that the killer was the one who wore the red shirt. What's the killer's code name?

202. Beth, Carl, Don, Ines and Mark were at a café a few days ago when they were approached by Inspector Moreau, who suspected one of them as the murderer in a cold case. She saw that each was wearing a different colored shirt (black, blue, green, orange, red) and that each one ordered a different drink (coffee, cola, hot chocolate, milk, tea). She suspected that the one who ordered milk was the killer. What was the name of her suspect? By the way, here's what took place at the café.

1. Beth wore the green shirt and she did not order the coffee.
2. Carl had the hot chocolate.
3. Don wore the blue shirt.
4. Mark did not order milk.
5. The person who ordered milk wore the orange shirt.

203. In another fascinating case, Inspector Moreau concluded that it was the accountant in a company who killed the CEO out of envy and revenge—both deadly sins! Initially she had suspected either the accountant, the designer or the engineer, whose names were Ben, Janine and Sophia, but not necessarily in that order. The accountant is an only child, and probably killed the CEO because he or she saw the CEO as a stern father figure. The accountant also earns the least of the three—another reason for revenge. Sophia is married to Ben's brother. She earns more than the engineer. Whodunit?

204. Mr. Chen, Mr. Davidoff and Ms. Fanucci are suspects in a cold case that Inspector Moreau has recently reopened. One of them is the murderer of an up-and-coming fashion model—an unsolved case that goes back ten years. Unfortunately Moreau has misplaced some of her notes, indicating where the suspects lived. She remembers that one lived in Cleveland, another in Palm Beach, and the third in Plymouth. The person living in Plymouth makes more money than the one living in Palm Beach. Ms. Fanucci makes more money than Mr. Davidoff. The resident of Palm Beach and the one who lives in Cleveland are members of the same criminal gang and know each other well. The one who lives in Cleveland and the one who lives in Plymouth have been friends since childhood. Ms. Fanucci has never met Mr. Davidoff. Now, Inspector Moreau has figured out that the killer lives in Palm Beach. So whodunit?

205. Last week, three gangsters and their girlfriends decided to go rob a bank together. One male gangster became too nervous and ended up shooting one of the tellers, wounding him critically. Inspector Moreau wanted to identify, above all else, who the shooter was. She interrogated several witnesses but their accounts varied. She was able to establish a few facts. She knew that one of the females was dressed in red, one in green, and one in blue. The male gangsters also wore outfits in the same three colors. While the three couples were robbing the bank, the male gangster dressed in red said to the girl in green and to her partner: "It is interesting that not one of us is coupled with a partner dressed in the same color." From accounts and forensic evidence, Moreau was able to figure out that the shooter was coupled with the girl who wore green. Whodunit?

206. Three people Inspector Moreau has identified as suspects in an ongoing murder investigation live on the same street. She has it from good sources that the killer is the oldest of the three. She doesn't know their ages and can't find them in her files. She does know that no two are the same age. The suspects' names are Sam, Ham and Ned. Ham is 27. In three years from now, Sam will be Ned's age today. They are all between 20 and 30 years of age and will remain so even three years from now. So whodunit?

207. Inspector Moreau has been assigned a truly hard case to solve. Here's what she knows. A musician murdered the beautiful soprano Maria Cantabile. She has identified Mr. Cellist, Mr. Mandolin and Mr. Saxophone, all musicians, as suspects. By a strange logic, the suspects play the cello, the mandolin and the saxophone, but none plays the instrument corresponding to his name. Each musician has a grown-up son who also plays one of these three instruments (Mr. Cellist Jr., Mr. Mandolin Jr. and Mr. Saxophone Jr.) and who also does not play the instrument that corresponds to his name. Moreover, no son plays the same instrument as his father. Moreau also knows that Mr. Mandolin is not the cellist. The Inspector has also figured out that the son who plays the mandolin is the killer. Whodunit?

208. Someone from her own court killed Judge Hilary Grumps. At least that is what Inspector Moreau suspects after being called in on the case. Moreau has identified three persons of interest. They are an attorney, a forensic scientist and another judge. Their surnames are Ms. Soo, Ms. Justice and Ms. Rook, but not necessarily in that order. Working in the same courthouse are three male custodians who have the same surnames (but who are not related or married to the three women)—Mr. Soo, Mr. Justice and Mr. Rook. Here's a list of the things Inspector knows about the six people.

1. Mr. Rook lives in Detroit.
2. The attorney lives halfway between Chicago and Detroit.
3. Mr. Justice earns exactly $4,000 a month.
4. Ms. Soo regularly works out with the forensic scientist, early in the morning before both head off to court.
5. The attorney's next-door neighbor, one of the male custodians, earns exactly three times more than one of the other male custodians.
6. The custodian who lives in Chicago has the same surname as the attorney.

After long deliberation Moreau comes to the conclusion that the killer is the forensic scientist. Whodunit?

209. Ben, Peter, Rick and Sasha are suspects in Inspector Moreau's most recent murder case. One of them murdered a famous jazz musician in a fit of envy. All of them are musicians, by the way. One is a drummer, one a pianist, one a saxophonist and one a guitarist, though not necessarily respectively. Being absent-minded and very busy, Moreau has forgotten who plays what. She can figure this out, however, from her notes.

1. Peter was in the audience when the saxophonist performed with his ensemble a while back.
2. Peter and Ben have played with the guitarist and the pianist on various occasions.
3. The guitarist often performs with Ben and Sasha.

Moreau has also determined that the killer was the pianist. Whodunit?

210. Four women and one man were recently invited as experts to an international conference on the state of the environment. One was a physicist. During the conference the organizer was brutally knifed to death. Inspector Moreau was called in and she quickly figured out that the killer was one of the experts, the urbanist, to be precise, but has not yet determined the motive. Can you figure out the name of the killer, given the following facts?

1. Kate, Laura and the meteorologist became good friends and went out frequently during the evenings of the conference.
2. Paul is the only male in the group.
3. Jasmine is neither the meteorologist nor the biologist.
4. Inspector Moreau interrogated the five experts at the same time. They were: the zoologist, Kate, Jasmine, the female urbanist and Sophia.
5. Kate was seen at a coffee shop with the urbanist a few hours before the organizer was murdered.

BRAIN FACT #21

The distinction between deductive and inductive logic is a conveniently reductive one in neurological terms. In fact, there are many degrees of logical thinking with deduction and induction being end points on a reasoning continuum. Technically speaking, deduction involves deriving a conclusion on the basis of specific premises, while induction involves the process of deriving general principles from particular facts or instances.

WHO'S WHO?

In her files, Inspector Moreau has ten cases going back a while involving family relations. They all concerned gruesome murders. She solved them all. See if you can, too. This genre of puzzle was introduced by Henry Dudeney. Some like it, some don't. But it will give your brain a good workout, no matter what your tastes in logic are. There is no need to go through a model puzzle in this case. This puzzle genre is self-explanatory.

211. Let's start off nice and easy. In the first case, Moreau's notes show that a vicious man, whose name was Cartwright, was killed by his wife's only brother. Cartwright's wife is named Rina. Cartwright's brother-in-law is named Mack. Cartwright was an only child. Who killed Cartwright?

212. In another case, Moreau investigated the murder of an elderly woman named Emilia. Emilia had only one child. His name is Peter. Emilia's granddaughter's name is Maria. Maria, by the way, also has one child. You should know as well that Emilia's great-grandson's name is Pascal. Emilia was killed by her son's daughter's son. Who was the killer?

213. In a third case, Moreau identified the killer of a man named Friedrich as one of his brother's or sister's own children. Friedrich's sister is named Frieda. The brother is named Jules. Jules has a daughter named Claudia and a son named Rinaldo. Frieda has two sons named Bruno and Dino. The killer does not get along with Claudia, his cousin. Bruno was out of the country when the murder occurred and thus could not have done it. Who killed Friedrich?

214. In a mystifying fourth case, Moreau identified the killer of a very elderly man named Carlo as his son's daughter's son's daughter. Carlo's son's name is James; his granddaughter's name is Naomi; his great-grandson's name is Brett; and Brett's daughter's name, who is Carlo's great-great-granddaughter of course, is Nicolette. Carlo was over one hundred when he was killed. Carlo, James, Naomi, Brett and Nicolette were only children, by the way. Who killed Carlo?

215. Moreau's fifth case was a baffling one. The victim, a woman named Julia, was killed by Frank's brother-in-law's older son. Steve is Frank's sister's husband. Frank's sister, by the way, is his only sibling. He has no other sister or brother. Her name is Norma Jean. Andrew and Billy are Steve's sons. Andrew always looks up to his older brother. Who killed Julia?

216. Inspector Moreau's sixth case is another one involving a complex kinship pattern. The killer was the victim's daughter's husband's sister's sister-in-law. The victim, a lady named Maria, had only one daughter. For the sake of clarity, Maria's daughter is named Dina, Dina's husband is named Harry, and Harry's sister is named Lydia. Who killed Maria?

217. In a seventh case, Moreau determined that the killer of a young man named Will was his father's brother's father's wife. Who killed Will? Here are their names. His father is named John. His only uncle, on his dad's side, is named Bill. His grandfather is named Herman, and his grandmother is named Helena.

218. In an eighth case, Moreau identified the killer of a young woman named Harriet, as her mother's brother's mother's husband. Here are the only living members of Harriet's family. Her mother is named Emma and Emma's parents are called Mina (a woman, of course) and Phillip (a man, of course). The other grandparents (on Harriet's father's side) are deceased. Emma's only uncle, on her mother's side, is named Arthur. Who killed Harriet?

219. Actually, Moreau's ninth case was a revisitation of her seventh one (puzzle number **217**). Recall that she determined that Will's killer was his father's brother's father's wife. Well, it was actually his father's brother's father's wife's son, which is even more gruesome to contemplate. She also knows that the father didn't do it. So who really killed Will?

220. Moreau's tenth case was also a revisitation of a previous case, number eight (puzzle number **218**). Originally she had concluded that Harriet's killer was her mother's brother's mother's husband. Now, she has come to the conclusion that it was, instead, her mother's brother's mother's husband's only daughter. So who really killed Harriet?

BRAIN FACT #22

In addition to deduction and induction, there is a process of reasoning called "insight thinking." Deduction and induction allow the brain to organize facts; insight thinking allows it to discover them. It involves brain areas that control inferences and hunches. Our brain is thus a "pattern-detecting" organ that searches out the hidden connections among things.

NAME DETECTION

In this next set of puzzles you will have to determine which of the four suspects is different, because he or she is the one Inspector Moreau believes to be the perpetrator of a crime. The solution is to be found in the actual names themselves. A model puzzle will suffice to show you what kind of forensic logic is involved.

One of four suspects surnamed Miller, Brunell, Geller and Diller is a murderer. Inspector Moreau has discovered that the killer's surname stands out in some way from those of the other suspects. Whodunit?

If you look at the names, you will see that all but one end in *-ller*. So the killer is *Brunell* because his name is different from all the others. In other cases, the difference may be more of a semantic nature. For example, which of the surnames *Fox, Elk, Trail, Wolf* is the different one? The only one that is different is *Trail*; the others are all words referring to animals.

That's all there is to it. Puzzle aficionados will instantly see that this is a version of the "odd one out" genre, but with a forensic twist. And as all you puzzle solvers will soon find out, unless you have a keen detective eye, these are rather tricky.

221. Inspector Moreau has determined that one of the four young women named Nora, Maria, Jill and Dianna is a murderer. The killer's name stands out in some way from the other names. Whodunit?

222. Moreau has rounded up four suspects, one of whom committed a bank robbery. They are Mack, Frankie, John and Andrew. Again, the criminal's name stands out in some way from the other names. Whodunit?

223. The Inspector has rounded up four more suspects surnamed Jones, Tailor, Cook and Clerk, one of whom committed a serious crime. Yet again, the criminal's surname stands out in some way from the other names. Whodunit?

224. This time Moreau is interrogating four suspects, one of whom is a murderer. Their names are Susan, Betty, Diana and Margaret. As in all this set of cases, the murderer's name stands out in some way from the other ones. Whodunit?

225. Of four murder suspects nicknamed Gig, Hap, Pip and Bab, Inspector Moreau has once more concluded that the killer's nickname stands out in some way from the other ones. Whodunit?

226. Moreau has rounded up four suspects nicknamed Bunny, Kiddie, Pippy and Kookie. One of them is a vicious murderer. As in her previous cases, she discovers that the killer's nickname stands out in some way from the other ones. Whodunit?

227. Moreau's next case involves extortion. She suspects one of four people whom she has been interrogating with respect to this case. Their names are Anna, Bob, Frank and Eve. As in her previous cases, she discovers that the extortionist's name stands out in some way from the other ones. Who is the extortionist?

228. In a recent case, a home robbery was involved. Moreau knows that one of four suspects named Beth, Nida, Sarah and Andra is the criminal. And as in all other cases of this kind, Moreau discovers that the robber's name stands out in some way from the other ones. Who's the robber?

229. Moreau is interrogating four suspects surnamed Mr. Powder, Mr. Pelt, Ms. Flake and Mrs. Sleet. Again, the one whose name stands out from the others is the guilty one, this time for perpetrating a fraudulent Ponzi scheme. Who's the fraudster?

230. For her final case, Inspector Moreau is interrogating four male suspects who spell their surnames as Poons, Cork, Finke and Bleat. By rearranging the letters in the surnames Moreau was able to determine that three of the surnames referred to kitchen items and one to something in nature instead. She concluded that the holder of that latter name is a killer. What's his surname?

BRAIN FACT #23

In real life, as in detective stories, accurate reckoning and insight thinking must be used together in the solution of all kinds of problems. In his *Murders in the Rue Morgue*, Edgar Allan Poe called this blend of thinking the human being's "bi-part soul," which, he suggested, produces in all of us the mind of a "poet-mathematician." The bi-part soul is the source of all great discoveries in science and mathematics, and it is one of the most important features of the human brain.

THE NEXT CLUE

The next set of cases constitutes a puzzle genre that involves a form of sequential logic that is known, colloquially, as "What comes next?" You are given four clues recovered from a crime scene. For example:

knife, blood, photo, watch, ___

You are then given two other items, one of which is recovered from the scene and thus constitutes a genuine clue and another one which is not, having gotten into the investigator's crime box erroneously: *scarf* and *tie*. The logic to be used is based, as above, on the actual clues themselves. The correct clue is *scarf* because like all the other clues it is made up of five letters; *tie* is not. Again, the pattern could be of any kind. For instance, if given the four clues *tooth, hair, earlobe* and *eyelash* and the options *fingernail* and *lip,* the fifth clue would be *lip,* because all the first four clues refer to parts of the body found in the head; *fingernail* is found in another part of the body, of course.

In sum, for each case you are given four clues and two options, one of which is a clue that can be connected to the other ones in some way, while the other is an intruder that does not belong. As you will soon see, your brain is in for quite a workout.

231. Here are four strange clues collected by Inspector Moreau at a murder scene: *ants, eggs, ink* and *oil*. She also finds two other clues, *paint* and a *ukulele*. She determines that only one of these two is relevant to the case and that, strangely, it has a logical linguistic connection to the others. Which clue is it?

232. The next four clues gathered by Moreau were from another murder scene: *wine, water, coffee* and *tea*. She collected two other clues, a *teaspoon* and *mineral water*. She concludes that only one of the two is part of the crime scene and, by pure happenstance, that it has a logical linguistic connection to the other four clues. Which clue is it?

233. A serial killer left four bizarre clues at his last crime scene, revealing a twisted mind: *acorns, beetles, crackers* and *detergent*. Inspector Moreau also finds two other clues, an *earring* and a *banjo*. She determines that only one of these two belongs to the scene and, again, that it has a logical linguistic connection to the other four clues. Which clue is it?

234. The Inspector is going over four clues she collected at a crime scene last week: a *pen*, a *paintbrush*, a *pencil* and a *crayon*. She also received two other clues from a partner, a *gun* and a *marker*. She decides, however, that only one of these two is pertinent to the case, noting that it also has a logical linguistic connection to the other four clues. Which clue is it?

> **BRAIN FACT #24**
> ● ● ● ● ● ● ● ● ● ● ● ● ● ● ● ● ● ● ●
> Solving puzzles mirrors how the brain's hemispheres interact, even though they might have a different structure. The right hemisphere has many associative connections, making it of the substrate for inductive logic and insight thinking. The left hemisphere, on the other hand, has a more sequential structure and is better at deductive logic tasks. Clearly both need to be "talking to each other" in order for us to carry out complex logical tasks, like solving the puzzles in this chapter.

235. Here are four clues collected by Inspector Moreau at the scene of a brutal killing: *fluff, a deed, a gag,* and strangely, *a window.* She looks in her evidence box and finds two other clues, *a bib* and *a sling.* She soon realizes that only one of these two is relevant to the case, and that it has a logical linguistic connection to the other four clues. Which clue is it?

236. In another interesting case involving the murder of a CEO, Moreau assembled four clues from the crime scene: a *hot dog,* a *hula hoop,* a *pet rock* and a *compact disc.* She also found two other objects, a *knife handle* and a *revolver.* But she determined that one of these two was the murder weapon and, as in previous cases, that it has a logical linguistic connection to the other four clues. Which one was it?

237. Inspector Moreau is stumped by the clues she collected at a recent murder scene. All of them were left by the killer in some kind of code: *A, DS, CTP* and *GHIR.* She also finds two other coded clues, *NMPRP* and *HTOP.* She determines that only one of these two belongs to the code, having also a logical linguistic connection to the others. Which clue is it?

238. Here are four clues picked up by the Inspector at yet another murder scene: a *box,* a *vase,* a *bottle* and a *purse.* She also finds two other clues, a *briefcase* and a *keychain.* She soon figures out that only one of these two is a pertinent clue. Again, she notes that it has a logical semantic connection to the other clues. Which clue is it?

239. At the murder scene of a famous industrialist, Moreau was able to assemble four clues: *pills, marbles, invoices* and *keys.* She also found two other clues, *pennies* and a *dollar.* She soon realizes that only one of these two is a relevant clue, and that it has a logical linguistic connection to the others. Which clue is it?

240. Inspector Moreau's keen eye spotted four alphanumeric clues left by the sadistic killer at a murder scene a few weeks ago: *1A, 3Dry, 5Never* and *2Be.* She also found two other coded clues, *6Killer* and *4Get.* She determines that only one of these two is part of the code. Which clue is it?

LIE DETECTION

How do you tell if someone is telling the truth or lying? Well, this next set of puzzles constitutes a genre that shows how truth and logic are related. The puzzles involve identifying who did what (steal something, murder someone, etc.) on the basis of certain statements made by various people, some of which are true and others false. Here's an example.

Inspector Moreau interrogated three suspects about a recent robbery. Here's what they said at certain points in the interrogation:

Mack: I didn't do it.

Jack: I confess. I did it.

Zack: No, no. Mack did it.

As it turns out, only one of these statements is false; the other two are true. Who was the robber?

First, let's take a close look at the nature of double negative logic, which is used a lot in solving these kind of puzzles. What's that, you may ask? When someone says "I didn't do it" and is telling the truth, then that person is innocent—that is, the person did not, in fact, do it, as he or she truthfully says. So far, so good. However, if the statement is false, then the opposite of what he or she says is true, and this means that he or she did, actually, do it and is lying to hide the truth. This is double negative logic: If you did not "not do something," then you did it. Confused? Try this. If you did not turn down ice cream—that is, if you did not "not have" ice cream—then you had it. See the logic? There's a little more to it than this for professional logicians, but for our intents and purposes this is what will be meant by double negative logic. Okay?

This kind of puzzle often requires hypothesis testing. Let's suppose that Mack's statement is one of the two true ones. This is our working hypothesis. What would be the logical result of this? Well, if he did not, in fact, do it, as he says, then he is innocent. Now, consider Zack's statement—"Mack did it." This is patently false, under our working hypothesis. We now have identified a true and a false statement. That means that the third statement—Jack's—must, under the conditions set by the puzzle, be true. Jack did indeed confess and is our robber. The hypothesis worked out.

Just for the sake of argument, let's try out a different working hypothesis. Let's suppose that Mack's statement is, instead, the only false one. If he says he did not do it, and this is false, then he, in fact, did it (using double negative logic). Then, Zack's statement—"Mack did it"—is clearly true. So far, we have one false and one true statement. This means that the third statement—Jack's—must be true, under the conditions of the puzzle. What's his statement? "I confess. I did it." Being true, this means that he actually did it. But under our new hypothesis we have just deduced that it was Mack who did it. We know that there was only one robber. So, the new hypothesis is wrong, since it led to deducing that there were two killers, not one. Back to the original one, which shows, conclusively now, that Jack is the one and only robber.

241. Inspector Moreau rounded up three suspects, one of whom she believes murdered a powerful socialite. Here's what they said during interrogation:

Mr. Stone: I didn't do it.

Mr. Rock: I didn't do it, either.

Mr. Pebble: Stone did it. Believe me.

Now, only one of these statements turned out to be true; the other two were false. Who's the killer?

242. Three suspects of a bank robbery were interviewed by Moreau yesterday. Here's what they said:

Gina: I didn't do it.

Pina: Neither did I.

Mina: One of us sure did it.

Interestingly, all three told the truth. Who's the robber?

243. Last night Moreau interviewed three people, one of whom is the leader of a car theft ring. Here's what they said to her:

Nubby: I admit it. I am the leader.

Tubby: No, I am.

Bubby: I don't know who the leader is.

All three lied. Moreau quickly figured out who the leader was. Can you?

244. Jane, Beth and Samantha were rounded up by the police yesterday, because one of them was suspected of having robbed a bank. The three suspects made the following statements under intensive questioning by Inspector Moreau:

Jane: I'm innocent. I am not the robber.

Beth: That's right. Jane is not the robber.

Sam: No, no. Jane is the robber.

If only one of these statements turned out to be true, who robbed the bank?

245. Someone robbed an armored car yesterday. Four suspects were rounded up by Inspector Moreau. Here's what they said to her under severe questioning:

Albert: Dick did it.

Dick: No, Tim did it.

Gaston: I certainly didn't do it.

Tim: Dick lied when he said that I did it.

Only one of these four statements turned out to be true. Who was the guilty man?

246. Four women, one of whom was known to have stolen a car, were brought in by the police this morning. The four suspects made the following statements when interrogated by the investigating detective, Inspector Moreau:

Amelia: Diana stole it.

Diana: Nah, Tara did.

Gillian: Well, I know I didn't steal it.

Tara: Diana lied when she said I did it.

Only one of these statements turned out to be false; the others were true. So, who stole the car?

247. Four well-known mobsters were brought in for questioning over the murder of another mobster. Here's what they told Inspector Moreau:

Curly: It was Baldy.

Baldy: No, it was Hairy.

Hairy: No way. It was Wavy.

Wavy: I agree with Baldy. It was Hairy.

All the statements turned out to be false. Through logic, Moreau figured out who the killer was. Who was he?

248. Four other mobsters were brought in the week after, killing the alleged killer of the previous case. Here's what they told Moreau:

Skinny: It wasn't Chubby.

Chubby: It wasn't Bubbly, either.

Bubbly: It wasn't Stubby.

Stubby: Yeah, that's right. It was not me.

This time around, all the statements turned out to be true. Again, through a use of steely logic, Moreau figured out who the killer was. Who was he?

249. Mobsters do not give up easily. This time four more suspects, all female gangsters, were brought in for having avenged the previous killing by murdering the killer in puzzle **248**. Here's the text of their statements to Moreau:

Bianca: Josie did it.

Josie: Nah, Nessa did it.

Nessa: No way. It was Caitlin.

Caitlin: Josie's wrong. Nessa didn't do it.

This time around, two of the statements were true and two were false. Who's the killer?

250. This last case was a tough one for Moreau to crack, but crack it she did. Five suspects were involved. One of them murdered a popular late-night TV comedian, perhaps to shut him up. Here are their alibis to Moreau. By the way, all the suspects lied. Can you figure out who the killer was?

Jack: I'm not sure who did it.

Mack: It was Hack.

Pack: It was Mack. I saw him.

Zack: It was the one who said he wasn't sure who did it.

Hack: It was the one who identified Mack as the killer.

6
PLACEMENT LOGIC

Sudoku is a simple exercise in the use of logical thinking.

WILL SHORTZ (B. 1952)

I N THE WINTER OF 2005, I was in my office early in the morning preparing my classes when I got an unexpected call from a reporter at the Associated Press who, having read my book *The Puzzle Instinct,* wanted to gauge my opinion on a new puzzle craze that was spreading throughout the world—sudoku. I had to humbly admit that I had never heard of sudoku. When the reporter explained the puzzle, however, it immediately became obvious to me why it would appeal so broadly. Like the crossword puzzle before it, sudoku has a simple structure, a simple set of rules for solving it, but it still presents a challenge. Unlike the crossword, however, it requires no "external knowledge" (names of people, events, linguistic knowledge, etc.). It just requires us to place symbols (usually the first nine digits) in cells in a logical way.

Sudoku is just that—a simple *placement* puzzle with no tricks or twists built into it. In its usual form, it is made up of a nine-by-nine grid, with heavy lines dividing it into nine three-by-three boxes. The challenge is to fill the layout with the digits from 1 through 9, so that every row, every column and every three-by-three box contains these digits, without repeating. The layout provides some of the numbers as the initial clues to be used in solving the puzzle. How is the level of difficulty determined? I am not sure, really, although the implicit principle seems to be that the fewer the initial clues given, the harder it is to solve the puzzle. What I can say, however, is that the logic centers of your brain are going to get a workout. This chapter will also give you other kinds of logical placement exercises.

The standard sudoku puzzle looks like this. If you have not done the puzzle before read on before starting.

4	9	7	1	8	3	6	5	2
2	8	1	9	6	5	4	3	7
3	5	6	4	7	2	1	9	8
1	2	9	5	4	7	8	6	3
7	6	5	8	3	9	2	1	4
8	3	4	2	1	6	9	7	5
9	4	3	6	5	8	7	2	1
6	7	8	3	2	1	5	4	9
5	1	2	7	9	4	3	8	6

There are nine cells in each marked box of the sudoku grid with the first nine digits (1, 2, 3, 4, 5, 6, 7, 8, 9) in them, some of which are missing. You have to insert the missing numbers in each of the boxes and in the rows and columns of the overall grid according to one simple rule—no repetitions of a digit are allowed in any box or in any row or column of the grid, but all nine digits must appear in the boxes and the rows and columns of the grid.

So let's look at the above grid, which is a really simple version of the classic puzzle. One obvious place to start is in the top left box. Why? Because it has only one cell to be filled. All the digits are there except 8, so that's the one to put into the empty cell. At the same time, if you look at the third row from the bottom of the grid, you will see eight digits there as well. In this case, the missing one is 2. Let's put these two digits in their appropriate cells, noting that there are no repetitions, as we do this.

By having inserted the 8 in the upper box, we have at the same time also completed the second row from the top and almost completed the second column from the left of the grid. Do you see that it is now missing one digit? What is that digit? It is 7. Let's put it in the appropriate empty cell.

This now allows us to fill in two cells at once. First, the lower left box now has only one missing digit and that digit is 5. The second row from the bottom also has one missing digit, and that digit is, as you can see, 2. Let's put them in.

4	9	7	1	8	3	6	5	2
2	8	1	9	6	5	4	3	7
3	5	6	4	7	2	1	9	8
1	2	9	5	4	7	8	6	3
7	6	5	8	3	9	2	1	4
8	3	4	2	1	6	9	7	5
9	4	3	6	5	8	7	2	1
6	7	8	3	2	1	5	4	9
5	1	2	7	9	4	3	8	6

These new placements now reveal the number missing from the left-most column. It is 7:

4	9	7	1	8	3	6	5	2
2	8	1	9	6	5	4	3	7
3	5	6	4	7	2	1	9	8
1	2	9	5	4	7	8	6	3
7	6	5	8	3	9	2	1	4
8	3	4	2	1	6	9	7	5
9	4	3	6	5	8	7	2	1
6	7	8	3	2	1	5	4	9
5	1	2	7	9	4	3	8	6

Now, it gets a little trickier. Look at the top row. It is missing two numbers: a 2 and an 8. If we put the 2 in the middle cell, then we would produce a repetition down lower in the column:

4	9	7	1	8	3	6	5	2
2	8	1	9	6	5	4	3	7
3	5	6	4	7	2	1	9	8
1	2	9	5	4	7	8	6	3
7	6	5	8	3	9	2	1	4
8	3	4	2	1	6	9	7	5
9	4	3	6	5	8	7	2	1
6	7	8	3	2	1	5	4	9
5	1	2	7	9	4	3	8	6

So we conclude that the 8 goes there and the 2 in the other cell, since this does not produce repetitions of any kind, as you can see:

4	9	7	1	8	3	6	5	2
2	8	1	9	6	5	4	3	7
3	5	6	4	7	2	1	9	8
1	2	9	5	4	7	8	6	3
7	6	5	8	3	9	2	1	4
8	3	4	2	1	6	9	7	5
9	4	3	6	5	8	7	2	1
6	7	8	3	2	1	5	4	9
5	1	2	7	9	4	3	8	6

These two placements now produce empty single-cell middle and right-most columns; the middle one is missing a 3 and the other one a 6:

4	9	7	1	8	3	6	5	2
2	8	1	9	6	5	4	3	7
3	5	6	4	7			9	8
1	2	9	5	4	7	8	6	3
7	6	5	8	3		2	1	4
8	3	4	2	1	6			5
9	4	3	6	5	8	7	2	1
6	7	8	3	2	1	5	4	9
5	1	2	7	9		3		6

Now, as you can see, the top middle box is missing a 2, the right-most upper box a 1, the middle box a 9, the box below it a 4, and the right-most lower box an 8. Let's put these in their cells:

4	9	7	1	8	3	6	5	2
2	8	1	9	6	5	4	3	7
3	5	6	4	7	2	1	9	8
1	2	9	5	4	7	8	6	3
7	6	5	8	3	9	2	1	4
8	3	4	2	1	6			5
9	4	3	6	5	8	7	2	1
6	7	8	3	2	1	5	4	9
5	1	2	7	9	4	3	8	6

Now, we can fill in the rest, since the third column from the right is missing a 9 and the second one from the right a 7. That completes the grid perfectly.

4	9	7	1	8	3	6	5	2
2	8	1	9	6	5	4	3	7
3	5	6	4	7	2	1	9	8
1	2	9	5	4	7	8	6	3
7	6	5	8	3	9	2	1	4
8	3	4	2	1	6	9	7	5
9	4	3	6	5	8	7	2	1
6	7	8	3	2	1	5	4	9
5	1	2	7	9	4	3	8	6

So, to sum up, no two identical digits are to appear in any box, in any row or in any column of the grid. The trick is to consider the placement of digits in the boxes and the grid at the same time, going back and forth as need be.

251.

7		3	1	6		4	8	5
5	4	6	2	3	8	7		9
8	9		4	5	7	3	6	2
2	6	4	8	7	3	9	5	1
1		7	9	2	4	6		8
3	8	9	6		5	2	4	7
	1	5	3	9	2	8	7	
4		2	7	8	1	5	9	6
9	7	8	5	4		1	2	

252.

	5	7	6		2	1	4	
1	3	2	4	7	5	9	6	8
9	6		1		3		7	2
3		9		5	6	2		1
6	2	5	8	4	1	7	3	
7	1	8		3			5	6
4	9		3	2	7		1	5
5	7	3	9		8	6	2	4
	8	1	5	6		3		

253.

7	6	4	5	8	2		3	9
5				1	6	2	4	8
2	8	1	9	4		5		6
	7	6	8	2	9		5	1
	4				1	6	8	
1	2	8	6	5	4	3	9	7
4		2	1	9	7	8		5
8		9	4					
6	5	7	2		8	9	1	4

254.

	9		1	8		3	2	7
	3	7	5		9	8		4
8	6	2	3		7	5		1
3	1	8		7	2	6	5	9
	5	6	8		1		4	2
7		4	6	9	5		3	8
	8	3	7	6		9	1	5
6		1		5	8			3
5		9	2	1	3	4	8	

255.

	4	5		3	9	8		6
8		6		1	4		3	5
7	9			6	8	2	1	
6	5	1	4			3	9	7
9			3	5	1	6		8
2	3		9	7		4		1
	8	9	1	4		7		2
4		2	6		7	5		3
5	6			2	3	1		9

256.

9		5		1	4	7	6	8
1		4		6	3	2		9
8		6	7	9		4	1	3
3		1	9		6	8	2	7
	8	9	1		2	3		6
	4	2	3		8	5	9	1
4	6	8			1	9	7	2
2		7	4	8				
5			6	2	7	1	8	4

257.

	8	7	6		4	3	2	
6		2		3	8	4		9
5	3		1	9	2		7	6
	5	1		8		6	3	
3		8	4		5	1	9	7
2	7			6			8	4
1	9			4	3		6	8
7		3	8		6	9		5
	4	6	5	7		2	1	

258.

	5	1	8	9		4	6	7
9		6	7		1	8		5
4	8			5	6	3	1	
	1	8		2			7	6
5		2	6		7	9		8
	7		3	8	5		4	
	2	4	5	6		7	9	
7		5	9		2	1		4
	9			7	4	6		2

259.

		7	4			5	8	3
6		8		7	2	9		4
3	4	9	1	8		7		
8			5	9	4	1		2
	9	6	8			3	4	5
5				3	1	8		
4			7			6		1
9			2	1	6		3	7
7		1	9	4	3		5	8

260.

4	8	6	9	2	7	3	1	5
3	1	2	8	5	6	9	4	7
5	7	9	4	3	1	2	6	8
8	5	3	2	6	4	7	9	1
1	2	7	5	8	9	4	3	6
6	9	4	7	1	3	5	8	2
2	4	1	3	7	8	6	5	9
9	6	5	1	4	2	8	7	3
7	3	8	6	9	5	1	2	4

Placement puzzles involving basic arithmetic have been around since time immemorial. They are, fundamentally, a type of sudoku, given that you have to place digits in cells, but this time according to the laws of arithmetic. We'll call this type of puzzle arithmedoku, for the sake of convenience. Let's do one together.

Place digits in the empty cells so that they make sense arithmetically. Unlike sudoku, not all the digits may be required, and some may have to be repeated. The bottom highlighted cell contains the sum of the numbers above it, and the numbers in the right-most column are the result of the indicated arithmetical operations in the rows.

2	x		=	4
	÷	1	=	
12	-		=	12
17	+		=	
				34

From the top row, it is easy to determine that the missing multiplicand (that is, number to be multiplied) is 2, because that is the only number that produces 4 ($2 \times 2 = 4$). Let's put that in.

2	x	2	=	4
	÷	1	=	
12	-		=	12
17	+		=	
				34

Now some real logical thinking is required. If you add up the vertical right-most column, you get $4 + 12 = 16$. The sum at the bottom shows 34. This means that the other two cells in the column have to add up to whatever is missing from 34, that is, $34 - 16 = 18$.

Look at the bottom row. There's a 17 in it. The maximum that can be put in the empty cell is 1, since this would make the row add up to 18 ($17 + 1 = 18$). But that would mean that the result of dividing something by 1 in the second row from the top would have to be 0, the only number now possible for the empty right cell, so that the total of the column adds up to 34: $4 + 0 + 12 + 18 = 34$. Let's put these in, just for the sake of clarity. They are shaded to indicate that they are simply trials:

2	x	2	=	4
?	÷	1	=	0
12	-		=	12
17	+	1	=	18
				34

But then, as you can see, what number could possibly be put in the cell with the questions mark? There is no such number. That means that the only possible number that can be added to 17 in the fourth row is 0, and the result of doing this is 17, of course:

2	x	2	=	4
	÷	1	=	
12	-		=	12
17	+	0	=	17
				34

Since now $4 + 12 + 17 = 33$ in the vertical right-most column, the only possibility for the empty cell in that column is 1:

2	x	2	=	4
	÷	1	=	1
12	-		=	12
17	+	0	=	17
				34

Now consider the second row. What number when divided by 1 produces 1? It is 1 itself:

2	x	2	=	4
1	÷	1	=	1
12	-		=	12
17	+	0	=	17
				34

The remaining empty cell can only be 0, since only that number fits arithmetically in the row, as you can see: $12 - 0 = 12$.

2	x	2	=	4
1	÷	1	=	1
12	-	0	=	12
17	+	0	=	17
				34

All the puzzles in this section are based on this kind of logic. However, some puzzles will add logical color by restricting the kinds of digits to be used (for example, they could be all even or include only the first 9). This will be indicated to you at the beginning of the puzzle.

261. Let's start off nice and easy with an arithmedoku that has no particular restrictions on it.

	x	2	=	6
4	÷		=	4
9	-		=	1
	+	1	=	2
				13

262. Here's another easy arithmedoku that also has no restrictions on it.

	x	3	=	15
15	÷		=	
7	-		=	5
1	+		=	6
				31

263. Here's one that will require a little more logic to solve. The two numbers in each row are identical digits (maybe two 1's, maybe two 6's, and so on) and the specific number twins in a row are not repeated in any other row.

	x		=	16
6	÷		=	
	-	2	=	
	+		=	26
				43

264. For this puzzle, the largest number to be inserted in the layout is 9 and the lowest is 2, so you cannot put any digit larger than 9 or smaller than 2 in any of the empty cells.

	x		=	4
	÷	3	=	3
5	-		=	
	+		=	18
				27

265. Now things get a little more interesting, since the only digits that have been used anywhere in the layout this time are even numbers (2, 4, 6, 8 and so on) with no repetitions of any digit: that is, no number has been used more than once in the layout. Also, the highest digit used (with the exception of the final tally of 64 in the right bottom box) is 28. Good luck!

	x	8	=	16
24	÷		=	
	-	12	=	14
	+	18	=	
				64

266. For this arithmedoku, only two even digits, 2 and 4, have been used; all the others are odd. The location of the even ones is shown by the shaded cells. Only one of the odd digits has been repeated.

5	x		=	45
	÷	3	=	7
19	-		=	▓
13	+	▓	=	17
				71

267. In this puzzle the number 3 appears once in each row.

	x	2	=	
12	÷		=	
	-		=	11
	+	9	=	**33**

268. This time the 8's are wild. That means that the number 8 appears once in every row.

2	x		=	
16	÷		=	
	-	8	=	
12	+		=	20
				39

269. This time the 9's are wild. The number 9 appears a number of times, but we won't tell you how many, although it will appear at least once in each row.

	x	2	=	
	÷		=	1
	-	1	=	
	+		=	18
				45

270. For this last one, you are not given any of the results of multiplying, dividing and so forth in the right-most column. There is only one solution. We will tell you, moreover, that the largest number anywhere in the layout is 9. Also, there is no 0 anywhere in the layout.

2	x		=	
6	÷		=	
	-	8	=	
	+		=	
				7

WORDOKU

A challenging version of sudoku can be called wordoku. You have to insert a nine-letter word (all letters being different) into each row, column and 3 × 3 box. Like the standard sudoku, no letter can occur in the same line (row or column) or box. No need to go through a model puzzle. The logic is exactly the same; instead of numbers you are going to use letters. That is, you have to insert the missing letters of the given word in each of the boxes and in the rows and columns of the overall grid according to one simple rule—no repetitions of a letter are allowed in any box or in any row or column of the grid, but all nine letters must appear in the boxes and the rows and columns of the grid.

271. The word whose letters are to be inserted in the grid and boxes according to the standard sudoku rules is *antipodes* (two things that are diametrically opposite each other). As before, we are going to start off nice and easy. Also, upon completing the puzzle the following words emerge as hidden among the letters. The words can be read from the top line down and from left to right only. Can you find them? There may be others (such as prepositions or words that can be read vertically), but these are the only ones we ask you to locate.

Hidden Words: NATO, SIP, PAN, SET, DAN, NOT, SOT

D	P	S	E		N	A	T	O
E		A	D	T	S		P	N
I	N	T	A		P	S	D	
A	D	P	N	S	I		O	
T		I		A		P	N	S
	S	O		P	E	D		I
P	A	N		E	T		I	D
O		E	I	D		N		P
S	I	D	P	N	O		E	

272. The word to be placed into the puzzle this time is *baritones.* In the completed puzzle the following words are hidden among the letters. The words we want you to find can be read from the top line down and from left to right only. Can you find them?

Hidden Words: BRATS, IRAN, SOB, BRO, BORN, SEAT, EON

	T	N	S		B	E		A
	B		I	R		N	S	T
S	A	I			N	B	R	O
I	O		N	S	E	A		B
B	N				R	O		S
T	E	S	A	B	O	R		I
A		E	O		I	T	B	R
O		T	B		S	I	A	N
N		B	R	A	T			E

273. The next word to put into the layout is *cabinetry*, and the difficulty level is going up just a tad. As in previous wordokus, upon completing the puzzle it turns out that words are hidden among the letters. The words we want you to find can be read from the top line down and from left to right only. Can you find them?

Hidden Words: CAT, CAR, BYE, ATE, RYE, CARE

		N	B	R	Y	C	E	A
		R	N		I	B	T	Y
B	Y	E	C		T			
A	E	C	Y			N		
R	N	I	A			Y	B	C
		T	I	N	C	A	R	E
N					B	T	A	I
E	I			Y	N	R		
T	C			I	A	E	Y	N

274. The relevant word to place in this next puzzle is *daughters.* As you know by now, upon completing the puzzle certain words emerge from hiding among the letters. They can be read from the top row down and from left to right only. Can you find them? There may be others, but these are the only ones we want you to find.

Hidden Words: ART, RAG, HUE, READS

		U	R	E			S	G
		R	T	G			A	H
G			H	S	D	U	T	R
H	U	E			T	G	D	S
D		T			G	H		
R		G	D	H	S	T		
E	T				H	R	U	D
		H	U	D	E			T
		D	S	T	R			E

275. The word to be put in the next puzzle is *facetious*. The hidden words, which can be read from the top line down and from left to right only, are the following ones. And again, these are the only ones we ask you to locate.

Hidden Words: SECT, SET (twice)

O	I	E	T	U				S
T			O	F				U
A					C	T	O	I
C				S	E	T	F	
	E	T	C	O	F	I	U	
F	A	U			E		S	O
E	C	A	F				I	T
				T	O	A	C	
I	T	O	A	C	U	S		

276. The next word to place in the puzzle is *globefish* (also known as porcupine fish). Upon completing the puzzle, certain words are hidden among the letters. The words we want you to find can be read from the top line down and from left to right only. Can you locate them?

Hidden Words: HOBS, IO (satellite of Jupiter), FOG, BIG, LOG

F	G	E		O	B	S		L
S					F	O		
I	O	H	G	L	S	F		B
	S			B	H	L	O	
L	H			G	E	B	F	I
B	I	G	O	F				S
O	L	B	F					E
		S	L	E	I	H	B	O
		I	B	S		G	L	F

277. The next word to be placed in the puzzle is *hairstyle,* and the difficulty level has gone up a notch, as you will discover. Once again, upon completing the puzzle, words appear hidden among the letters. The words we want you to find can be read from the top line down and from left to right only. Can you find them?

Hidden Words: HAIL, ASH, HEY, HIS, LAY, THE

				T	R	I	L	A
T			A	I	Y	H		
H	A	I			S	Y	T	R
I	S	R			H		Y	L
E		T	Y	R	I		S	
	H	Y		L				
R	E	H		S	T	L		Y
L		S		Y		T	H	E
Y		A	E		L	S		I

278. The next word is *interflow* (to merge into a single stream). As you know, upon completing the puzzle you will find words hidden among the letters. The words we want you to find can be read from the top line down and from left to right only. Can you find them this time as well?

Hidden Words: WOE, NIT (insect egg), TOE (twice), LIE, OFT

L	R		O	E			T	
O		I	T	W		R	N	
E			F	R	W	L	O	
I	L		N	W	E			
T		E	F		L			W
N	W		T	R	O			E
	I		W	O		F	E	
F		O	E		I	N		R
W	E			N	F		O	I

279. The next word to be placed in the puzzle is *preachify.* The difficulty level continues to rise. Again, upon completing the puzzle the following words are hidden among the letters. The words we want you to find (there may be others) can be read from the top line down and from left to right only. Can you find them?

Hidden Words: ARC, AERY, CHIP

Y		A	R		I	P	E	F
	I		P		E			C
P		C	H	Y				R
E	C	P	F		H	R		A
		H	Y		R	F	C	E
R	F		A		C	H		P
	Y	I	E		F	C	P	H
C		F		H		E		Y
H		E	C		P	A		I

280. The last word is *watchdogs*. Once again, upon completing the puzzle the following words are hidden among the letters. The words we want you to find can be read from the top line down and from left to right only. Can you find them?

Hidden Words: SOT, AGO (twice), HOG, WATS (Buddhist temples), DAG, SAG, DOT, SO, DO, COATS

G		T	S				D	O
A			O	T	D	G		W
D		O	G			A	T	S
H	D	W		A		O		T
		C		W		D		G
S	A	G					W	C
	S		A		O		C	H
T		H	W	D		S		A
	O		T		H	W	G	

SQUAREDOKU

Have you ever heard of a magic square? This is the original placement puzzle. It consists in arranging the first nine integers (1, 2, 3, 4, 5, 6, 7, 8, 9) in a square pattern so that the sum of the numbers in each row, column, and diagonal is the same. It is called *Lo Shu* in China. Since its discovery over 4000 years ago, the arrangement has always been perceived as magical—hence the name *magic square*. The Chinese continue to ascribe mystical properties to it. It is thought to provide protection against the Evil Eye when placed over the entrance to a dwelling or room. Fortunetellers use it to cast fortunes. Amulets and talismans are commonly designed with Lo Shu inscribed in them.

The three rows, three columns and two diagonals of Lo Shu add up to 15. This is known as the *magic constant*. Here's one version of the original magic square:

8	3	4
1	5	9
6	7	2

In our version, you are given some of the numbers of a given set and told what the magic constant is. The main difference is that only the rows and columns will add up to that constant, *not the diagonals*. A second difference is that only a subset of numbers (not the first nine digits) will be used. This means that numbers can be repeated. We call it "Squaredoku." It is actually much harder than it looks and can be quite challenging. Here's a tip. Many of the harder ones are solved by trial and error. You try certain numbers in certain cells and see which trial is possible under the given conditions.

281. Let's start off nice and easy with a Squaredoku consisting of the numbers 0, 1, 2, 4, 5 and 8. These are to be placed in the square in such a way that the three rows and three columns always add up to 10. Some numbers have already been inserted. By the way, you might need to use a number more than once, but each number must be used at least once. There is a single solution. Can you reconstruct the square?

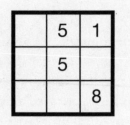

282. In the next puzzle, just three numbers, 2, 4 and 6, are to be placed in the square in such a way that the three rows and three columns add up to 12. Each number must be used at least once and any number can be repeated. Some numbers have already been inserted for you. Can you reconstruct the square?

283. In the next puzzle, the numbers 0, 2, 3, 5 and 7 are to be placed in the square in such a way that the three rows and three columns add up to 12. And remember that any number can be repeated and that each number must be used at least once. Some have already been inserted for you. Can you reconstruct the square?

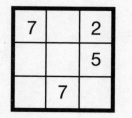

284. In the next puzzle, the numbers 2, 3, 7 and 8 are to be placed in the square in such a way that the three rows and three columns add up to 13. Can you reconstruct the square? Again, don't forget that each number must be used at least once and that any number can be repeated. Some numbers have already been placed for you.

285. Now things get a little bit harder. This time you are given numbers to put into a four-by-four square, rather than a three-by-three one. Again, the numbers are to be placed in the square in such a way that the four rows and four columns add up to 11. The numbers to use are 0, 1, 2, 3, 4, 5, 6, some of which have already been placed for you. The numbers may be repeated, but each number must be used at least once. Can you reconstruct the square?

1		5	2
	1		2
	1	1	
2			3

286. The numbers 0, 1, 2, 3, 4, 5, 6, 8, 9 and 11 are to be placed in the four-by-four square in such a way that the four rows and four columns always add up to 18. Some have already been placed for you. The numbers can be repeated but each one must be used at least once. Can you reconstruct the square?

9	8		
	6	3	
		9	3
0			11

287. The numbers 2, 3, 4, 5, 8, 9 and 10 are to be placed in the next four-by-four square in such a way that the four rows and four columns add up always to 20. Can you reconstruct the square? Remember that each number must be used at least once and that any number can be repeated. Some numbers have already been placed for you.

5			5
	9	2	
	2	10	
5			8

288. The numbers 0, 1, 2, 4, 5 and 8 are to be placed in this last four-by-four square in such a way that the four rows and four columns always add up to 10. Can you reconstruct the square? Again, remember that each number must be used at least once and that numbers can be repeated. Some numbers have already been placed for you.

		8	1
5		0	
4	1		
	8		0

289. Now, for the next two puzzles, try your hand at a five-by-five square. In this particular one the five rows and five columns add up to 14 and the numbers used are 0, 1, 2, 3, 4 and 6. Remember that you must use each number at least once (producing a singular solution) and that numbers can be repeated. Some numbers have already been placed for you. Can you reconstruct the square?

1		6	1	6
0	1			3
	6		3	
4		3		2
6		1	2	

290. The numbers 1, 2, 3, 7, 8 and 9 are to be placed in the five rows and five columns of this last five-by-five square in such a way that each row and column in the square adds up to 21. Again, the numbers must be used at least once, but each number can be repeated. Some numbers have already been placed for you.

7	8			1
		3	7	1
8	3	1		
2			1	9
	1	8	9	

ALPHADOKU

Remember word squares (chapter 1)? Well, here is a version of that genre which involves placement logic. You are given a series of letters to place in a square arrangement. The letters are to be placed horizontally (in a row line and read from left to right) only. You are not told what the words are. We call it alphadoku.

For example, place the letters *E, I, L, N, O, U, P, T* and *G* in the following square to make three words, read in the rows from left to right. Some of these—*L, I, N, E, T*—have already been placed for you. That leaves just *O, U, P* and *G* to place in the empty cells:

L	I	
	N	E
T		

Look at the top row. The final cell in it can be filled with either *P* (= *LIP*), *T* (= *LIT*) or *E* (= *LIE*) from the list to produce a legitimate word. However, the *E* and the *T* have already been used in the square (as you know), so the only candidate for that cell is *P*:

L	I	P
	N	E
T		

It is now obvious that the *O* from the remaining letters—*O, U* and *G*—is to be placed before the ___*NE* in the second row to produce *ONE*:

L	I	P
O	N	E
T		

Placing the remaining *U* and *G* in the last two cells produces the third word: *TUG*.

The three hidden words are *LIP, ONE* and *TUG*. That's all there is to it.

291. Place the following letters in the square to produce three words read in the rows from left to right only: *A* (twice), *B, C, E* (twice), *R, S, T.* Note that some of these have already been placed in cells for you.

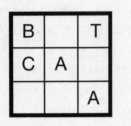

292. Place the following letters in the square to produce three words read in the rows from left to right: *A, D, E, M, N, O* (twice), *U, Y.* Note that some of these have already been placed in cells for you.

293. Place the following letters in the square to produce three words read in the rows from left to right only: *A, D, E* (three times), *I, N, P, R*. Some of these have already been placed in cells for you.

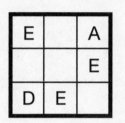

294. Place the following letters in the square to produce three words read in the rows from left to right only: *A, E* (twice), *G, N, R, S, U, Y*. Note that some of these have already been placed in cells for you.

	U	
		E
	Y	E

295. The difficulty level is going up a notch or two. This time, place the following letters in the square to produce four words read in the four rows from left to right only: *A* (twice), *B, E* (four times), *H, L, O, R, S, T* (twice), *V, Y*. Note that some of these have already been placed in cells for you.

B		A	
L		V	
	T	A	Y
H	E		

296. Place the following letters in the square to produce four words read in the rows from left to right only: *A, C* (twice), *E* (four times), *G, H, I, L, M, N, T, U* (twice). Note that some of these have already been placed in cells for you.

M		L	
	U	T	
N		C	
H		G	

297. Place the following letters in the square to produce four words read in the rows from left to right only: *A, E* (twice), *H* (twice), *I, L* (four times), *N, T, W* (four times). Note that some of these have already been placed in cells for you.

	H		N
W		A	
	I		L
	E	L	

298. Again, place the following letters in the square to produce four words read in the rows from left to right only: *D* (three times), *E* (twice), *F* (twice), *G, L, M, O* (six times). Note that some of these have already been placed in cells for you.

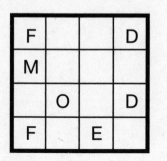

F			D
M			
	O		D
F		E	

299. The difficulty is going up again. Place the following letters in the square to produce five words read in the five rows from left to right only: *A* (three times), *B, C, E* (five times), *F, H* (three times), *L, O, R* (four times), *S* (twice), *T* (three times). Note that some of these have already been placed in cells for you.

C	L			R
H				T
	H		O	B
F			S	H
	E			

300. Place the following letters in this last square to produce five words read in the five rows from left to right only: *A* (three times), *C* (three times), *E* (twice), *G, I* (four times), *K, M* (three times), *N, O* (twice), *P, R, S, U, V.* Some of these have already been placed in cells for you.

	U			C
M		K		R
	A	G		C
P		A		
	O		C	

7
VISUAL LOGIC

One eye sees, the other feels.

PAUL KLEE (1879–1940)

THE BRAIN IS AN "organizing organ." It sees wholes where there may not even be wholes. Experiments have shown, in fact, that the perception of form does not depend on the perception of individual elements making up the form. For instance "squareness," or a square figure, can be perceived in any figure made up of four lines as well as in one of black dots. Indeed, this tendency of the brain can be seen in a classic puzzle that readers may have come across, a puzzle, incidentally, that gave origin to the expression "thinking outside the box." Here's an example:

Without letting your pencil leave the paper, can you draw four straight lines through the following nine dots?

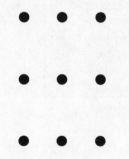

If you haven't seen this puzzle before, you might tend to solve it by joining up the dots as if they were located on the perimeter of an imaginary box figure. That is what your brain is accustomed to "seeing." But this reading of the puzzle will not yield a solution, no matter how many times you try. A dot will always be left over. However, the brain is also a creative organ. All you have to do is ask the right question: "What would happen if I think outside the box?" That turns out to be the relevant insight. One possible solution is as follows:

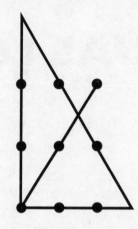

Another example of a visual logic puzzle is the tangram, whose origin is uncertain. The puzzle consists of a square cut into five triangles, a smaller square and a rhomboid. The challenge is to reassemble them into different given figures. Below is an example of how the pieces of the tangram puzzle (on the left) can be reassembled to produce the figure for a cat (on the right).

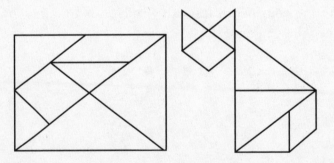

Puzzles such as these are perfect examples of what "visual thinking" involves. This is a major function of the right hemisphere of the brain, also called the visual hemisphere. The puzzles in this chapter are designed to activate that hemisphere, since they will get you to count figures (triangles, rectangles, etc.) hidden in other figures, rearrange figures, and so on. To solve them you will have to visualize, for example, how parts can be assembled to form wholes and how figures can be separated logically. Some people find these among the most frustrating of all types of puzzles. But they are worth the effort, since they activate whole-part thinking, one of the brain functions that needs to be exercised regularly.

STICK FIGURES

Stick figures are puzzles that get you to use given sticks to produce certain numbers or numerical statements—in other words, to make number figures from the sticks. Here's a simple example.

With these three sticks can you make a digit indicating the number four?

Below is the simple solution.

The basic idea here is to get your brain to envision or picture a numerical concept in your mind with given visual materials (in this case sticks). Given their nature, the ten puzzles in this section cannot really be arranged in any order of increasing difficulty or complexity. You either can envision a solution or not. Thus, they are either all easy for you or all challenging. You will find, though, that the last puzzles in this section might be harder to envision. Good luck!

301. Can you turn three sticks into a numerical figure indicating the number nine?

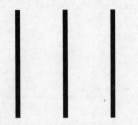

302. Can you turn two sticks into a numerical figure indicating the number ten?

303. Can you make a numerical expression standing for the value of one with three sticks?

304. Can you make the number seven with two sticks?

305. Can you make the number five with the same two sticks?

306. Can you turn three sticks into nothing, or more specifically a numerical statement standing for zero?

307. Now, with four sticks can you make an arithmetical expression standing for one?

308. Can you make an arithmetical expression that stands for ten with just four sticks?

309. Can you make the number seventeen with just three sticks?

310. Finally, can you make an expression standing for twelve with five sticks?

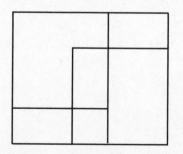

V I S U A L   L O G I C

FIGURE COUNTING

The idea in this next set of visual logic puzzles is to identify how many of a certain type of figure there are in a given diagram or shape.

How many four-sided, 90° figures (squares and rectangles) are in the diagram below?

The best way to solve puzzles like this one is to number all the segments.

As you can see, the twelve squares and rectangles are:

1. 1 + 2
2. 1 + 2 + 5 + 6
3. 1 + 2 + 3 + 4 + 5 + 6 (the overall diagram is itself a square)
4. 2
5. 2 + 6
6. 2 + 4 + 6
7. 3
8. 3 + 4
9. 4
10. 5
11. 5 + 6
12. 6

Be careful not to count the same figure more than once. For example, when considering figure 4 (number 9), you might be tempted to make it part of the figure 4 + 2 + 6. But this has already been identified as 2 + 4 + 6 (number 6).

311. Let's start with a similar puzzle. How many four-sided, 90° figures (squares and rectangles) are in the diagram below?

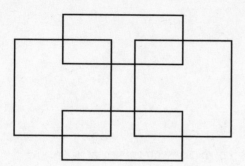

312. Now let's put our focus on triangles. How many triangles are there in this diagram?

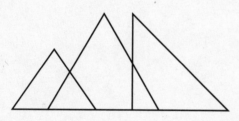

313. This is a bit trickier than the previous one. How many triangles are there in the diagram?

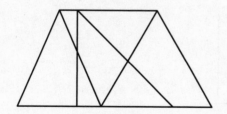

314. One last triangle puzzle. How many do you see in the diagram below?

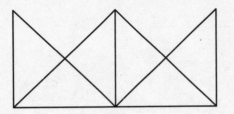

315. Here's one involving circles. How many circles, not ovals, segments or arcs, are there in the diagram?

316. Let's do another rectangle- and square-counting exercise. How many four-sided, 90° figures (squares and rectangles) are in the diagram below?

317. Here's another rectangle- and square-counting exercise. How many four-sided, 90° figures (squares and rectangles) are in the diagram below?

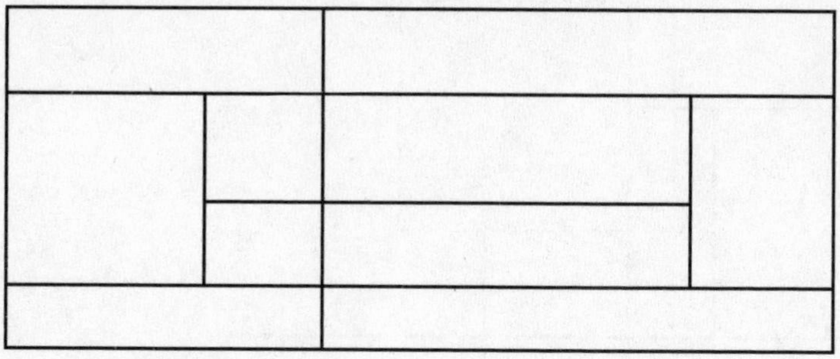

318. Let's continue with this kind of puzzle. How many four-sided, 90° figures (squares and rectangles) do you see in the diagram below?

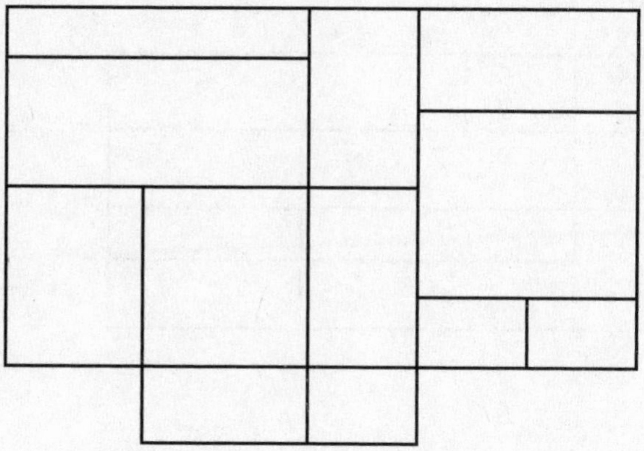

319. Here's yet another puzzle of this type, which looks much easier than it is. How many four-sided, 90° figures (squares and rectangles) do you see in the diagram below?

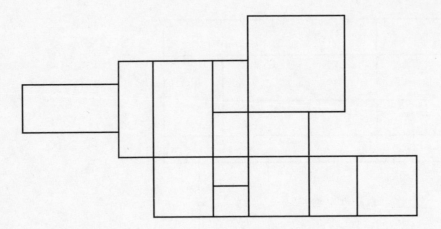

320. Here's the last puzzle in this genre, which, again, looks much easier than it really is. How many four-sided, 90° figures (squares and rectangles) do you see in the diagram below?

MATCHSTICK PUZZLES

A classic genre of visualization puzzle involves matchsticks in an arrangement that you are supposed to change in some way. Here's a simple example.

The 10 matchsticks below have been arranged to make three square figures. Remove just two matchsticks to produce two identical squares. There can be no partial squares remaining.

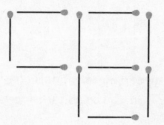

Simply remove the matchsticks marked as 1 and 2 and you will get the two squares.

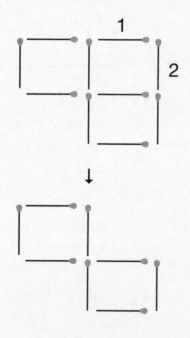

321. As always, let's start off nice and easy. The 12 matchsticks below have been arranged to make four square figures. Remove just two matchsticks to produce three identical squares. There can be no partial squares remaining.

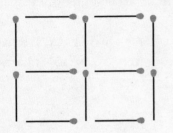

322. Consider the same 12-matchstick arrangement. This time remove just two matchsticks to produce two identical rectangles. There can be no partial rectangles remaining.

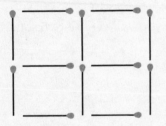

323. Consider the same 12-matchstick arrangement one more time. This time remove just three matchsticks to produce one rectangle and one square. There can be no partial squares or rectangles remaining.

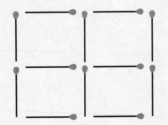

324. The 15 matchsticks below have been arranged to make five square figures. Remove just two matchsticks to produce two identical rectangles and one square. There can be no partial squares or rectangles remaining.

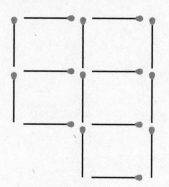

325. The 16 matchsticks below have been arranged to make five square figures. Remove just two matchsticks to produce four identical squares. There can be no partial squares remaining.

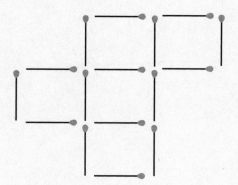

326. Consider the same arrangement. This time remove just two matchsticks to produce two identical rectangles and one square. There can be no partial squares or rectangles remaining.

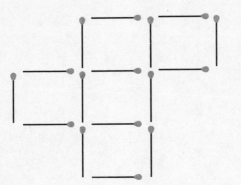

327. Now consider the following 20-matchstick arrangement of seven identical squares. Remove four sticks to produce a "cross figure" made up of five identical squares.

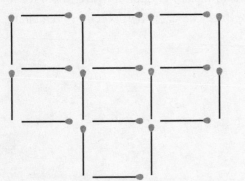

328. Consider the same 20-matchstick arrangement of seven identical squares. Remove four sticks to produce two rectangles and one square. There can be no partial squares or rectangles remaining.

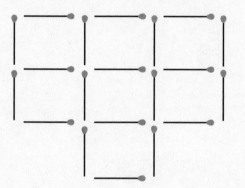

329. The 16 matchsticks below have been arranged to make five square figures. Remove just two matchsticks to produce four identical squares. There can be no partial squares remaining.

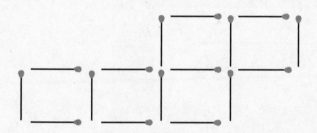

330. Now consider the same 16 matchsticks arranged to make five square figures. This time *move*, rather than remove, just two matchsticks to produce four identical squares. There can be no partial squares remaining.

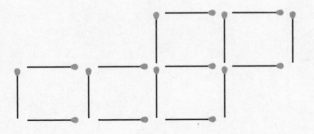

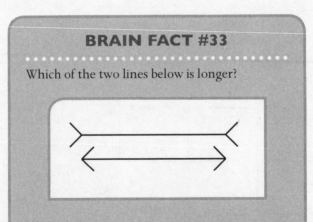

Can you spot anomalies in figures? In these puzzles you will have to do exactly that, but on the basis of logical deduction. This set is a version of the "odd one out" type of puzzle in the visual realm. Here's an example.

Which figure does not belong?

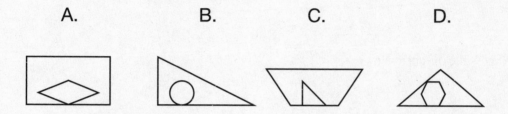

The answer is **b**. Each figure is made up of two shapes. In **a**, **c** and **d** the two shapes are straight-edged. The exception is **b**, in which the internal shape is a smooth, round one (a circle).

331. As always, we will start you with an easy one. Pick the intruder.

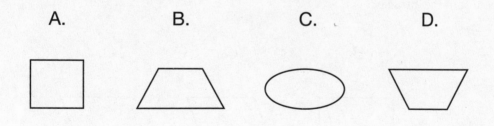

332. Which is the intruder now?

A.   B.   C.   D.

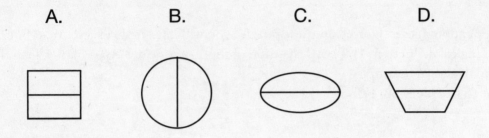

333. Where's the intruder below?

A.   B.   C.   D.

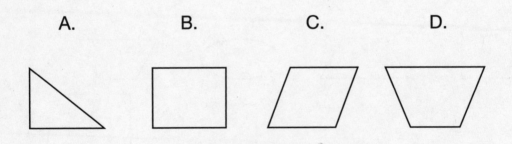

334. Can you spot the intruder?

A.   B.   C.   D.

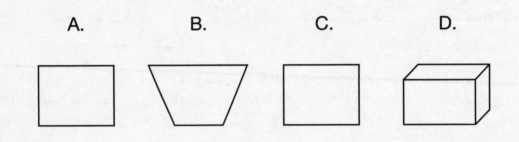

335. This is trickier than the previous ones. Which one is the intruder?

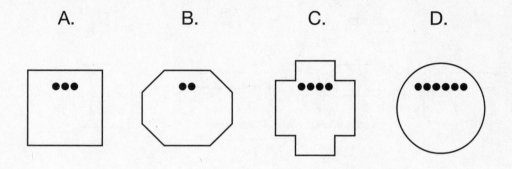

A.   B.   C.   D.

336. Picking out the intruder is starting to become a little more difficult. Where is it this time?

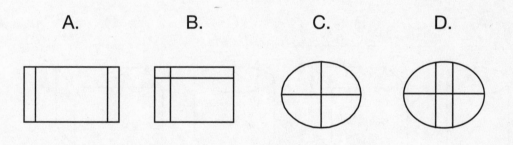

A.   B.   C.   D.

337. Now try your hand at this one, picking out the intruder again.

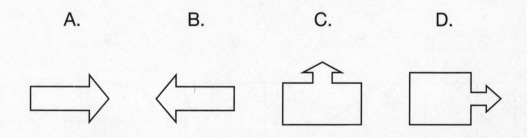

A.   B.   C.   D.

338. Here's a rather tricky one. Where's the intruder below?

A.   B.   C.   D.

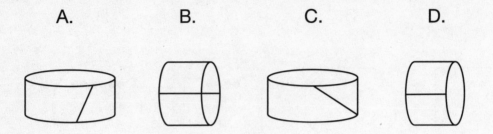

339. Here's another tricky one. Can you pick out the intruder?

A.   B.   C.   D.

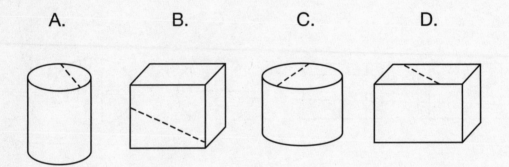

340. Here's the last one in this genre. Needless to say, it is trickier than the others. Can you pick out the intruder?

A.   B.   C.   D.

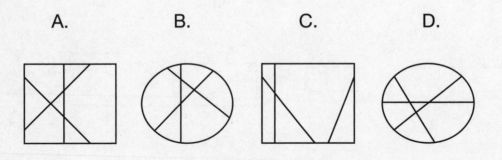

DISSECTION PUZZLES

In the remaining set of ten puzzles, you will have to use both your visual logic and a little knowledge of basic geometry. You will be asked to dissect some figure to produce some other figure or form. Here's a very simple example.

With two straight lines, dissect the circular pie into four equal slices.

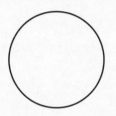

The best way to achieve this is to make the two lines across the diameter of the circle, intersecting at right angles. They can slant in any direction.

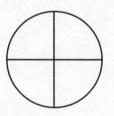

As you can see, this produces four equal slices in the circle.

As you do these puzzles, note that nobody is telling you what the length of the line should be. Make no assumptions.

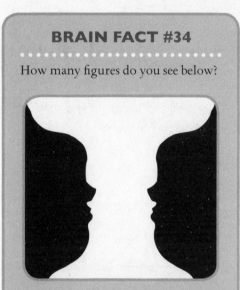
VISUAL LOGIC

341. Let's start off with a triangle dissection puzzle. With three lines dissect the triangle below to produce six new triangles inside such that four also make two equal triangles. It is not as tricky as it seems.

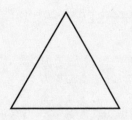

342. Here's another triangle puzzle. With one other line can you produce three internal triangles in the figure below?

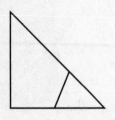

343. Now try your hand at a circle dissection puzzle. As you can see there are four slices inside the circle. With one other line can you produce six?

344. Here's another circle dissection puzzle. As you can see, the two lines produce three slices in the circle below. With one more line make it six.

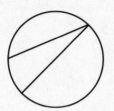

345. Now, using the same figure, can you produce only five slices this time with one new line?

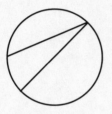

346. Let's move on to a square-dissection puzzle. The line in the square below produces one internal triangle. With two more lines can you produce four and only four triangles (including the original one)?

347. Here's a similar puzzle. The line in the figure below produces one internal triangle. With two more lines can you produce eight and only eight triangles (including the original one)?

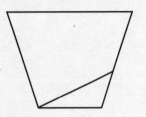

348. In the hexagon below, the two lines produce one single triangle, numbered as **1**. With four other lines can you produce eight and only eight triangles?

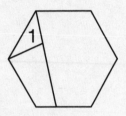

349. There are no triangles in the pentagon below with its internal line. Can you produce five and only five triangles by adding three new lines to it?

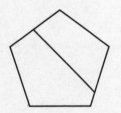

350. With two new lines can you produce seven and only seven triangles in the figure below? Note that smaller triangles can be components of larger triangles or figures.

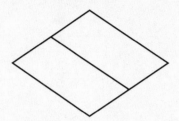

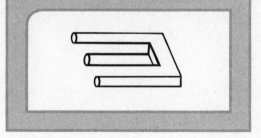
VISUAL LOGIC

8
MIND BOGGLERS

Puzzle-solving, like virtue, is its own reward.

HENRY E. DUDENEY (1847–1930)

MIND BOGGLER. WHAT AN interesting term—a puzzle that boggles the mind. And it is an appropriate one for the kinds of puzzles that you will be solving in this chapter. The term actually comes out of the mathematics field, where bogglers are used primarily for illustrative and pedagogical reasons. In some ways, the term is a generic one for puzzles, since the two are often used synonymously. But here it will be restricted to the more boggling aspects of certain puzzles, which entail facts, figures or situations that seem overwhelming and can only be sorted out by clear, logical thinking.

Are mind bogglers good for the brain? As with other puzzles, the research seems to answer with a resounding yes. The memory systems of those who do these puzzles seem to resist the ravages of aging. Scientists hypothesize that this may be due to the reinforcement of the brain cell pathways. As you solve a boggler, messages move along the overall network of brain cells. When a brain cell is stimulated, it releases chemicals called neurotransmitters. Some carry messages to neighboring cells. Others maintain the strength and longevity of the connections. Still others encourage the growth of new synapses (cell connections) to produce even more robust pathways. So by solving such puzzles, an assortment of thinking pathways are activated, allowing you to sustain and improve the overall functioning of your brain.

The first set of ten bogglers involves foot races, requiring you to figure out who finished in what order, or who won the race, and so on. Here's a very simple example.

Mark, Jane and Sarah had a race yesterday. Sarah came ahead of Jane and Mark came after Jane. Who won the race?

Mark came after Jane, so he did not win the race. Either Sarah or Jane won the race. We are told that Sarah came ahead of Jane, so Sarah is the winner. The order is: Sarah (first), Jane (second), Mark (third).

351. Here's a very simple puzzle in this genre. Three runners, Fred, Holly and Gillian, raced against each other at a high school meet. Fred beat Holly, but not Gillian. Who came in first?

352. Four runners met at a competition last week. Mary beat Shamila who beat Natasha. Bettina beat Mary. In which order did they finish?

353. At the same competition, four other runners competed in a separate race. Anoush beat Lenny, who beat Joshua. Tom came in right after Anoush. In which order did they finish?

354. In an Olympic 100-meter tryout event, Chloe beat Jasmine and Sally. Dana came in right after Sally but ahead of Jasmine. In which order did they finish?

355. Alexander, Chris, Sarah, Danielle and Ethan competed against each other at a local community race for charity. Ethan beat Chris, Sarah beat Ethan, Danielle came in right after Sarah and just ahead of Ethan, and Alexander beat Sarah. In which order did they finish?

356. At the same meet another five people competed. Rick came in right after Miriam and just ahead of Jameel. Wes came in right after Jameel. Tyrell beat Miriam. In which order did they finish?

357. Five professional runners squared off at a recent competition. On their shirts they bore the numbers 1, 2, 3, 4 and 5. Here's what happened. No runner came in according to his or her number; that is, the one who wore number 1 did not come in first, the one who wore number 2 did not come in second, and so on. Numbers 3, 4 and 5 finished one after the other, with 3 coming in just ahead of 4 who came in just ahead of 5. But 3 was not the overall winner. In which order did they finish?

358. Five other professional runners competed at the same competition. Again they bore the numbers 1, 2, 3, 4, 5 on their shirts. Number 1 did not end up first and Number 5 did not end up fifth. However, 1 came in just ahead of 5. Number 4 did not win the race, nor did she end up second or fourth. Number 3 came in right after 5. In which order did they finish?

359. Six runners competed at an international meet. Corey came in just ahead of Allan, who came in just ahead of Betty. Everett came in just ahead of Corey. Dale came in right after Betty and just ahead of Frank. In which order did they finish?

360. At the same meet, six other runners squared off. Jake beat Buck who beat Pam who beat Sheila who beat Tyler. Lenny came in right after Tyler. In which order did they finish?

BRAIN FACT #36

Why are we so intrigued and also frustrated by puzzles? The answer might lie in the origin of the English word *puzzle* itself, which comes from the Middle English word *poselen*, which means "to bewilder, confuse." And indeed, puzzles generate bewilderment and confusion, because they cannot be solved by applying any formula or method mindlessly. They always require a dose of creative, unconventional thinking, which psychologists call "insight thinking." Puzzles are like vitamins for our brains.

These puzzles involve simply, yet maddeningly, the ability to count and figure out how old people are. Here's an example.

Annie, Nicky and Mary are three children. Nicky is twice as old as Annie, but half the age of Mary. The sum of their ages totals just 14. How old is each one?

Perhaps trial and error is the best way to approach this puzzle unless you are interested in using algebra. If we assign the age of 1 to Annie, then Nicky would be 2 (twice her age) and Mary would be 4, since Nicky's age of 2 would be half of this age. Adding them up, however, makes $1 + 2 + 4 = 7$, which is not 14. The ages that work under these conditions, therefore, are Annie = 2, Nicky = 4 (twice Annie's age and half Mary's age) and Mary = 8. Add them up and you get 14.

These can really get to be quite challenging, as you will see, and really boggle your brain. Good luck; you'll need it!

361. Becky, Tricia and Frieda are teenage friends. No one is older than 18 or younger than 13. Tricia is five years older than Becky and Frieda is one year younger than Tricia. How old is each one?

362. In the Younger family there are two brothers and two sisters. The sum of their ages is 32. The two brothers differ in age by one year, as do the two sisters. The sum of the brothers' ages is 11. How old is each one?

363. By subtracting the ages of three brothers, from the oldest to the youngest in that order, the result is 10 years. No one is older than 40. The middle brother is half the age of the oldest brother, and the youngest brother is half the age of the middle brother. How old is each one?

364. The ages of a brother and sister are digit reversals (for example, if one were 14, the other would be 41, if one were 16, the other would be 61, and so forth). The sum of their ages is 33. The sister, who is the younger of the two, is not older than 14. How old is each one?

365. There are four brothers in a family. Amazingly, one is three times older than the youngest, and the oldest is three times older than this brother is. A fourth brother is twice as old as the youngest. Yet, not one of the four is older than 10. How old is each one?

366. Two sisters' ages are digit reversals of each other (that is, if one is 13 the other is 31, and so on). If you add the ages up, you'll get 55. Neither sister is older than 20. What are their ages?

367. The ages of four brothers are consecutive prime numbers and the sum of these numbers is 36. What is a prime number? It is a number, other than 1, that can only be divided by itself (and 1, of course). For example, 3 is a prime, but 4 is not because it can be divided by 2. Also, 11 is a prime because it can only be divided by itself and 1. So what are their ages?

368. Four sisters are exactly two years apart in age, from the youngest to the oldest. For example, if the youngest sister were 2 years old, the next one would be 4, the third oldest would be 6, and the oldest would be 8. The total of their ages is 44. One of the sisters is 12 years old. How old is each one?

369. The Green family consists of a father, mother, son and daughter. The mother is exactly two years younger than the father. Strangely the father is exactly twice his son's age and the mother exactly twice her daughter's age. One of the two siblings is 24 years old. The siblings differ in age by one year. The sum of all their ages is 147. How old is each one?

370. Four online gamers challenge each other every day. Their names are Gina, Jake, Sophie and Roy. The youngest is 10 and the oldest is 26. A third gamer is half one of these ages, and the last of the four gamers is one year older than one other gamer. All together their ages add up to 60. Gina is not the oldest or the youngest. Jake is not the oldest or the youngest either. Sophie is older than Roy and Gina is older than Jake. How old is each one?

ARITHMETIC BOGGLERS

The next set of bogglers involves basic knowledge of arithmetic (addition, subtraction and so on). Here's a simple example:

Using exactly three 2's and choosing from only four basic arithmetic operations (+, −, ×, ÷) make the number 2 again.

There are two answers: (1) $2 + 2 \div 2 = 2$ or (2) $2 \times 2 \div 2 = 2$. Simple enough, right? It gets much harder as you progress through the puzzles.

371. Using exactly three 1's and only four basic arithmetic operations (+, −, ×, ÷) make the number 2.

372. Using exactly four 2's and only four basic arithmetic operations (+, −, ×, ÷) make the number 3.

373. Using exactly three 3's and only four basic arithmetic operations (+, −, ×, ÷) make the number 6.

374. Using exactly four 4's and only four basic arithmetic operations (+, −, ×, ÷) make the number 3.

375. Using exactly four 5's and only four basic arithmetic operations (+, −, ×, ÷) make the number 3.

376. Using exactly four 6's and only four basic arithmetic operations (+, −, ×, ÷) make the number 11.

377. Using exactly five 7's and only four basic arithmetic operations (+, −, ×, ÷) make the number 7.

378. Using exactly seven 8's and only four basic arithmetic operations (+, −, ×, ÷) make the number 40.

379. Using exactly four 3's and the basic arithmetic operations (+, −, ×, ÷) as well as exponent notation, make the number 3. An exponent is a superscript number written above and to the right of a number to show how many times the number is to be multiplied (used as a factor). For example, $3^4 = 3 \times 3 \times 3 \times 3$ and $5^6 = 5 \times 5 \times 5 \times 5 \times 5 \times 5$.

380. Using exactly six 2's and the basic arithmetic operations (+, −, ×, ÷) as well as exponent notation, make the number 2.

This next set of puzzles are true mind bogglers. You will be asked where certain people sit at a table. You will have to keep in mind what left and right, for example, entail when sitting around a table. Here's an example.

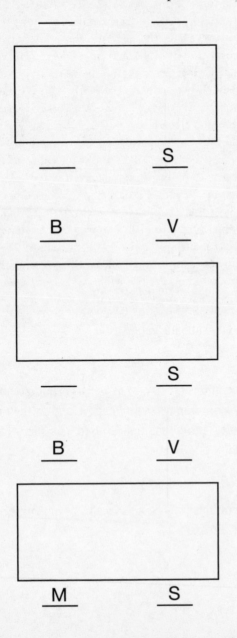

Bill, Mimi, Valerie and Samantha were seated at dinner last night. They paired off on two sides of a rectangular table. No one sat at either head of the table. Bill sat to Valerie's right. Samantha (S) was seated as shown. What was the seating arrangement?

Note that you are looking down at the table from above. Clearly, Bill (B) and Valerie (V) sat next to each other and on the other side from S, since we are told that "Bill sat to Valerie's right." The trick now is to envision what "to Valerie's right" would mean in terms of the diagram. You have to consider where Valerie's right arm is in your mind, sitting next to Bill on the side opposite Samantha. The only possible arrangement of B and V that is consistent with this position of Valerie's right arm is shown in the second diagram.

Just think about it (or go to a table and lay out the people as required) and you will see that in this configuration, B is seated to the right of V (even though it appears as to the left in the diagram). Mimi (M) sat, of course, in the remaining spot.

For all of these puzzles, you will be looking down at the table from above. As always we will start you off nice and easy, gradually turning up the difficulty level a notch or two as you progress through the puzzles.

381. Four people sat facing each other at a rectangular table to play cards. They were Alex (A), Fred (F), Bertha (B) and Tina (T). Tina sat as shown below. Alex sat diagonally across from Tina (not right in front of her). Bertha sat to Alex's immediate left. How were the four seated?

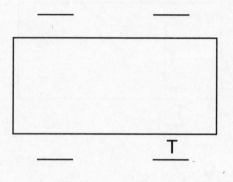

382. Katharine (K), Cailin (C), Bianca (B), Vanessa (V) and Sara (S) were playing cards around a rectangular table yesterday. Bianca took one of the head table spots as shown below. To her immediate left sat Katharine and to her (Bianca's) immediate right sat Sara. Vanessa did not sit on the same side as Katharine. How were they seated?

383. Six guys—Andrew (A), Peter (P), Tom (T), Larry (L), Sid (S) and Rick (R)—get together every Monday to play poker. They also sit in the same spots each time. Andrew and Tom are partners (and thus sit facing each other), as are Peter and Larry (who also face each other) and Rick and Sid (who also face each other). Tom and Sid always sit as shown below. Peter sits to Sid's immediate right. With these few facts you should be able to indicate where the guys sit every time they get together to play poker.

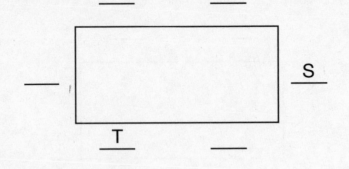

384. Seven people were seated at a dinner party. Their names are Beth (B), Caitlin (C), Ned (N), Mark (M), Zooey (Z), Dina (D) and Wes (W). Wes sat at one of the two head table spots, as did Zooey. Caitlin sat as shown below (and thus faced no one). Ned sat to Zooey's immediate left and across the table from Caitlin's side. Beth sat to Caitlin's immediate right, and she did not face Dina. Can you figure out how the seven were seated?

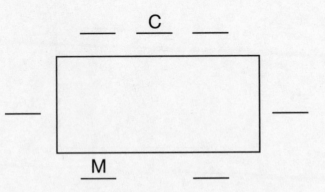

385. Four people—Chris (C), Alex (A), Danielle (D) and Sarah (S)—sat around a circular table. Chris took up the seat shown below. Alex did not sit next to Danielle and Sarah did not sit next to Chris. Alex sat to Sarah's immediate left. How were they seated?

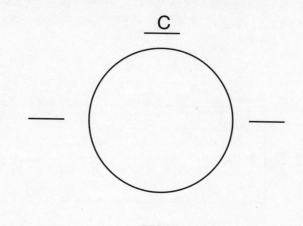

386. Three singers and a pianist sat around a circular table to discuss a rehearsal. Their names are Marcel (M), Sophia (S), Vanessa (V) and Bianca (B). Marcel sat as shown below. Neither Vanessa nor Bianca are the pianist. Sophia sat to the immediate right of the pianist and Bianca sat right across from the pianist. How were the four seated?

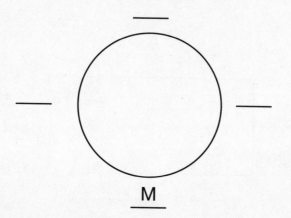

387. Inez (I), Edward (E), Rita (R), Alex (A), William (W), Matt (M) and Terry (T) sat around a rectangular table yesterday for a regularly scheduled meeting at work. We will show you only where Alex sat. Matt was the only one who did not sit directly across from anyone. Inez and Edward sat right next to each other on the same side of the table. Edward and Terry sat directly across from each other, and William sat to Matt's immediate right. Can you determine what the seating arrangement was?

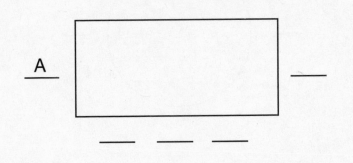

388. Seven female friends were seated for dinner at a posh restaurant the other night. Their names are Cynthia (C), Ariana (A), Dina (D), Louise (L), Martha (M), Shirley (S) and Yvonne (Y). We will show you where Shirley and Ariana were seated. Across from Ariana sat Louise and Yvonne. But neither one sat directly across from Ariana. Louise sat to Shirley's immediate right. Dina sat directly across from Yvonne. Cynthia sat on the same side as Dina. How were the women seated?

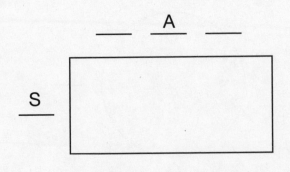

389. Four couples went out to dinner to celebrate their anniversaries. The couples were Jack (J) and Vanessa (V), Frank (F) and Quentina (Q), Helen (H) and Omar (O), and Peter (P) and Mariana (M). We will show you only where Jack and Vanessa sat, opposite each other. Peter and Mariana, as well as Helen and Omar, sat right next to each other on opposite sides of the table: that is, Peter sat next to Mariana on one side of the table and Helen sat next to Omar on the other side of the table. Mariana sat on the same side as Jack and to Quentina's immediate right. Vanessa sat to Frank's immediate right and Helen's immediate left. How were the couples seated?

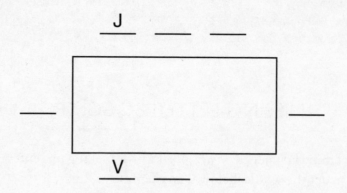

390. Eight friends went out to dinner at an expensive restaurant. Their names are Asha (A), Kevin (K), Trinity (T), Misha (M), Rona (R), Sabrina (S), Pat (P) and Lucy (L). We will show you only where Rona sat. Asha, Kevin and Pat sat on the same side of the table, and Trinity, Misha and Lucy sat on the other side. Pat sat to the immediate right of Sabrina and directly across from Lucy. Asha sat directly across from Trinity and to Rona's immediate left. How were the friends seated?

MISSING-LETTER BOGGLERS

For your final set of mind bogglers, you are given words making up sentences, but with missing letters. Reconstruct the words. Below is an example.

L _ V _   _ V _ R Y   D _ Y   _ S   _ F   _ T

W _ R _   T H _   L _ S T   D _ Y   _ F

Y _ _ R   L _ F _

This is the saying *Live every day as if it were the last day of your life*. The words are missing vowels. You will be told what the expression concerns at the beginning. Good luck!

391. Title of a hymn and popular Christmas song. As you can see, the first letters of the words are missing:

_ O Y   _ O   _ H E   _ O R L D

392. Common expression referring to the weather. As you can see, the vowels of the words are missing:

_ T ' S   R _ _ N _ N G   C _ T S   _ N D

D _ G S

393. Common proverb related to appearance. As you can see, the second and last letters of every word are missing. Sometimes these are one and the same.

B _ A U T _   I _   I _   T _ _   E _ _

O _   T _ _   B _ H O L D E _

394. Common proverb. As you can see, the first and last letters of every word are missing (thus, both letters of two-letter words will be missing):

_ _   _ N _   _ N O W _   _ H A _   _ H _

_ U T U R _   _ I L _   _ R I N _

395. Another common proverb. Some vowels are missing, but not all.

T H _   B _ S T   T H _ N G S   _ N

L _ F _   A R _   F R _ _

396. Good advice. As you can see, only the first and last letters of each word are given:

Y _ U   S _ _ _ _ D   A _ _ _ _ S   H _ _ E

F _ R   T _ E   B _ _ T

397. Movie title (1967). As you can see, the last two letters of every word are missing:

Y _ _   O N _ _   L I _ _   T W I _ _

398. Common saying. As you can see, the first two letters of every word are missing:

_ _ U   _ _ W A Y S   _ _ R T   _ _ E

_ _ E   _ _ U   _ _ V E

399. Title of a famous play and movie. Letters have been removed randomly.

S _ _ E   L _ K _   _ _   _ O T

400. A well-known saying. Letters have been removed randomly.

A   P _ _ _ _ _ _   _ _   W _ R _ _   _

T H _ _ _ _ N _   W _ _ D _

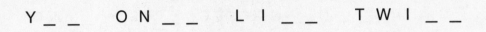

BRAIN FACT #40

Following up on the previous sidebar, we tested puzzles on the interviewees that expressed a preference for another genre. For example, those who disliked crosswords were trained to do crosswords. And those who hated math puzzles were given a number of math puzzles to do. At the end of the period we found that a significant number claimed that they started to like the puzzle genre they once disliked. So by simply being trained to do puzzles, our puzzle instinct seems to kick in and allow us to enjoy all genres.

9
MISCELLANEOUS LOGIC PUZZLES

A child asked, "Can God do everything?"
On receiving an affirmative reply, she at once said:
"Then can He make a stone so heavy that He can't lift it?"

HENRY DUDENEY (1847–1930)

LOGIC. THAT WORD IS AN AMBIVALENT TERM, referring to many aspects of thinking. But what is logic really? Henry Dudeney, one of the greatest puzzle makers of all time, presents us with a truly enigmatic conundrum, reproduced in the epigraph above. The child's question is similar to a classic question: What would happen if an irresistible moving body came into contact with an immovable body? Such bizarre paradoxes arise only because we take delight in inventing them. In actual fact, if there existed such a thing as an immovable body, there could not at the same time exist a moving body that nothing could resist.

Logic puzzles allow you to hone your puzzle-solving skills in a systematic fashion. This chapter covers a wide variety of logic puzzles. The work in neuroscience has been confirming that all areas of the brain are involved in producing complex thought. In other words, by doing puzzles such as those in this chapter you will be exercising your whole brain. In the same way that exercising your whole body (not just the hands or the feet, for example) produces many benefits—called whole-body exercise—so too will exercising the whole brain produce many benefits. By analogy, this can be called "whole-brain exercise."

You've probably heard of the term *lateral thinking*. This now covers a broad range of meanings. It refers especially to the use of logic in nontraditional ways and it is also used to warn you about being careful about facts, scrutinizing them in an observant way. It is in this latter sense that we use the term *lateral*. Here's an example of the kind of puzzle you will be facing in this section.

Maria's dad has five daughters.
The first four are named Ada, Ede, Idi and Odo.
What is the name of the fifth daughter?

Because the first four daughters all have names that start and end with the first four vowels in order *(a, e, i, o, [u])*, surrounding a *d*, you might have been easily duped into thinking that the fifth daughter's name starts and ends with the fifth vowel: *Udu*. The fifth daughter's name is *Maria*, as given to you at the beginning of the puzzle. Did you miss it?

Some of these are classic nuts in this genre. You are really going to have to pay attention to the wording of the puzzles. Good luck!

401. I have two current U.S. coins, one in my right and one in my left hand. The two coins add up to 15¢. I opened one hand and, to my surprise, saw that it was not a nickel. So what two coins do I have?

402. A man has three daughters, each of which has a brother. How many children did he have altogether?

403. Frank's widow Maria got remarried, and he didn't even put up a fuss, even though Frank and Maria had been passionately in love for years. Can you figure out why he didn't?

404. The other day Armand, who is quite big, weighed himself on a scale. He was shocked at what he saw. He weighed 400 pounds! To make himself feel better, he lifted one leg, hopefully to get a smaller weight measurement for his sanity. How much did he weigh with his one leg lifted up?

405. If it takes twelve one-dollar bills to make a dozen, how many two-dollar bills does it take?

406. I love cooking spaghetti. However, I find that cooking without my glasses on takes one hour and twenty minutes; with them off it takes me 80 minutes. Can you explain why?

407. There are seven tomatoes in a box. Without cutting up any of the tomatoes, they were divided among seven family members, and yet one tomato was left in the box. How could this be?

408. Mary and Frank are married and have a son, but Mary has never seen the son. How could this be?

409. Gina and Sophie are sisters, and yet they have two mothers. How could this be?

410. A two-ton truck got stuck under a bridge that was too low for it to make it through. The driver clearly underestimated the height. However, he had a flash of insight whereby he got the truck through the bridge without having to destroy or damage either the truck or the bridge. How did he do it?

LOGIC WHEELS

Logic wheels are circles divided into six segments. Five of these have words or symbols of various kinds in them. On the basis of reasoning alone you should be able to figure out what is missing from the sixth segment so as to complete the wheel logically. Here's a simple example.

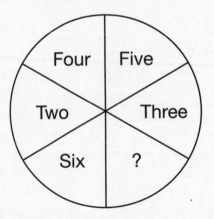

There are two answers here. One possible answer is *one*, since the words in the wheel refer to the first six numbers, but *one* is missing. Another answer is *seven*. Why? Because the wheel contains number pairs that differ by one (2 and 3; 4 and 5), and which start with the same letter when written (*Four* and *Five*; *Two* and *Three*). So, *Six* and *Seven* form a pair differing by one and starting with the same letter.

Anything goes here, as you will soon discover. Sometimes even the position of the symbols matters. You'll just have to put on your logical thinking cap.

411.

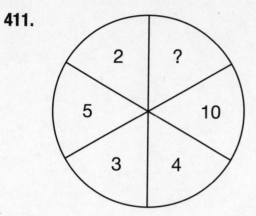

412.

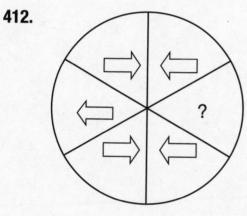

413.

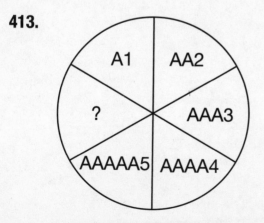

414.

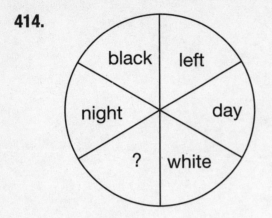

415.

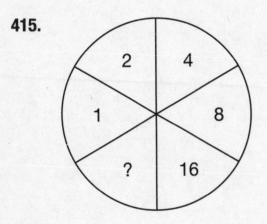

416.

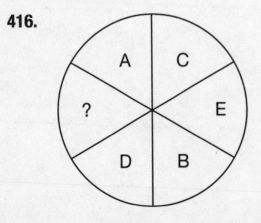

417.

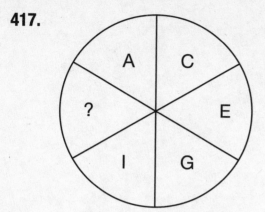

418.

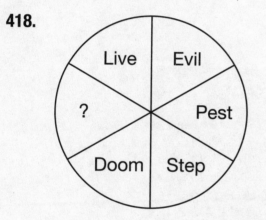

419.

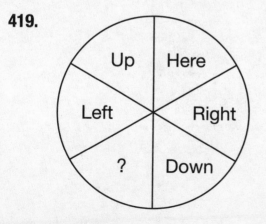

420.

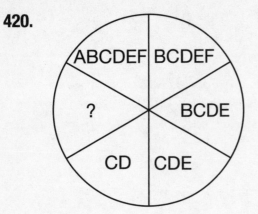

In the next set of puzzles, you are shown three boxes with labels designating the coins supposedly contained therein. But all or some of the labels are marked incorrectly; that is, they might or might not indicate the amount of coins in each box. You have to figure out where the coins are. Here's an example:

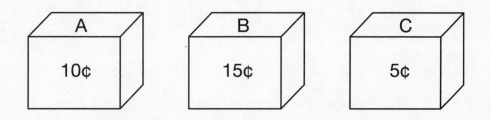

Each box is labeled incorrectly; that is, it does not contain the amount it shows. The amounts shown are distributed differently. You are told that the actual amount in C is 15¢. How much is in A and B?

First, as you can see, there is a total of 30¢ in the three boxes (10¢ + 15¢ + 5¢). Box C contains 15¢. We can easily deduce that A contains 5¢, since it contains neither the 15¢ (which is in C), nor the 10¢ (which is what its label wrongly indicates, as we know). By the process of elimination, B contains the 10¢. In sum: A = 5¢, B = 10¢, C = 15¢.

421. Let's start off really easy. The labels of two of the boxes below have been attached incorrectly, thus indicating the wrong amount of coins in each. One is labeled correctly. The total amount of coins in the three boxes is 55¢ (as the sum of the labels indicates). Box A is opened up and it is shown to contain 5¢. How much is in each box?

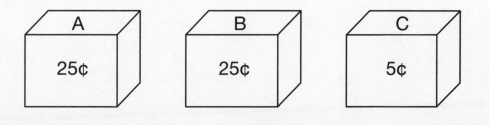

422. The labels of the three boxes below have been switched, thus indicating the wrong amount in each. The total amount of coins in the three boxes is 30¢ (as the sum of the labels indicate). Box A is opened up and it is shown to contain 15¢. How much is in each box?

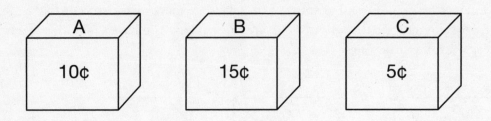

423. Two of the three labels below are correct. Someone labeled a third one incorrectly. In total the amount in the three boxes is actually 50¢, not the 45¢ you get by adding the amounts shown on the labels. As it turns out, the label figure of the one labeled incorrectly is a divisor of the figure on one of the two correctly labeled boxes. Which box is labeled incorrectly and how much is in it?

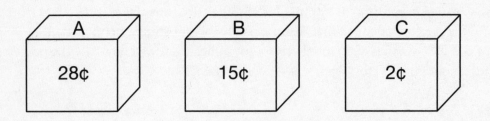

424. The labels of A and B below are both incorrect. We are told, however, that they contain equal amounts of money. C is labeled correctly. The total amount in the three boxes is 50¢. How much money is in each box?

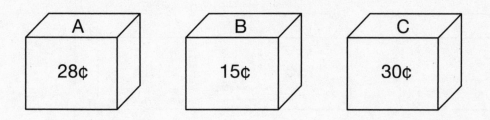

425. The three labels below are incorrect, having been switched around. The total amount in the three boxes is 90¢, with one of them being empty, as you can see. If you add the real contents in C to those in one other box you get 40¢. How much money is in each box?

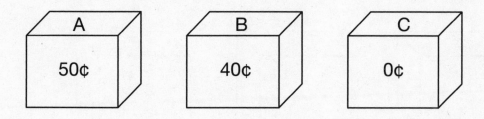

426. All three boxes have had their labels switched around and, thus, no box shows the correct amount. The difference in actual money between Box B and C is 5¢ nonetheless, with B having the larger amount. How much is in each box?

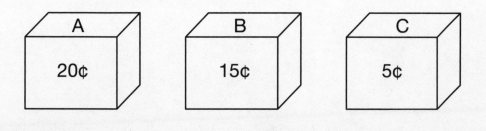

427. Someone forgot to put the label on Box A and also put incorrect labels on both B and C. The total amount in the three boxes is 40¢. One of the two labels found on B or C is actually the amount in A. B does not contain the lowest amount of money. How much is in each box?

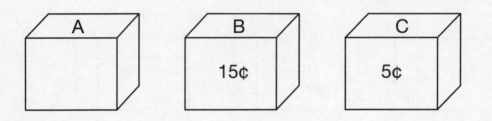

428. This time someone forgot to label two boxes, A and B. The total amount in the three boxes is 50¢. The label put on C shows an incorrect amount for that box. C's label shows an amount that belongs actually to either A or B. Someone attempts to take out the amount of money in C and finds that it is empty. How much is in the two other boxes?

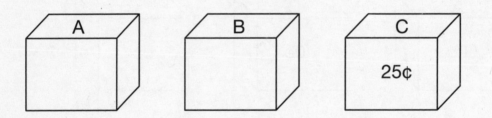

429. Someone forgot to label all three boxes. We are told that each box contains three times the one before it alphabetically (or from left to right): that is, Box B contains three times the amount in Box A and Box C contains three times the amount in Box B. The total amount in the three boxes is 39¢. How much money is in each box?

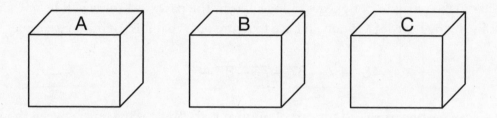

430. Someone forgot to label the amount of money contained by Boxes A and C and put a label on Box B that is either 5¢ more or 5¢ less than the amount shown. The total amount contained by the three boxes is 35¢. Boxes A and C are not empty and contain the same amount of money. How much money is in each box?

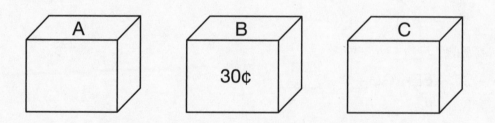

30¢

PASSWORD CODES

Everything is done with passwords nowadays. The internet age could actually be characterized as the password age. In this set of puzzles you are given a series of numbers, letters or symbols that make up a kind of password logic. From the password there will be one element missing. Using pure logic, you will have to figure out what it is. Here's an example:

$$45-54-67-76-85-\underline{\quad}$$

As you can see, the password consists of number pairs. What is the link between them? If you look closely, you will see that the pairs are reversals; that is, they are written with the same digits in reverse: 45 and 54, 67 and 76 and, thus, 85 and 58. So 58 is the answer.

431. Let's start off nice and easy.

$$1A-2B-3C-4D-5E-\underline{\qquad}$$

432. Here's another fairly easy one.

$$AA-CC-EE-GG-II-\underline{\qquad}$$

433. This one is still relatively easy.

$$TEN-NET-BUT-TUB-PAL-LAP-DAM-\underline{\qquad}$$

434. The code-breaking logic is starting to get harder with this one.

$$A1-D4-G7-I9-M13-X\underline{\qquad}$$

435. The difficulty continues to rise.

112—235—336—437—516—63_____

436. This next one is equal in difficulty level to the previous one.

725—936—541—743—853—65_____

437. The difficulty level is going up a bit, but this puzzle is based on a code that is similar to the previous two, although not identical.

2510—4520—3618—8432—7428—5315—93_____

438. This next one is not really that difficult, but it is rather tricky.

RAT1—BOOR2—HAIL2—TEASE3—EASIEST4—SCREAM_____

439. The trickiness continues.

BILL4—TOM3—PENNY5—NATASHA7—GILLIAN7—MARTIN_____

440. Try your hand at this last one, which is, needless to say, quite challenging.

AB3—CF9—EF11—GR25—IJ19—BZ_____

BRAIN FACT #45

The great philosopher Gottfried Leibniz was among the first to forge a link between logic and the brain. Calling logical reasoning a *lingua universalis* (a "universal language" of mind), Leibniz claimed that it could be used to great advantage in the betterment of the human condition for the simple reason that "errors" in thinking could be reduced to errors in logic and thus easily fixed. I am not as confident about this as Leibniz was, but certainly the connection between brain and logic that he indicated is unquestionable.

There are many two-word expressions. In this set of puzzles, you are given two words separated by a space. That space contains a word that completes the two-word expression associated with the first word and starts the two-word expression associated with the second word. Here's an example:

KEY _____ LINK

What word fits logically in the space? That word is *CHAIN* and the two relevant expressions are *KEY CHAIN* and *CHAIN LINK*. That's all there is to it, but the challenge is undeniable. You will really have to put your thinking cap on here.

441. TRUE _____ AFFAIR

442. NEW _____ WAR

443. LIFT _____ BASE

444. WILD _____ SHARK

445. RED _____ BEETLE

446. BLUE _____ PHASE

447. DOG _____ BOAT

448. SUN _____ CHECK

449. REAL _____ TAX

450. TRIAL _____ AROUND

PART III

IQ
and the Brain

FACTS ABOUT IQ

⌘ IQ, which stands for Intelligence Quotient, is a relative measure of intelligence.

⌘ The first true IQ test was invented in 1905.

⌘ During the 1930s, controversy over the definition of IQ led to the development of the Wechsler-Bellevue Intelligence Scale, which was designed to provide an index of general mental ability and reveal intellectual strengths and weaknesses.

⌘ The most important aspect of IQ testing is the interpretation of the results. Various scoring techniques are used for comparing an individual's score with the scores of a larger group. This is why it is called a "relative" measure of intelligence.

⌘ The test has changed considerably over the years because of criticism leveled against it that it is biased towards certain groups. It may, in fact, be impossible to come up with a test that is based on true intelligence, since we really do not know what intelligence is anyhow.

⌘ Puzzles are part of the fun of being a member of Mensa, an international high IQ society that has over 100,000 members worldwide, with 57,000 in the U.S. Mensa has only one requirement for membership, a score in the top 2 percent on a standardized and supervised intelligence test or equivalent.

10
IQ TESTS

There are three kinds of intelligence:
one kind understands things for itself, the other appreciates what others can understand,
the third understands neither for itself nor through others.
This first kind is excellent, the second good, and the third kind useless.

NICCOLÒ MACHIAVELLI (1469–1527)

THE FIRST INTELLIGENCE TEST for standardized use was devised in 1905 by the French psychologist Alfred Binet (1857–1911) and his colleague Théodore Simon (1873–1961). Binet wanted to ensure that no child would be denied instruction in the Paris school system, no matter what socioeconomic class the child came from. In 1916, the American psychologist Lewis Madison Terman (1877–1956) revised the Binet-Simon test, adapting it specifically to the needs of American society. Terman believed that the test would provide a scientific basis for comparing the intelligence levels of individuals. But what Terman failed to see was that his test measured only what he himself believed was intelligence. Its validity was therefore called into question almost from the moment it was devised. But even before Terman, the notion that intelligence testing could predict success consistently revealed itself to be flawed. Poet Ralph Waldo Emerson, for instance, always scored at the bottom of tests designed to test intelligence as it was conceived during his era. Thomas Edison was told he was "too stupid" to do anything in life because of his inability to do well on school tests; Albert Einstein performed poorly on mathematics tests; and the list of such cases could go on and on.

People of all eras, cultures and educational backgrounds have made and solved puzzles. Hundreds of thousands of puzzle books are sold every year, and almost every one of the nearly two thousand newspapers published in the United States alone carries a puzzle. Let's not even mention the internet sites containing puzzles. That number is beyond comprehension. Clearly, puzzle-solving is hardly the exclusive domain of high-IQ achievers. But an IQ test is, in a fundamental way, a puzzle test of a certain kind. In this chapter, I have concentrated on the most common type of problems found on various IQ tests throughout the world.

It goes without saying that the same benefits that accrue to general puzzle-solving also apply to the kinds of puzzles contained in this last chapter. In short, they're good for your brain!

WORD SEQUENCES

In this typical IQ exercise, you are asked what word comes logically next, (a) or (b). Here's a very simple example.

> new, old, right, left, true, ___
> (a) false
> (b) real

If you look at the words, they form pairs of opposites: *new—old, right—left,* thus *true—false.* So, the answer is (a). Be careful, since the pattern may be semantic, orthographic or some other logical one.

451. bill, tell, stall, well, ___
   (a) rail
   (b) spill

452. morning, noon, afternoon, evening, ___
   (a) day
   (b) night

453. baseball, soccer, football, tennis, ___
   (a) basketball
   (b) hockey

454. one, four, seven, eleven, ____
  (a) fifteen
  (b) fourteen

455. automobile, bus, truck, van, ____
  (a) bicycle
  (b) skateboard

456. bad, set, lit, won, ____
  (a) sun
  (b) den

457. ant, bake, cream, dove, ____
  (a) easy
  (b) bird

458. sun, tree, lake, star, ____
  (a) roof
  (b) pebble

459. bean, team, treat, seat, ____
  (a) retreat
  (b) week

460. place, stop, frank, create, ____
  (a) try
  (b) make

NUMBER SEQUENCES

A counterpart to the word sequence in IQ tests is the number sequence. In this case you have to figure out what number comes logically next, (a) or (b). Here's a very simple example.

1, 2, 4, 8, 16, 32, ___

(a) 64

(b) 58

Each number in the sequence is double the one before it, so the answer is (a). Not all sequences are this easy. They may have alternating patterns, reversals and all other kinds of forms that will truly test your logic skills. As always, we will start off nice and easy, gradually increasing the difficulty level.

461. 1, 4, 7, 10, 13, 16, ___
  (a) 19
  (b) 18

462. 31, 27, 23, 19, 15, 11, ___
  (a) 9
  (b) 7

463. 2, 3, 5, 8, 12, 17, ___
  (a) 22
  (b) 23

464. 12, 34, 56, 78, 910, 1112, ___
  (a) 1214
  (b) 1314

465. 1, 1, 2, 3, 5, 8, 4, 5, 9, 6, 3, ___
(a) 9
(b) 10

466. 2, 1, 1, 8, 5, 3, 9, 5, 4, 9, 3, ___
(a) 4
(b) 6

467. 1, 2, 2, 3, 2, 6, 4, 5, 20, 5, 5, ___
(a) 10
(b) 25

468. 8, 4, 2, 12, 6, 2, 25, 5, 5, 32, 8, ___
(a) 40
(b) 4

469. 123, 234, 345, 456, 567, 678, ___
(a) 789
(b) 723

470. 224, 339, 4416, 5525, 6636, 7749, ___
(a) 8864
(b) 8852

A second counterpart to the word sequence in IQ tests is the symbol sequence. Here you have to figure out what symbol comes next logically, (a) or (b). Here's a very simple example.

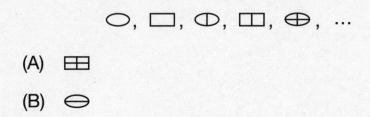

(A)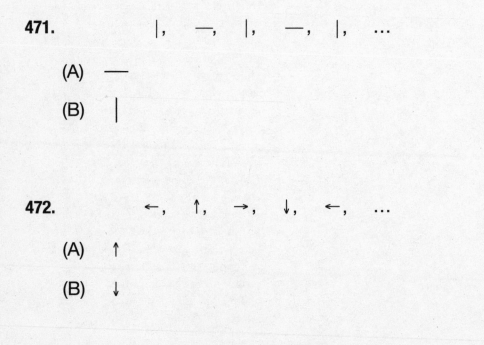

(B)

The answer is (a) because the sequence consists of ellipse and rectangle pairs, in that order. The first pair has no lines inside, the next one has one, so the third will have two. As always, we will start you off very easily, gradually turning up the difficulty level.

471. |, —, |, —, |, ...

(A) —

(B) |

472. ←, ↑, →, ↓, ←, ...

(A) ↑

(B) ↓

473. ←, ↓, →, ↑, ←, ...

(A) ↑

(B) ↓

474. ∠, △, □, ⬠, ...

(A) ⬡

(B) ▱

475. ∩, ∪, ⊃, ⊂, ⊇, ...

(A) ∈

(B) ⊆

476. ●, ■, ▲, ◆, ○, □, △, ...

(A) ▼

(B) ◇

477. ◀ , ▶ , ◀◀ , ▶▶ , ▲ , ...

(A) ▼

(B) ◀

478. 1@, 2##, 3$$$, 4%%%%, 5*****, ...

(A) 6++++

(B) 6&&&&&&

479. O, T, T, F, F, ...

(A) O

(B) S

480. T, ▲ , S, ■ , D, ♦ , C, ...

(A) ●

(B) ▼

MISCELLANEOUS SEQUENCES

For your last set of sequences, we are going to really challenge you. You will be given a sequence (verbal, numerical or symbolic) with a missing term, as before. This time, however, you are not given any options. You will have to figure out for yourself what comes next.

481. angle, triangle, square, pentagon, ___

482. stop, pots, spin, nips, pans, ___

483. 23, 32, 45, 54, 67, ___

484. 9, 18, 27, 36, 45, ___

485. ⇐, ⇑, ⇒, ⇓, ⇐, ___

486. ⊂, ⊃, ⊒, ⊆, ∪, ___

487. clean, dirty, near, far, here, ___

488. M, T, W, T, F, S, ___

489. AZ, BY, CX, DW, ___

490. 43=A, 51=D, 63=C, 71=F, 92=___

PROPORTIONS

Proportions are found commonly on IQ tests. You are asked to figure out what completes a proportion such as the following very simple one:

White *is to* Day *as* Black *is to* ?

The answer is *Night,* of course, since we are dealing here with opposites (White—Black and Day—Night) in a proportional relation.

491. Left *is to* Right *as* Up *is to* ?

492. Triangle *is to* Three *as* Rectangle *is to* ?

493. Hat *is to* Head *as* Glove *is to* ?

494. Walk *is to* Legs *as* Crawl *is to* ?

495. Meat *is to* Chew *as* Water *is to* ?

496. Eight *is to* Even *as* Nine *is to* ?

497. Page *is to* Book *as* Leaf *is to* ?

498. Daisy *is to* Flower *as* Water *is to* ?

499. Ate *is to* Before *as* Eating *is to* ?

500. Puzzles *is to* Brain *as* Food *is to* ?

BRAIN FACT #50

It has been found by neuroscientists that a significant injury to the brain at a young age does not necessarily affect IQ. It has also been found that brain size does not correlate positively with IQ, although there also exists some research which suggests that doing IQ tests may increase brain size. Whatever the case, it is obvious that doing IQ-type puzzles can only be of benefit to the overall functioning of the brain.

Answer Key

1. (a) den (You can also make the name "Ned")

   (b) ram (You can also make the word "mar")

   (c) mace (You can also make the word "acme")

   (d) name (You can also make the words "mean" and "amen")

2. (a) cheat

   (b) trail

   (c) resist (You can also make the phrase "is rest/rest is")

   (d) react (You can also make the words "trace" and "crate")

3. (a) tape (You can also make the word "pate" and the phrase "a pet;" adding an accent produces "paté")

   (b) paste (You can also make the words "peats" and "tapes" and the phrases "a pest" and "a step")

   (c) satin (You can also make the phrases "sat in" and "as tin")

   (d) boredom

4. (a) the rate (You can also make the phrase "a tether")

   (b) her tab (You can also make the phrases "the bar," "the bra" and "her bat")

   (c) dog sigh (You can also make the unusual phrase "gosh dig")

   (d) fuel vent

5. (a) beat (You can, of course, also make the single word "bate")

   (b) reboot (You can also make the phrase "to bore")

   (c) threat (You can, of course, also make the phrase "the art")

   (d) inspire (You can, of course, also make the unusual phrases "pin sire/sire pin")

6. (a) shellfish (You can also make the unusual phrase "hell's fish")

(b) therapeutic

(c) troublesome (You can also make the unusual phrase "some blue rot")

(d) kilometer (You can also make the unusual phrases "or like met/like or met")

7. (a) Madam Curie (in French spelling it would be "Madame Curie")

(b) Madonna Louise Ciccone

(c) Elvis Aaron Presley

(d) Vin Diesel

8. (a) a model

(b) the hair

(c) the meaning of life

(d) the countryside

9. (a) directory

(b) the cockroach

(c) lovable

(d) vile conversation

10. (a) silent lives

(b) discreet

(c) musical

(d) monastery stone

11. There are two possible answers.

ANSWER 1

MAD

bad (Result of changing *m* to *b*)

BED (Result of changing *a* to *e*)

ANSWER 2

MAD

med (Result of changing *a* to *e*)

BED (Result of changing *m* to *b*)

12. NONE

lone (Result of changing the first *n* to *l*)

LOVE (Result of changing *n* to *v*)

13. EASE

east (Result of changing second *e* to *t*)

past (Result of changing *e* to *p*)

PEST (Result of changing *a* to *e*)

14. There are two possible answers in this case.

ANSWER 1

SPOON

swoon (Result of changing *p* to *w*)

swoop (Result of changing *n* to *p*)

stoop (Result of changing *w* to *t*)

SCOOP (Result of changing *t* to *c*)

ANSWER 2

SPOON

spool (Result of changing *n* to *l*)

stool (Result of changing *p* to *t*)

stoop (Result of changing *l* to *p*)

SCOOP (Result of changing *t* to *c*)

15. There are three possible answers in this case.

ANSWER 1

DUST

lust (Result of changing *d* to *l*)

lost (Result of changing *u* to *o*)

lose (Result of changing *t* to *e*)

hose (Result of changing *l* to *h*)

HOME (Result of changing *s* to *m*)

ANSWER 2

DUST

rust (Result of changing *d* to *r*)

ruse (Result of changing *t* to *e*)

rose (Result of changing *u* to *o*)

hose (Result of changing *r* to *h*)

HOME (Result of changing *s* to *m*)

ANSWER 3

DUST

must (Result of changing *d* to *m*)

most (Result of changing *u* to *o*)

host (Result of changing *m* to *h*)

hose (Result of changing *t* to *e*)

HOME (Result of changing *s* to *m*)

16. WHITE

while (Result of changing *t* to *l*)

whale (Result of changing *i* to *a*)

shale (Result of changing *w* to *s*)

shake (Result of changing *l* to *k*)

slake (Result of changing *h* to *l*)

FLAKE (Result of changing *s* to *f*)

17. SCARE

score (Result of changing *a* to *o*)

store (Result of changing *c* to *t*)

stone (Result of changing *r* to *n*)

NOTES (Result of rearranging the letters of *stone*)

18. There are three ways to solve this (and there may be others). Answer 1 involves rearrangement; the other answers do not.

ANSWER 1

TOPS

pots (Result of rearranging the letters of *tops*)

rots (Result of changing *p* to *r*)

rote (Result of changing *s* to *e*)

rate (Result of changing *o* to *a*)

FATE (Result of changing *r* to *f*)

ANSWER 2 (NO REARRANGEMENT NECESSARY)

TOPS

tope (Result of changing *s* to *e*)

tote (Result of changing *p* to *t*)

rote (Result of changing the first *t* to *r*)

rate (Result of changing *o* to *a*)

FATE (Result of changing *r* to *f*)

ANSWER 3 (NO REARRANGEMENT NECESSARY)

TOPS

tots (Result of changing *p* to *t*)

tote (Result of changing *s* to *e*)

rote (Result of changing *t* to *r*)

rate (Result of changing *o* to *a*)

FATE (Result of changing *r* to *f*)

19. I

in (Result of adding *n*)

sin (Result of adding *s*)

sing (Result of adding *g*)

sting (Result of adding *t*)

STRING (Result of adding *r*)

20. Two answers are possible.

ANSWER 1

STONED

stone (Result of subtracting *d*)

tone (Result of subtracting *s*)

ton (Result of subtracting *e*)

ON (Result of subtracting *t*)

ANSWER 2

STONED

toned (Result of subtracting *s*)

tone (Result of subtracting *d*)

ton (Result of subtracting *e*)

ON (Result of subtracting *t*)

21.
1. to stand firmly against (resist)
2. the color of blood (red)
3. period of rule (reign)

22.
1. awe, amazement (wonder)
2. period comprising Saturday and Sunday (weekend)
3. to stay in one place (wait)
4. H_2O (water)

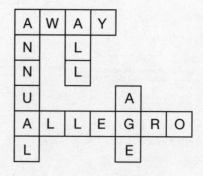

23.
1. the years you have lived (age)
2. quick, lively musical tempo (allegro)
3. once a year (annual)
4. not here (away)
5. every one (all)

24. 1. to lay a wager (bet)
2. lacking originality (banal)
3. cake and bread maker (baker)
4. sport played by Hank Aaron and Mickey Mantle (baseball)
5. intense in color (bright)
6. curved (bent)

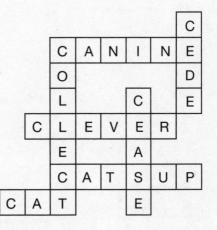

25. 1. another name for ketchup (catsup)
2. sharp of mind (clever)
3. to stop (cease)
4. feline (cat)
5. dog-like (canine)
6. to give up something (cede)
7. to gather together (collect)

26. 1. Australian wild dog (dingo)
2. to swindle someone (diddle)
3. European artistic movement (Dada)
4. Disney character (Dopey)
5. to be excessively fond of (dote)
6. decorative sticker (decal)
7. a complete failure, fiasco (debacle)
8. punctuation mark (dot)

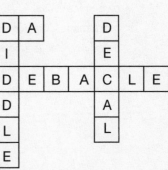

27.
1. illegal drug (dope)
2. loud persistent noise (din)
3. corruption, debauchery (decadence)
4. boring (dull)
5. easily led or managed (docile)
6. pronunciation or accent mark (diacritic)
7. drawn conclusion (deduction)
8. to give a speech (deliver)
9. persistent false belief (delusion)

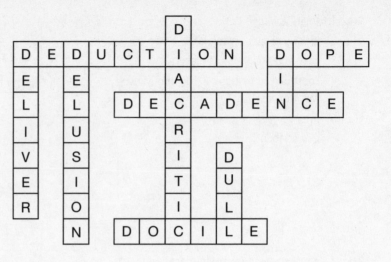

28.
1. irony or sarcasm that exposes or denounces (satire)
2. impudent (sassy)
3. sexual male (stud)
4. biological subdivision (species)
5. apparently true, but actually false (specious)
6. different from what it claims to be (spurious)
7. male or female (sex)
8. consequently (so)
9. board game (Scrabble)
10. messily written (scribbled)

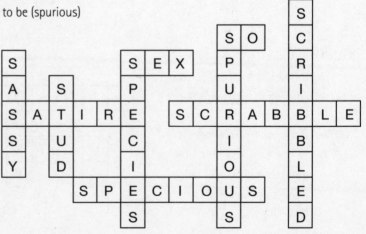

29.
1. to move slowly (trundle)
2. brass instrument (trumpet)
3. showing great resolve (tough)
4. child (tot)
5. this evening (tonight)
6. number of digits in the decimal system (ten)
7. type of bag with handles (tote)
8. aggressive, sullen (truculent)
9. musical speed (tempo)
10. figure of speech (trope)
11. to tangle or ruffle hair or fur (tousle)

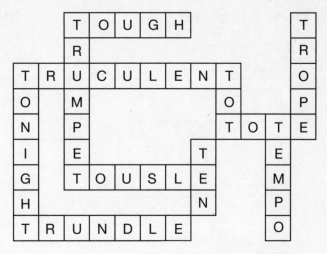

30.
1. twining plant (vine)
2. the age of a wine, high quality wine (vintage)
3. full name of the cello (violoncello)
4. soft, lustrous fabric (velvet)
5. by word of mouth, or "... voce" (viva)
6. used in making plastics (vinyl)
7. in truth (verily)
8. with the voice (vocal)
9. lively, vigorous spirit (verve)
10. blood vessel (vein)
11. to subject someone to scrutiny (vet)
12. offered in fulfillment of a vow (votive)

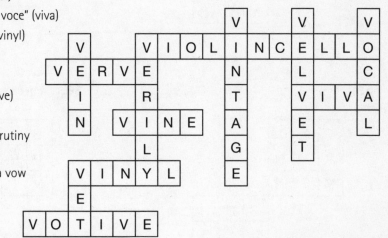

31. *Hidden Word:* TABLET

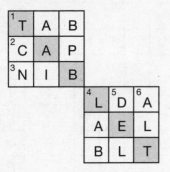

¹T	A	B
²C	A	P
³N	I	B

⁴L	⁵D	⁶A
A	E	L
B	L	T

34. *Hidden Word:* ZENITH

¹Z	E	N
²P	E	W
³T	E	N

⁴I	⁵S	⁶B
C	T	A
E	E	H

32. *Hidden Word*: LITTLE

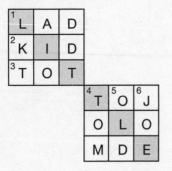

¹L	A	D
²K	I	D
³T	O	T

⁴T	⁵O	⁶J
O	L	O
M	D	E

35. *Hidden Word:* PANTRY

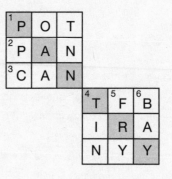

¹P	O	T
²P	A	N
³C	A	N

⁴T	⁵F	⁶B
I	R	A
N	Y	Y

33. *Hidden Word:* GINGER (ROGERS)

¹G	A	L
²K	I	N
³M	E	N

⁴G	⁵D	⁶H
U	E	E
Y	N	R

36. *Hidden Word:* SERENE

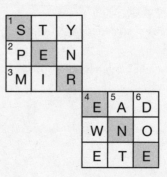

¹S	T	Y
²P	E	N
³M	I	R

⁴E	⁵A	⁶D
W	N	O
E	T	E

37. *Hidden Word:* (SAMUEL) BARBER

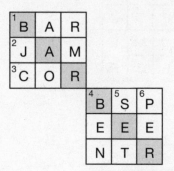

¹B	A	R
²J	A	M
³C	O	R

⁴B	⁵S	⁶P
E	E	E
N	T	R

38. *Hidden Word:* ENGINE

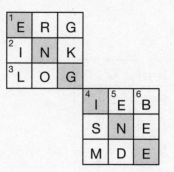

¹E	R	G
²I	N	K
³L	O	G

⁴I	⁵E	⁶B
S	N	E
M	D	E

39. *Hidden Word:* LESSEN

¹L	O	T
²F	E	W
³C	O	S

⁴S	⁵T	⁶T
I	E	O
N	N	N

40. *Hidden Word:* RESCUE

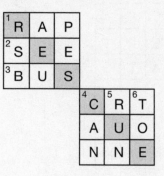

¹R	A	P
²S	E	E
³B	U	S

⁴C	⁵R	⁶T
A	U	O
N	N	E

41.

O	N	E
N	O	R
E	R	A

42.

T	O	P
O	A	R
P	R	Y

43.

S	O	R	E
O	P	E	N
R	E	A	D
E	N	D	S

44.

J	U	D	O
U	V	E	A
D	E	F	T
O	A	T	S

45.

F	R	O	M
R	A	R	E
O	R	A	L
M	E	L	T

46.

B	E	A	T
E	A	S	E
A	S	I	A
T	E	A	M

47.

S	O	N	G
O	P	A	L
N	A	T	O
G	L	O	W

48.

R	O	C	K
O	B	O	E
C	O	M	E
K	E	E	P

49.

C	A	D	S
A	M	E	N
D	E	C	O
S	N	O	B

50.

V	E	N	O	M
E	R	A	S	E
N	A	V	A	L
O	S	A	G	E
M	E	L	E	E

CHAPTER 2

51. one in a million

52. for instance ("four+ in + stance"; *four* and *for* are pronounced the same way)

53. foreign language ("four + in + language")

54. sitting on top of the world

55. Read between the lines.

56. History repeats itself.

57. Excuse me ("x + q's + me"; *x* is pronounced like *ex,* and *q's* like *cuse*)

58. travel overseas ("travel" over "c's"; *c's* is pronounced like *seas*)

59. I am under pressure (👁 = "eye" = "I"; eye and *I* are pronounced the same way)

60. Go, go, go, go around me! or Goes around me!

61. *Proverb:* To everything there is a season.

T	O	C	A	D	S	V	B	N	M	M	O
P	O	I	U	Y	T	R	E	V	B	N	N
E	V	E	R	Y	T	H	I	N	G	B	M
B	G	R	T	G	M	K	I	E	V	R	T
E	T	H	E	R	E	T	Y	U	I	O	P
N	M	K	L	P	O	I	U	Y	T	R	F
N	I	S	M	A	N	B	M	L	O	P	D
M	K	O	P	L	M	K	J	H	G	T	R
S	E	A	S	O	N	P	B	N	M	O	P
N	M	K	L	P	O	R	D	S	E	S	A
N	M	K	L	O	P	N	M	K	I	O	L
M	N	B	V	C	F	R	G	T	H	U	P

62. *Saying:* It is vain to do with more what can be done with less.

```
I  T  A  I  S  C  V  A  I  N  D  S
Q  E  W  S  D  C  V  B  N  H  J  M
K  T  O  G  D  O  M  L  P  O  T  R
S  B  N  M  K  L  P  Y  T  R  D  S
W  I  T  H  N  M  O  R  E  M  K  L
Q  S  C  E  D  V  R  F  B  T  G  H
M  K  O  P  Y  T  I  K  L  F  G  M
W  H  A  T  V  C  A  N  B  E  M
B  G  T  Y  H  N  M  J  U  K  I  L
D  O  N  E  N  W  I  T  H  M  N  B
V  B  N  M  J  K  L  L  P  O  M  N
N  M  L  E  S  S  B  N  M  K  L  P
```

63. *Saying:* Bad art is a great deal worse than no art at all.

```
B  S  V  V  D  V  V  V  R  T  Y  P
A  N  A  M  E  B  T  N  M  A  R  T
D  B  N  M  A  N  H  L  P  T  R  W
N  B  G  M  L  B  A  T  F  V  C  B
N  N  R  M  N  B  N  V  B  A  Y  T
A  M  E  B  W  N  M  K  L  L  O  A
R  K  A  B  O  N  N  N  M  L  V  C
T  L  T  G  R  H  O  H  J  K  L  M
N  O  G  O  S  O  D  C  A  D  S  L
M  P  B  N  E  M  A  L  O  P  M  A
I  W  N  B  M  N  R  M  K  L  N  V
S  S  C  A  D  S  T  C  A  D  S  T
```

64. *Line:* Charity begins at home and justice begins next door.

N	C	Q	S	V	H	G	T	R	C	N	R
M	H	A	B	L	O	J	G	F	A	E	T
K	A	Z	E	Y	M	U	B	V	D	X	Y
L	R	X	G	L	E	S	N	B	S	T	H
O	I	S	I	V	T	T	M	N	C	G	Y
P	T	W	N	L	A	I	K	M	A	J	U
R	Y	E	S	V	N	C	L	B	D	H	O
T	B	D	E	L	D	E	P	E	S	N	P
G	N	C	A	V	P	B	O	G	V	M	D
H	M	V	T	L	Q	N	I	I	V	L	O
Y	K	F	V	V	W	M	U	N	L	P	O
R	I	R	V	L	S	K	Y	S	L	U	R

65. *Lines:* Parting is all we know of heaven/And all we need of hell.

P	A	R	T	I	N	G	V	I	S	V	V
V	V	C	A	D	S	B	N	M	M	L	P
V	A	L	L	M	W	E	N	K	N	O	W
B	V	L	M	D	V	L	M	D	S	O	M
B	N	M	K	O	P	I	U	Y	T	G	F
O	F	R	H	E	A	V	E	N	Q	W	S
Q	A	Z	X	C	D	E	R	G	B	N	W
P	A	N	D	B	A	L	L	M	W	E	Q
X	C	V	B	N	M	K	L	O	P	R	T
N	E	E	D	B	O	F	N	J	I	O	P
Q	A	Z	X	D	E	R	F	V	B	G	F
N	H	Y	U	M	H	E	L	L	N	O	P

66. *Saying:* New York will be a great place when they finish it.

```
Q  N  V  W  P  H  A  P  P  T  W  F
W  E  L  I  L  G  L  L  L  H  Q  I
S  W  V  L  M  F  G  A  M  E  S  N
D  R  L  L  N  R  R  C  N  Y  D  I
C  V  V  G  B  W  E  E  B  D  P  S
V  Y  V  B  V  Z  A  G  V  F  L  H
F  O  D  E  H  P  T  W  D  P  M  J
R  R  W  N  G  L  M  W  B  L  N  I
T  K  S  M  F  M  Q  H  N  M  B  T
G  V  C  L  R  N  W  E  M  N  V  I
B  V  V  K  W  B  S  N  K  B  B  L
N  I  B  P  Z  V  X  V  I  V  N  D
```

67. *Quotation:* Life is not a dress rehearsal.

```
A  W  C  V  L  B  N  N  M  P  Q  A
C  V  W  S  I  Q  Z  O  S  R  O  P
P  H  I  Z  F  I  A  T  C  E  H  A
D  S  C  A  E  V  L  B  N  H  M  P
Q  W  S  D  F  H  B  A  W  E  Q  R
Q  A  Z  X  D  E  R  V  B  A  M  P
W  T  Y  I  O  N  M  B  N  R  M  O
C  V  B  N  M  P  R  D  Q  S  C  V
B  N  M  N  I  M  P  R  F  A  S  C
G  H  K  L  S  P  Q  E  W  L  X  C
B  N  M  K  L  P  O  S  V  B  C  X
Z  S  Q  W  R  T  H  S  H  V  V  I
```

68. *Quotation:* The boisterous sea of liberty is never without a wave.

N	M	B	V	L	V	N	V	W	V	V	V
C	M	O	S	I	M	E	M	I	F	X	M
V	N	I	E	B	N	V	N	T	N	W	N
T	B	S	A	E	B	E	B	H	M	A	B
H	V	T	C	R	V	R	V	O	B	V	V
E	C	E	O	T	C	B	C	U	V	E	C
O	X	R	F	Y	X	Q	X	T	C	C	X
W	Z	O	B	S	Z	A	Z	B	X	A	Z
S	A	U	N	I	A	C	A	A	S	D	A
C	F	S	M	S	F	D	F	N	D	S	F
V	D	R	T	I	D	V	D	M	F	V	D
G	B	V	Y	V	B	L	B	V	R	B	B

69. *Line:* Comedy is tragedy that happens to other people.

A	S	Q	W	X	Z	C	V	F	R	T	H
M	P	V	L	V	L	V	L	G	B	V	I
N	M	C	O	M	E	D	Y	B	N	K	I
M	P	V	L	V	L	V	L	G	B	V	I
C	V	W	C	I	S	D	A	C	S	B	N
A	S	Q	W	X	Z	C	V	F	R	T	H
V	T	R	A	G	E	D	Y	L	P	N	N
B	N	T	H	A	T	V	C	B	N	R	T
M	P	V	L	V	L	V	L	G	B	V	I
H	A	P	P	E	N	S	K	T	O	P	M
B	N	M	O	T	H	E	R	B	N	M	P
B	P	E	O	P	L	E	V	L	V	L	E

70. *Line:* Man consists of two parts, his mind and his body, only the body has more fun.

71. Foreign language

72. Theodore Roosevelt

73. *Jailhouse Rock*

74. Albert Einstein

75. Galapagos (or Galápagos) Islands

76. *Gone with the Wind*

77. Fork and spoon

78. *All in the Family*

79. Ingrid Bergman

80. *The Da Vinci Code*

81. *The Gold Bug*
Code: Each letter in the title has been replaced by the second one after it in the alphabet.

82. Living high off the hog

Code: Each letter in the expression has been replaced by the fourth one after it in the alphabet.

83. Seeing is believing

Code: Each letter in the expression has been replaced by the one before it in the alphabet.

84. Ask not what your country can do for you—ask what you can do for your country.

Code: Each letter in the expression, except for *C* (which has been preserved), has been replaced by the third one after it in the alphabet. Note that *Y* is replaced by *B* because you start counting over at the end of the alphabet.

85. Germaine Greer

Code: As in the model puzzle, each letter of the alphabet has been replaced with the digits in numerical order—*A* = 1, *B* = 2, and so on. Of course, if a letter does not occur, then its numerical equivalent is skipped. For example, in the expression B does not occur, so the number 2 does not occur.

86. The day after tomorrow

Code: Each letter of the alphabet has been replaced with the even digits only in order—*A* = 2, *B* = 4, *C* = 6, *D* = 8 and so forth. Again, if a letter does not occur, then its numerical equivalent is skipped. For example, in the expression B does not occur, so the number 4 does not occur.

87. Life loves the liver of it.

Code: Each letter of the alphabet has been replaced with the odd digits only in order—*A* = 1, *B* = 3, *C* = 5, *D* = 7 and so on. Again, if a letter does not occur, then its numerical equivalent is skipped. For example, in the quotation A does not occur, so the number 1 does not occur.

88. *The Adventures of Huckleberry Finn* (by Mark Twain)

Code: Each vowel in order *(A, E, I, O, U)* has been replaced with the even digits in numerical order—*A* = 2, *E* = 4, *I* = 6, *O* = 8 and *U* = 10; the consonants have been replaced by the odd digits in order: *B* = 1, *C* = 3, *D* = 5, *F* = 7, etc. Again, if a letter does not occur, then its numerical equivalent is skipped. So here's what the substitution system looks like. I have highlighted the vowels.

2	1	3	5	4	7	9	11	6	13	15	17	19
↑	↑	↑	↑	↑	↑	↑	↑	↑	↑	↑	↑	↑
A	B	C	D	E	F	G	H	I	J	K	L	M

21	8	23	25	27	29	31	10	33	35	37	39	41
↑	↑	↑	↑	↑	↑	↑	↑	↑	↑	↑	↑	↑
N	O	P	Q	R	S	T	U	V	W	X	Y	Z

89. I am fond of music because it is so amoral. (The full quotation is actually "I am fond of music because I think it is so amoral.")

Code: Each vowel in order (A, E, I, O, U) has been replaced with the first five digits in order, A = 1, E = 2, I = 3, O = 4, U = 5, and each consonant has been replaced with the second letter after it in the alphabet: for example, M is replaced by O, F by H, and so on.

90. To talk without thinking is to shoot without aiming.

Code: It is the reverse of the previous code. Each vowel in order (A, E, I, O, U) has been replaced with the second letter after it in the alphabet, A = C, E = G, I = K, O = Q, U = W, and each consonant has been replaced with digits in order: for example, B = 1 and C = 2. Below is the complete substitution cipher:

C	1	2	3	G	4	5	6	K	7	8	9	10
↑	↑	↑	↑	↑	↑	↑	↑	↑	↑	↑	↑	↑
A	B	C	D	E	F	G	H	I	J	K	L	M

11	Q	12	13	14	15	16	W	17	18	19	20	21
↑	↑	↑	↑	↑	↑	↑	↑	↑	↑	↑	↑	↑
N	O	P	Q	R	S	T	U	V	W	X	Y	Z

91. trap—rap—reap

92. grape—gape—gap

93. slate—late—plate

94. be—bet—beat

95. red—read—bread

96. plane—plan—plant

97. blame—lame—flame

98. see—seed—steed

99. chair—hair—air

100. steep—seep—see

CHAPTER 3

101. Jack Lemmon

102. Elvis Presley

103. Oprah Winfrey (The staged musical genre is "opera")

104. Angelina Jolie (Her father is Jon Voight)

105. Marilyn Monroe

106. Tom Cruise

107. Brad Pitt

108. Paris Hilton

109. Sophia (Sofia) Loren

110. Morgan Freeman

For puzzles 111–120, the code is shown below:

8	10	21	3	11	15	6	13	5	20	23	1	16
↑	↑	↑	↑	↑	↑	↑	↑	↑	↑	↑	↑	↑
A	B	C	D	E	F	G	H	I	J	K	L	M

9	14	22	--	19	17	12	2	7	4	--	24	18
↑	↑	↑	↑	↑	↑	↑	↑	↑	↑	↑	↑	↑
N	O	P	Q	R	S	T	U	V	W	X	Y	Z

111. Ludwig van Beethoven

112. Wolfgang Amadeus Mozart

113. Johann Sebastian Bach

114. Peter Ilich Tchaikovsky

115. Jerome Kern

116. Henry Mancini

117. Madonna Louise Ciccone

118. George Gershwin

119. Willie Nelson

120. Andrew Lloyd Webber

121. Francis Ford Coppola

```
V  S  A  X  D  C  A  G  R  C  A  B  S  C
→F  R  A  N  C  I  S  S  T  D  S  G  R  C
A  E  T  B  A  Q  F  M  G  A  C  G  V  T
N  V  D  B  S  C  O  P  P  O  S  S  B  A
B  E  F  R  M  M  R  C  B  A  D  M  B  S
I  N  S  P  I  E  D  C  O  P  P  O  L  A→
S  F  O  R  D  P  M  T  Y  C  S  A  M  D
E  B  O  O  M  I  S  E  H  Q  Q  D  S  C
C  D  A  N  A  M  E  M  B  W  W  D  Q  V
```

122. Orson Welles

```
G  V  D  S  O  B  E  H  Q  H  O
A  N  S  P  R  N  L  B  N  R  I
O  D  I  S  S  M  Q  Q  B  W  W
E  B  O  O  O  K  S  E  H  Q  Q
F  T  J  R  N  W  E  L  L  E  S→
J  E  T  S  O  Q  E  M  P  A  C
R  U  Y  M  O  P  M  T  Y  C  S
K  S  A  N  N  W  E  L  T  E  S
Z  E  F  R  M  I  S  E  H  Q  Q
```

123. Tinsel town

```
A  V  D  B  S  C  D  Q  V  D  S
A  N  S  P  I  E  L  B  E  R  G
C  D  A  N  A  M  E  M  B  W  W
E  B  O  O  M  L  L  T  O  W  N→
J  T  J  V  T  P  E  S  T  D  S
J  E  T  B  A  Q  S  M  G  A  C
J  U  Y  T  O  P  N  T  Y  C  S
M  S  A  X  D  C  I  G  R  C  A
Q  E  F  R  M  M  T  C  B  A  D
                 ↑
```

124. Academy Awards

```
               ↑
J  T  O  V  T  P  S  S  T  D  S  S  S
J  E  J  S  O  P  D  D  G  A  C  D  M
A  V  D  B  S  C  R  F  Z  D  B  C  D
Q  E  F  R  W  M  A  A  B  A  D  B  N
A  N  S  P  I  E  W  W  S  Z  G  J  K
J  C  K  A  D  N  A  A  Y  C  S  L  B
→A  C  A  D  E  M  Y  E  H  Q  Q  M  D
D  D  A  N  A  M  E  M  B  W  M  S  C
W  S  B  X  D  Z  A  G  R  C  A  C  T
```

125. *The Ten Commandments*

```
→T  H  E  X  D  C  A  G  R  C  C  S  O  P  H
H  T  T  V  T  P  R  S  T  D  S  C  H  A  D
R  T  E  B  A  Q  E  M  G  A  C  H  W  L  S
A  V  N  C  O  M  M  A  N  D  M  E  N  T  S→
Q  E  F  R  M  M  G  C  B  A  D  A  W  Y  T
A  N  S  P  I  E  L  B  E  R  G  D  I  D  Y
J  U  Y  T  O  P  M  T  Y  C  S  S  C  I  U
E  B  O  O  M  I  S  E  H  Q  Q  A  K  A  O
D  D  A  N  A  M  E  M  B  W  A  R  I  O  M
```

126. Alfred Hitchcock

```
C S T P I E L P R C A
J T A V T P R S T D S
J F S Y T D E R F L A ←
A V M B S H D Q V D S
Q P L R M I E B F L A
A T O P L T L V R R S
J E Y T O C M T Y C S
E V O O M H S E H Q Q
D D A N A C E M B W S
F R M M G O F R M M G
Q Q A K A C Q Q A K A
S O P H I K C H A D W
            ↓
```

129. *Close Encounters of the Third Kind*

```
  ↓
C S A M C D Q M J C G I
L P J V T P R S Y D S P
O E T B A Q E S D A C Q
S R D B S V D Q F D S C
E E N C O U N T E R S C
A N S P I E L R Y R O R
J U Y T O Y L E H T F P
E B O O S I S T H Q Q L
C D D C M C D H C W K A
D A S C D D F I P O N N
B O N M T S M R D R S S
N M T S E D R D K I N D →
```

127. Federico Fellini

```
  N V A W F L A G R L J
  J T J V T P R V T D V
→ F E D E R I C O G A L
  A V D B V L D F V D V
  Q G F R L L G E B A D
  A N V P I G L L G R F
  J U Y T O P L L Y L V
  G B O O L L S I H Q F
  L D A N A C F N B L L
  M M G O F P N I N O P
                ↓
```

130. Vanessa Redgrave

```
    ↓
V V V A X D C A V R C
J M A J V T P R M T D
J C N Y B A Q E M G A
A V E D B M C D Q V D
V D S F R M M G C B A
A G S M P I E L K E J
J M A R E D G R A V E →
E Q B O O M I M E H Q
V W D A N A M E S B V
```

128. Judy Garland

```
  C S A U J T O J J C A
→ J U D Y T P R S T D S
  A E T G A Q E M C A C
  S V D A S C D Q T D J
  M E F R M C D C A A D
  A N S L I R L B S R G
  J I E A O P M T M C S
  E B O N M T S E H Q J
  C D A D A M E J B J W
        ↓
```

131. If **par is** a criterion, then this French city is above par for beauty, history and importance, alongside many other great cities of the world.

par + is = Paris

132. As a capital city and hub of secret government information, it is not unusual to find much "laundering" there of the information that is made public, as if **washing ton**s of bad information out of government documents, so to speak, could ever keep the truth from coming out in the end.

washing + ton... = Washington

133. Francis, my brother, does not like Parme**san; Francis co**uld eat any other cheese, however, especially in his favorite delicatessen in the West Coast city, by the bay, where he lives.

san; + Francis + co... = San Francisco

134. If you are **new, have n**o fear; you will still be welcomed by the students of this friendly and distinguished Ivy League university located in this city.

new, + have + n... = New Haven
(The university is Yale.)

135. After both **wars, aw**ful things happened to many cities, including this Eastern European capital city.

wars, + aw = Warsaw

136. No matter how you inter**pret or I a**nalyze our current situation, we cannot travel to this Southern Hemisphere city, which is the administrative capital of the country.

pret + or + I + a... = Pretoria (The country is South Africa.)

137. If you're often **mad, rid** yourself of all your frustrations by visiting this beautiful Spanish city.

mad, + rid = Madrid

138. If you feel a little tired from jetlag, first take a b**ath, ens**uring that you will feel better; and then go out to see the historical delights of this great ancient city.

ath, + ens = Athens

139. In a beautiful gar**den, ver**dant in the summer but snow-covered in the winter, I met the love of my life in this west central U.S. city.

den, + ver = Denver

140. In this West German city, women wore beautiful **bonn**ets on Sunday strolls in the eighteenth century.

bonn = Bonn

141. Hula Hoop

142. *The Blair Witch Project*

143. *All in the Family*

144. Pet Rock

145. Edsel

146. *Mister Ed*

147. Frank Sinatra

148. *Jurassic Park*

149. *The War of the Worlds*

150. Pulp fiction

CHAPTER 4

151. Blue (B) Bunt
Trap (A) Pad
Tall (T) Chat

152. Judge (J) Jade
Truck (U) Hunt
Great (G) Glint

153. Spy (Y) Why
Ploy (O) Ton
Muck (U) Trust

154. Bent (N) Grant
Ether (E) Fleck
Lend (E) Mean
Dove (D) Dry

155. Spool (L) Glow
Toy (O) Chop
Live (V) Verve
Bend (E) Whet

156. Chat (T) Mitt
Flair (or Frail) (R) Spare
Hue (U) Trump
Well (E) Sweet

157. Sheer (H) Halted
Vast (A) And
Plan (or Clap) (P) Ape
Spy (P) Ply
Mayor (Y) Yell

158. Crew (C) Sock
Humor (H) When
Quack (A) Rave
Wear (R) Blur
Same (M) Storm

159. Clout (T) Out
Chair (R) Scar
Union (U) Truck
Fuse (S) Sorry
Bet (T) Duty

160. Tow (W) Would
Lovely (O) Over
Sneak (or Spank) (N) Nor
Tweed (D) Endure
Tee (E) Gel
Reign (R) Enrage

161.

	¹A	M	P	L	E		
²P	E	R	I	M	E	T	E	R
	³F	I	E	L	D		
⁴S	Q	U	A	R	E		

162.

	¹H	O	M	E			
²D	O	O	R				
	³F	U	S	E			
		⁴S	H	E	L	V	E	S
	⁵B	E	D	R	O	O	M	

163.

```
        ¹S K I I N G
²O L Y M P I C S
      ³F O O T B A L L
      ⁴R O W I N G
      ⁵T E N N I S
      ⁶S O C C E R
```

166.

```
      ¹C A T
      ²H Y E N A
³F E L I N E
⁴P E R S I A N
      ⁵T I G E R
⁶S I A M E S E
      ⁷H A I R
```

164.

```
      ¹Y O L K
²R E D
³F L A X E N
⁴B L U E
⁵D A F F O D I L
⁶T A W N Y
```

167.

```
      ¹C H E S T
      ²L E G S
³M A N D I B L E
      ⁴V E I N S
⁵B R A I N
⁶N E C K
⁷E A R L O B E S
      ⁸T E E T H
```

165.

```
¹P I A N O
²V I O L I N
³A C C O R D I O N
⁴C O N D U C T O R
⁵S W I N G
⁶S Y M P H O N Y
⁷T A N G O
```

168.

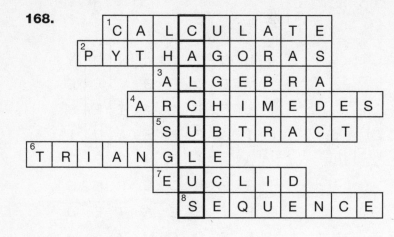

```
¹C A L C U L A T E
²P Y T H A G O R A S
    ³A L G E B R A
  ⁴A R C H I M E D E S
    ⁵S U B T R A C T
⁶T R I A N G L E
    ⁷E U C L I D
    ⁸S E Q U E N C E
```

169.

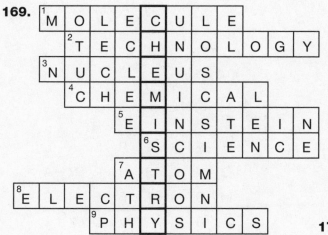

```
¹M O L E C U L E
  ²T E C H N O L O G Y
³N U C L E U S
  ⁴C H E M I C A L
    ⁵E I N S T E I N
      ⁶S C I E N C E
    ⁷A T O M
⁸E L E C T R O N
    ⁹P H Y S I C S
```

170.

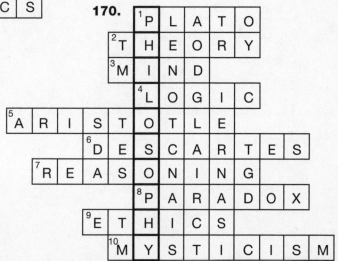

```
¹P L A T O
²T H E O R Y
³M I N D
  ⁴L O G I C
⁵A R I S T O T L E
  ⁶D E S C A R T E S
⁷R E A S O N I N G
    ⁸P A R A D O X
⁹E T H I C S
¹⁰M Y S T I C I S M
```

171. ear—eat

172. rash—dash

173. sweat—swear

174. clean—clear

175. simple—dimple

176. bottle—battle

177. peddle—meddle

178. verify—verily

179. lobster—mobster

180. leaning—meaning

182. deed

```
L O V E A N D Y
M F O R E V E E
I C R E A T E S
T W O H E A D T
A X I O M S G E
T E N D E R R R
E T R E A T E D
E B O O M P A A
C D A N A M T Y
```

181. madam

```
I C J E C T S Y
N O O N T U E S
F M I N L O V E
A M A D A M D C
T O M O R R O W
U N B E A T E N
A T T I T U D E
T B O O M I N G
E N L I S T E D
```

183. level

```
R E V E R S A L
O N U S R P R A
M O S T E E R S
A B R O V C I T
N A A O I L V I
C I C N V A A N
E L E V E L I G
S E N S U A L Q
C A R N A L E A
```

184. tenet

```
D E C I S I O N
R O M A N T L C
M U S I C I A N
S C H O L A R C
R E M O T E L Y
A V B N E T B A
J H H A N S S S
N J O K E R S E
H E A R T M E A
```

186. toot

```
H E A R T S L Y
A A M E R P R S
P G A N O O E M
P E T O O T D C
L R E V P M A D
N N U A E T R Y
E E R T R S A Y
S O B V U O U S
S S A N L T Y A
```

185. sagas (Plural of "saga")

```
S I N G I N G S
A M A T O R Y M
G L A D N E S S
A W E S O M E H
S V B N R T B A
A W K W A R D P
A P P R O A C H
R E T U R N E D
```

187. solos (Plural of "solo")

```
M M I S S I O N
A P R O F M E R
T H L L I P E M
E L D O S E D C
R O O S T L G H
N V B N R I B A
A U T H O R M P
L O V I N G L Y
C A R E S S E S
```

188. peep

```
S  O  P  H  I  S  T  Y
J  B  R  N  T  P  R  E
A  E  O  N  S  Q  E  A
P  I  M  L  S  C  A  R
E  E  I  O  M  M  D  N
P  V  S  O  R  T  B  I
P  E  E  P  E  T  M  N
E  C  L  E  A  R  L  G
R  D  A  N  E  S  A  T
```

190. pullup (pull-up)

```
F  P  O  W  E  R  L  Y
M  U  S  T  E  R  R  S
V  L  I  K  I  N  G  M
A  L  I  K  E  C  D  C
L  U  S  C  L  O  U  S
A  P  E  A  C  H  Y  A
I  M  P  O  R  T  M  P
E  X  P  O  R  T  S  E
T  O  U  C  H  I  N  G
```

189. terret

```
H  R  I  V  E  C  P  S
I  E  B  I  X  O  R  S
G  V  E  M  T  R  E  M
M  O  T  O  R  R  D  C
R  I  T  T  E  E  G  H
A  V  E  O  M  C  B  A
T  E  R  R  E  T  M  P
E  R  O  O  M  I  S  E
T  O  U  C  H  L  N  G
```

191. dam—mad

192. stop—pots

193. buns—snub

194. tool—loot

195. rats—star

196. trap—part

197. slap—pals

198. tram—mart

199. devil—lived

200. stressed—desserts

CHAPTER 5

201. Mr. G

We know that Ms. B did not wear the brown shirt (because none of the colors of the shirts matched the letters of the code names). She did not know the suspect who wore the red shirt, as told. This means that she did not wear the red shirt, another suspect did. So, by the process of elimination, we can deduce that Ms. B wore the green shirt:

GREEN SHIRT	BROWN SHIRT	RED SHIRT
Ms. B	_____	_____

We know that Ms. R did not wear the red shirt and, of course, she did not wear the green one, since we just figured out that Ms. B did. So that leaves only the brown shirt for Ms. R:

GREEN SHIRT	BROWN SHIRT	RED SHIRT
Ms. B	Ms. R	_____

Now, as you can see, Mr. G wore the red shirt (the only shirt left for him to wear), and thus he is the killer, since we are told that the person who wore the red shirt was the killer.

GREEN SHIRT	BROWN SHIRT	RED SHIRT
Ms. B	Ms. R	Mr. G

202. Ines

By figuring out who wore the orange shirt we will unravel who our suspected killer is, since he or she, who is also our milk drinker (the suspected killer), wore it (statement 5). Don wore the blue shirt (statement 3). We can thus eliminate him as our suspected killer. Mark did not order milk (statement 4). And thus he too is not our killer (who, as you know from statement 5, ordered milk). Carl had the hot chocolate (statement 2). We can thus eliminate Carl as well as our killer for the same reason (that is, he is not the one who ordered milk). This leaves Beth or Ines as the suspected killer. From statement 1 we can deduce that Beth is not our killer, because the statement tells us that she wore the green shirt, not the orange one worn by the killer. That leaves Ines, who by deduction wore the orange shirt, drank milk and was the suspect Inspector Moreau had in mind.

203. Janine

The accountant is an only child. Ben has a brother (to whom Sophia is married). So, by elimination, Ben is not our accountant. We deduce this because Ben, having a brother, is not (like the accountant) an only child. That leaves either Sophia or Janine as the killer accountant. We are told that the accountant earns the least of the three. Sophia earns more than the engineer. So, by simple deduction, she cannot be the one who earns the least (she earns more than someone else). By further deduction, we can conclude that Sophia is also not the accountant (who, as told, is the one who earns the least). That leaves, by elimination, Janine as our accountant killer. By the way, you may have figured out as well that Ben is the engineer and Sophia the designer.

204. Mr. Davidoff

The first part of the reasoning is tricky. Here's how it goes. The one who lives in Cleveland knows both the Palm Beach resident and the one who lives in Plymouth—that is, both the other suspects. Why? Because we are told that he or she knows one since childhood and the other through gang membership. We are told that Ms. Fanucci has never met Mr. Davidoff. So, she can't be the one living in Cleveland. Why? Because we have just deduced that the Cleveland resident knows both the other residents. But Ms. Fanucci has never met Mr. Davidoff, one of the other two. As a simple corollary, neither can Mr. Davidoff be the one living in Cleveland because he too does not know one other person—Ms. Fanucci. This is just a different way of saying that they do not know each other. So, by the process of elimination, it would seem that Mr. Chen is the person who lives in Cleveland. Fanucci and Davidoff thus live in Palm Beach and Plymouth in some order. We are told that the Plymouth resident makes more than the one living in Palm Beach. Ms. Fanucci makes more than Davidoff. Connecting these two facts, we can now see that Ms. Fanucci is the one who lives in Plymouth. That leaves Mr. Davidoff as the Palm Beach resident and the killer of the fashion model.

205. The gangster dressed in blue

As in puzzle 201, it is useful to use a system of recording the deductions, referring to the gangsters as Mr. R (who wore red), Ms. R (who also wore red), Mr. G (who wore green), Ms. G (who also wore green), Mr. B (who wore blue) and Ms. B (who also wore blue). Mr. R is not coupled with Ms. R since, as he pointed out, no one is coupled with a partner dressed in the same color. We can also deduce that he was not coupled with the girl in green, or Ms. G, since he made the statement to her and her partner. To summarize, Mr. R was not coupled with either Ms. R or Ms. G. By elimination, Mr. R was coupled with Ms. B:

MS. R	MS. G	MS. B
_____	_____	Mr. R

Mr. G cannot be coupled with Ms. G, of course, because no couple wears the same colored outfit. And he is not coupled with Ms. B, since we just deduced that Mr. R was. So, by elimination, Mr. G is coupled with Ms. R:

MS. R	MS. G	MS. B
Mr. G	_____	Mr. R

So, again by elimination, it is Mr. B who is coupled with Ms. G:

MS. R	MS. G	MS. B
Mr. G	Mr. B	Mr. R

We now know that it was the gangster dressed in blue who shot the teller, since he is the one coupled with Ms. G, the girl dressed in green.

206. Ham

This puzzle might seem confusing, but it really is not. It is obvious that Sam is not the oldest, since he will be Ned's age in three years. This means that he is younger than Ned. So, we can eliminate Sam as the culprit, since the killer is the oldest. The killer is thus either Ham or Ned. We are told that Ham is 27. Three years from now he will, of course, be 30. No one exceeds that age even three years from now, because we are told that the three are between 20 and 30 now and remain so three years from now. Thus, since no two are of the same age and no one is older than 30 or will be older than 30 in three years, this means that only Ham reaches the limit of 30 in three years, not Ned. In three years, Ned will be less than 30 and, thus, younger than Ham. Ham is thus the oldest. As such, he is the killer.

207. Mr. Saxophonist Jr.

Mr. Mandolin does not play the mandolin, since the musician's name and the instrument he plays never match. We are told that he is not the cellist. Let's summarize. Mr. Mandolin is not the mandolinist and he is not the cellist. So, by elimination, he is the saxophonist:

CELLIST	MANDOLINIST	SAXOPHONIST
_____	_____	Mr. Mandolin

Mr. Cellist does not play the cello, of course, and, as we just deduced, he is not the saxophonist (Mr. Mandolin is). So he is the mandolinist.

CELLIST	MANDOLINIST	SAXOPHONIST
_____	Mr. Cellist	Mr. Mandolin

By elimination, this leaves Mr. Saxophonist as the cellist:

CELLIST	MANDOLINIST	SAXOPHONIST
Mr. Saxophonist	Mr. Cellist	Mr. Mandolin

Now, let's turn our attention to the three children of the musicians, Mr. Cellist Jr., Mr. Mandolinist Jr. and Mr. Saxophonist Jr. Mr. Cellist Jr. does not play the cello, of course. His father, Mr. Cellist, plays the mandolin (as you can see in the chart above). So, junior does not play the mandolin either, because no son plays the same instrument as his father. Thus, by elimination, he plays the saxophone.

CELLIST	MANDOLINIST	SAXOPHONIST
_____	_____	Mr. Cellist Jr.

Now, Mr. Mandolinist Jr. does not play the mandolin, as you know. He does not play the saxophone either. As we just found out, Mr. Cellist Jr. does. So, he is a cellist.

CELLIST	MANDOLINIST	SAXOPHONIST
Mr. Mandolinist Jr.	_____	Mr. Cellist Jr.

This leaves Mr. Saxophonist Jr. as the mandolinist.

CELLIST	MANDOLINIST	SAXOPHONIST
Mr. Mandolinist Jr.	Mr. Saxophonist Jr.	Mr. Cellist Jr.

Thus, our killer is Mr. Saxophonist Jr., since he is the son who plays the mandolin.

208. Ms. Rook

This is easier than what it seems. But you will have to use a large dose of logical thinking, nonetheless. The first line of reasoning is a bit complicated, but not that difficult to follow. You can identify the attorney's surname by finding out the surname of the custodian who lives in Chicago. This is because we are told that the custodian who lives there has the same surname as the attorney (statement 6). That surname is certainly not Rook, because the custodian named Mr. Rook lives in Detroit (statement 1), while the attorney lives halfway between Detroit and Chicago (statement 2). We are told that the attorney's next-door neighbor earns three times as much as someone else does (statement 5). Since Mr. Justice earns $4,000 a month (statement 3), it is obvious that he cannot be that person. Why? Because $4,000 cannot be exactly three times any figure: that is, there is no salary which when multiplied by 3 equals exactly $4,000. So, Mr. Justice is not the attorney's next-door neighbor. To summarize, we have deduced that the attorney's neighbor is neither Mr. Rook nor Mr. Justice. Her neighbor is, by elimination, Mr. Soo. From all this, we can conclude that Mr. Soo is not the one who lives in Chicago, because as the attorney's neighbor he lives, like her, halfway between Chicago and Detroit (statement 2). Therefore, we now know that neither Mr. Soo nor Mr. Rook live in Chicago—the former lives halfway between Chicago and Detroit and the latter lives in Detroit. So, it is Mr. Justice who lives in Chicago (by elimination). Thus, Justice is the attorney's surname, since as statement 6 informs us, she has the surname that he does:

ATTORNEY	FORENSIC SCIENTIST	JUDGE
Ms. Justice	_____	_____

Statement 4 tells us that Ms. Soo and the forensic scientist work out regularly. So, Ms. Soo is definitely not the forensic scientist. She is also not the attorney—we just found out that Ms. Justice is. So, she is the judge:

ATTORNEY	FORENSIC SCIENTIST	JUDGE
Ms. Justice	_____	Ms. Soo

This leaves Ms. Rook as the forensic scientist:

ATTORNEY	FORENSIC SCIENTIST	JUDGE
Ms. Justice	Ms. Rook	Ms. Soo

Ms. Rook, according to Inspector Moreau, is thus our killer.

209. Sasha

Neither Ben nor Sasha is the guitarist. Why? Because the guitarist, whoever he is, often performs with Ben and Sasha (statement 3). Peter is not the guitarist either, because he has played with the guitarist on various occasions (statement 2). So has Ben (same statement). So, the guitarist is not Ben, Sasha or Peter. He must be Rick:

DRUMMER	PIANIST	SAXOPHONIST	GUITARIST
_____	_____	_____	Rick

Peter is not the pianist, since he (and Ben) has played with the pianist on various occasions (statement 2). He is also not the saxophonist, because he was an audience member when the saxophonist performed with his own ensemble (statement 1). He is not the guitarist either, as just concluded. So, the only possibility left for Peter is that of drummer:

DRUMMER	PIANIST	SAXOPHONIST	GUITARIST
Peter	_____	_____	Rick

Of the remaining two suspects, Ben and Sasha, one of whom is the pianist and the other the saxophonist (the only two possibilities left), we know that Ben is not the pianist, because Ben, we are told, has played with him on various occasions (statement 2). Thus, he is the saxophonist:

DRUMMER	PIANIST	SAXOPHONIST	GUITARIST
Peter	_____	Ben	Rick

As you can see, the only possibility left for Sasha is as the pianist. He is thus our killer.

DRUMMER	PIANIST	SAXOPHONIST	GUITARIST
Peter	Sasha	Ben	Rick

210. Laura

This puzzle is a bit complicated, but not more difficult than the other ones. We can quickly figure out that Paul is the zoologist from statement 4. How? We are told that there are four women and one man, and that his name is Paul (statement 2). In statement 4, Moreau interviews the five, four of whom are women—Kate, Jasmine, the female urbanist, and Pina. The other interviewee is the zoologist. So, that means that the zoologist is the only male—namely, Paul:

METEOROLOGIST	ZOOLOGIST	BIOLOGIST	URBANIST	PHYSICIST
_____	Paul	_____	_____	_____

From statement 1, we can easily determine that neither Kate nor Laura is the meteorologist—since the two of them became good friends with the meteorologist; and from statement 3 we are told that neither is Jasmine. Summarizing, there are four possibilities for the meteorologist and we have just determined that the meteorologist is not Kate, Laura or Jasmine. So, by elimination, Sophia is the one:

METEOROLOGIST	ZOOLOGIST	BIOLOGIST	URBANIST	PHYSICIST
Sophia	Paul	_____	_____	_____

From statement 3 we know that Jasmine is not the biologist either, and from statement 4, we can see that she is not the urbanist (who is another one in the list). So, not being the biologist nor the urbanist, she must be the physicist (the only profession left for her):

METEOROLOGIST	ZOOLOGIST	BIOLOGIST	URBANIST	PHYSICIST
Sophia	Paul	_____	_____	Jasmine

There are two professions left to be assigned to Kate and Laura. From statement 5, we can eliminate Kate as the urbanist, since she was seen with the urbanist at a coffee shop. She is thus the biologist.

METEOROLOGIST	ZOOLOGIST	BIOLOGIST	URBANIST	PHYSICIST
Sophia	Paul	Kate	_____	Jasmine

So, that leaves Laura as our urbanist and killer.

METEOROLOGIST	ZOOLOGIST	BIOLOGIST	URBANIST	PHYSICIST
Sophia	Paul	Kate	Laura	Jasmine

211. Mack

Cartwright's wife is named Rina. Rina's brother is, of course, Cartwright's brother-in-law, Mack. There is no other possibility, because Rina has only one brother (Mack) and Cartwright is an only child. So, Mack is the killer.

212. Pascal

The killer is Pascal. Why? In the words of the puzzle, the killer was Emilia's son's (Peter's) daughter's (Maria's) son (Pascal). Another way to figure this out is as follows. Maria is Peter's daughter. That makes her Emilia's granddaughter. Her son is the killer. Who is her son? It is Pascal, who is, of course, Emilia's great-grandson.

213. Dino

The killer is one of the four cousins mentioned, since they are the children of Friedrich's brother and sister. We are told that the killer does not get along with his cousin, Claudia. So, it is not Claudia. Claudia has two cousins, Bruno and Dino. The killer is one or the other. Since Bruno was out of the country at the time of the murder, the killer was Dino.

214. Nicolette

Let's give names to the people mentioned in the relevant phrase, numbering each one as shown: "his (1) son's (2) daughter's (3) son's (4) daughter." Who is Carlo's son (1)? It is James (his only son, by the way). Who is James's daughter (2)? She is Carlo's granddaughter, of course. Her name is Naomi (again, an only child). Next, who is Naomi's son (3)? He is Carlo's great-grandson, of course. His name is Brett (again, an only child). And who is Brett's daughter (4)? She is Carlo's great-great-granddaughter. Her name is Nicolette. We have now identified the killer. By the way, Moreau was shocked to find that Nicolette was barely 18 when she killed Carlo in a moment of anxiety.

215. Billy

Let's break up the relevant phrase into numerical parts: Julia was killed by "Frank's brother-in-law's (1) older son (2)." Who is Frank's brother-in-law (1)? Frank's brother-in-law is Frank's only sister's (Norma Jean's) husband, Steve. Steve has two children, Andrew and Billy. The older son is named Billy. Why? Because we are told that Andrew looks up to him. So Billy, the older son, is the killer (2).

216. Dina

Again, let's break up the relevant statement into numerical parts as follows: The killer was Maria's daughter's (1) husband's (2) sister's (3) sister-in-law (4). Who is Maria's daughter (1)? Dina. Who is Dina's husband (2)? Harry. Who is Harry's sister (3)? Lydia. Who is Lydia's sister-in-law (4)? Dina (who, being married to Lydia's brother, Harry, is Lydia's sister-in-law). This is a roundabout way of saying that Dina killed her own mother.

217. Helena

Let's use the same "numerical approach" of previous puzzles. The relevant statement can be broken down numerically as follows: The killer is Will's father's (1) brother's (2) father's (3) wife (4). Who is Will's father (1)? John. Who is John's brother (2)? It is Will's only uncle on his dad's side. What's his name? Bill. Who is Bill's father? By the way, it is also John's father, since Bill and John are brothers (given that we are told that Bill is Will's only uncle on his dad's side). Who is Bill's or John's father (3)? It is Will's grandfather, of course. What's his name? It is Herman. Who is Herman's wife (4)? It is, of course, Will's grandmother. Her name is Helena. That's who killed Will.

218. Phillip

The relevant statement can be broken down numerically as follows: The killer is Harriet's mother's (1) brother's (2) mother's (3) husband (4). Who is Harriet's mother (1)? Emma. Who is Emma's brother (2)? It is Emma's only uncle on her mother's side (recall that those mentioned in the statement are Harriet's only living relatives). What's his name? Arthur. Who is Arthur's mother (3)? Being Emma's brother, Arthur's mother is also Emma's mother. So, she is Harriet's only living grandmother. What's her name? Mina. Who is Mina's husband (4)? It is, of course, Harriet's only living grandfather. What's his name? Phillip. That's who killed Harriet.

219. Bill

In **217** we figured out that Will's grandmother, Helena, was the killer. Now we are told that it was her son. She has two sons, Will's father, John, and his brother, Bill, who is Will's only uncle and thus John's only brother. So, the killer was either John or Bill. We're told it was not the father, so it was Bill, the uncle.

220. Emma

In **218** we figured out that Harriet's grandfather, Phillip, was the killer. Phillip's only daughter would thus be Harriet's mother, Emma. And that's who killed Harriet.

221. *Jill* is the only name that does not end in *a*. So she's the killer.

222. *Andrew* is the only name that does not begin with a consonant. So he's the robber.

223. All the surnames, except Jones, are words referring to jobs or avocations. So Jones is the criminal.

224. *Margaret* is the only name with more than five letters in it; all the others are made up of five letters. So she's the murderer.

225. *Gig, Pip* and *Bab* are all palindromes (that is, they can be read forward and backward); *Hap* is the exception, and so Hap is our killer. Another explanation is that all names but Hap begin and end with the same consonant.

226. *Bunny, Kiddie and Pippy* all have double consonants in them; *Kookie* has a double vowel. So Kookie is our killer.

227. The names *Anna, Bob* and *Eve* start and end with the same letter; *Frank* does not. So Frank is our extortionist.

228. *Beth* is the only name with one vowel in it; all the others have two vowels. Beth is our robber.

229. The fraudster is Mr. Pelt. His name is a word referring to rain; the others are words referring to types of snow or snow conditions.

230. The letters of *Poons* can be rearranged to produce the word *spoon;* the letters of *Finke* can be rearranged to produce the word *knife;* and the letters of *Bleat* can be rearranged to produce the word *table.* The letters of *Cork* can be rearranged to produce the word *rock,* which is something in nature. So Cork is our killer.

231. The ukulele. All the other clues—ants, eggs, ink and oil—start with a vowel in order *(a, e, i, o).* Ukulele starts with the last vowel, *u,* in the order *(a, e, i, o, u).*

232. The mineral water. The previous clues are all liquids. Teaspoon is not a liquid.

233. The earring. All the clues begin with the first five letters of the alphabet in order: *a, b, c, d, e* (acorns, beetles, crackers, detergent, earring).

234. The marker. Like all the other clues, the marker is a writing utensil; the gun is not.

235. The bib. Like the other four clues, the word *bib* begins and ends with the same consonant; *sling* does not.

236. The knife handle. Like the other clues, this clue consists of two words; *revolver* does not.

237. *NMPRP.* Each clue increases by one letter: *A* (one), *DS* (two), *CTP* (three), *GHIR* (four), *NMPRP* (five). On the other hand, *HTOP* has four letters.

238. The briefcase. All the clues, except the keychain, are types of containers.

239. The pennies. All the clue words are in the plural. *Pennies* is in the plural, but *dollar* is not.

240. 6Killer. The numeral indicates the number of letters in each clue. *Killer* has six letters, as indicated by the numeral 6 before it, but *4Get* has three, not four, letters.

241. Mr. Rock

Since there is only one true statement and one killer, Mr. Stone's and Mr. Rock's statements cannot both be false. Why? Because if they were both false, then, using double negative logic for both, it would mean that they both did it. If Mr. Stone's statement "I didn't do it" is false, then contrary to his statement, it implies that he did do it. The same reasoning applies to Mr. Rock's statement, and thus leads to the conclusion that Mr. Rock also did it. That means that both would be the killers, and this contradicts the conditions given by the puzzle. Clearly, then one of these two statements must logically be true and the other one false. Since there is only one true statement in the set, and two false ones, the third statement, by Mr. Pebble, is, by the process of elimination, one of the two false ones. This means that his accusation of Mr. Stone is false. It is, in other words, a lie. That means that Mr. Stone is, on the contrary, innocent. So, Mr. Stone's statement turns out to be the only true one, since he says in fact he didn't do it, confirming our deduction. Thus, Mr. Rock's statement is the other false one (remember that there are two false statements in the set). So, by elimination, the killer is Mr. Rock, who thus lied saying that he didn't do it.

242. Mina

Since all three told the truth the contents of their statements are true. So, Gina and Pina, having told the truth, are not the robbers, since they said they didn't do it, and we know this is true. Mina made no such admission, so, by elimination she's the robber, even if her statement is true.

243. Bubby

We know that all three statements are false. So, Nubby's statement that he is the leader is false. This means he's certainly not the leader. Similarly, Tubby is not the leader. We can easily deduce this because his statement is false. What's his statement? "I am." So, the statement being a lie, we can see that, contrary to what Tubby says, he is not the leader. That leaves Bubby as the ringleader by the process of elimination. And even though his statement—"I don't know who the leader is"—is false, it does not contradict anything we have deduced so far; it just shows that he is a liar.

244. Jane

Let's start by assuming that Jane's statement is the only true one of the set. What is it? "I am not the robber." Being true, this implies that she is, of course, not the robber. Now, Beth's statement "Jane is not the robber" simply confirms this. This means that it too is true, of course. But, then, we have two true statements under this working hypothesis—Jane's and Beth's—contrary to the given fact that there is only one in the set. So, our working hypothesis is clearly wrong. This means that Jane's statement is actually false (since it cannot be true, as shown). Being false it identifies her, by double negative logic, as being the robber—if her statement "I am not the robber" is false, then she is the robber. That's our first false statement. Look at Beth's statement now under the new hypothesis. Beth says that Jane is not the robber. But, as we have just discovered, Jane actually is. So, Beth's statement is false as well. This means that Samantha's statement is the only true one. And in it she confirms, truthfully, that Jane is the robber.

245. Gaston

Albert's statement cannot be the true one. Why? If it is, then it means that Dick is indeed the robber, as he says. However, this would also mean that Gaston's statement—"I certainly didn't do it"—is true, since he would indeed not be the robber, as he says. But, there is only one true statement in the set. This would make two. So, we have indirectly deduced that Albert's statement can only be false. He says that "Dick did it," but contrary to what he says, Dick did not rob the armored car. Let's assume, under our next hypothesis, that Dick's statement is the only true one. Identifying Tim is the robber, this means that Tim actually did it. But, then again, Gaston's statement would turn out to be true, since he would not have done it, as he says. Again, there would be two true statements, not one in the set. So, we can only conclude that

Dick's statement is also false. That means that Tim's statement is true, since, as he correctly says, Dick lied. We have, by the way, just identified the only true statement in the set. So, Gaston's statement turns out to be false, since there cannot be two true statements. And, in contrast to what he says (since it is false), Gaston is the robber.

246. Diana

Diana's and Tara's statements cannot both be true; otherwise they would be contradictory. And, of course, they cannot both be false, since there is only one false statement in the set. So, one is true and one is false. Diana's statement is "Tara did (it)." For our first hypothesis, let's assume it is the true one of the two. If it is true, then Tara did indeed do it, as Diana points out. This means that Tara's statement—"Diana lied when she said I did it"—is the false one, since, as just discovered from Diana's supposedly truthful statement, she is the car thief. For our second hypothesis, let's assume that Diana's statement is, instead, the only false one. This means that, contrary to what she says, Tara did not steal the car. Tara's statement confirms this, so her statement is the true one of the two. So far, both hypotheses hold. Since we have allocated the only false statement in the set to Diana or Tara, the remaining statements are necessarily true. Look at Amelia's statement: "Diana stole it." Being true, it confirms the second hypothesis, namely that Diana lied, thus identifying Diana indirectly as the car thief. Gillian's statement does not contradict this in any way, since, being true, all it says is that she, Gillian, didn't do it.

247. Curly

This is actually easier than it seems. All statements were false. So, from Curly's statement, we can deduce that it was not Baldy, contrary to what Curly says. Similarly, from Baldy's statement, we can conclude that it was not Hairy, again contrary to what he says. From Hairy's false statement, we can similarly deduce that it was not Wavy, contrary to what Hairy says. Wavy's statement is also false. He identifies Hairy as the murderer, but this is false. So, who's left? If it wasn't Baldy, Hairy or Wavy, it was Curly.

248. Skinny

Since all the statements are true, from the first three, we can easily see that the murderer wasn't Chubby, Bubbly or Stubby. Being all true, they simply confirm these facts. Stubby's statement, being true, also confirms that he was not the murderer. Who does that leave? It leaves Skinny as our killer. He told the truth that Chubby wasn't the killer, but that does not absolve him from the crime.

249. Josie

Josie's and Caitlin's statements contradict each other. So, they cannot both be true. Nor can they both be false. Try out the logic for yourself, if you don't believe me. So, one of the statements is true and the other false. Now, if Bianca's statement is true, then it means that Josie was the killer and thus that Josie's statement is false. Josie denied being the killer, but this is false. Consequently, Nessa's statement is false, because Nessa identified Caitlin as the killer. We have now identified one true and two false statements. Caitlin's statement is thus the other true statement in the set. It simply confirms that Nessa didn't do it. Thus, Josie was the killer.

250. Zack

Jack's statement tells us essentially nothing. We know that he, like the others, is just a liar. Ignore it. Because Mack's statement, like all the others, is false, this means that the person he identifies, Hack, is not the killer, contrary to what he says. Because Pack's statement is false, we also know it was not Mack (the one he mendaciously blames). Zack identifies Jack indirectly as the killer, since Jack is the one who said "I'm not sure who did it." But Zack is a liar like the rest of them. So, it is not Jack, as he wants Moreau to believe. Hack identifies Pack indirectly as the killer, since it was Pack who claimed Mack was the killer. But since he is a liar, we can conclude that it is not Pack. In sum, it's not Hack, Mack, Jack or Pack, so it leaves Zack as the killer.

CHAPTER 6

251.

7	2	3	1	6	9	4	8	5
5	4	6	2	3	8	7	1	9
8	9	1	4	5	7	3	6	2
2	6	4	8	7	3	9	5	1
1	5	7	9	2	4	6	3	8
3	8	9	6	1	5	2	4	7
6	1	5	3	9	2	8	7	4
4	3	2	7	8	1	5	9	6
9	7	8	5	4	6	1	2	3

253.

7	6	4	5	8	2	1	3	9
5	9	3	7	1	6	2	4	8
2	8	1	9	4	3	5	7	6
3	7	6	8	2	9	4	5	1
9	4	5	3	7	1	6	8	2
1	2	8	6	5	4	3	9	7
4	3	2	1	9	7	8	6	5
8	1	9	4	6	5	7	2	3
6	5	7	2	3	8	9	1	4

252.

8	5	7	6	9	2	1	4	3
1	3	2	4	7	5	9	6	8
9	6	4	1	8	3	5	7	2
3	4	9	7	5	6	2	8	1
6	2	5	8	4	1	7	3	9
7	1	8	2	3	9	4	5	6
4	9	6	3	2	7	8	1	5
5	7	3	9	1	8	6	2	4
2	8	1	5	6	4	3	9	7

254.

4	9	5	1	8	6	3	2	7
1	3	7	5	2	9	8	6	4
8	6	2	3	4	7	5	9	1
3	1	8	4	7	2	6	5	9
9	5	6	8	3	1	7	4	2
7	2	4	6	9	5	1	3	8
2	8	3	7	6	4	9	1	5
6	4	1	9	5	8	2	7	3
5	7	9	2	1	3	4	8	6

255.

1	4	5	2	3	9	8	7	6
8	2	6	7	1	4	9	3	5
7	9	3	5	6	8	2	1	4
6	5	1	4	8	2	3	9	7
9	7	4	3	5	1	6	2	8
2	3	8	9	7	6	4	5	1
3	8	9	1	4	5	7	6	2
4	1	2	6	9	7	5	8	3
5	6	7	8	2	3	1	4	9

257.

9	8	7	6	5	4	3	2	1
6	1	2	7	3	8	4	5	9
5	3	4	1	9	2	8	7	6
4	5	1	9	8	7	6	3	2
3	6	8	4	2	5	1	9	7
2	7	9	3	6	1	5	8	4
1	9	5	2	4	3	7	6	8
7	2	3	8	1	6	9	4	5
8	4	6	5	7	9	2	1	3

256.

9	3	5	2	1	4	7	6	8
1	7	4	8	6	3	2	5	9
8	2	6	7	9	5	4	1	3
3	5	1	9	4	6	8	2	7
7	8	9	1	5	2	3	4	6
6	4	2	3	7	8	5	9	1
4	6	8	5	3	1	9	7	2
2	1	7	4	8	9	6	3	5
5	9	3	6	2	7	1	8	4

258.

2	5	1	8	9	3	4	6	7
9	3	6	7	4	1	8	2	5
4	8	7	2	5	6	3	1	9
3	1	8	4	2	9	5	7	6
5	4	2	6	1	7	9	3	8
6	7	9	3	8	5	2	4	1
1	2	4	5	6	8	7	9	3
7	6	5	9	3	2	1	8	4
8	9	3	1	7	4	6	5	2

259.

2	1	7	4	6	9	5	8	3
6	5	8	3	7	2	9	1	4
3	4	9	1	8	5	7	2	6
8	7	3	5	9	4	1	6	2
1	9	6	8	2	7	3	4	5
5	2	4	6	3	1	8	7	9
4	3	2	7	5	8	6	9	1
9	8	5	2	1	6	4	3	7
7	6	1	9	4	3	2	5	8

260.

4	8	6	9	2	7	3	1	5
3	1	2	8	5	6	9	4	7
5	7	9	4	3	1	2	6	8
8	5	3	2	6	4	7	9	1
1	2	7	5	8	9	4	3	6
6	9	4	7	1	3	5	8	2
2	4	1	3	7	8	6	5	9
9	6	5	1	4	2	8	7	3
7	3	8	6	9	5	1	2	4

261.

3	x	2	=	6
4	÷	1	=	4
9	-	8	=	1
1	+	1	=	2
				13

262.

5	x	3	=	15
15	÷	3	=	5
7	-	2	=	5
1	+	5	=	6
				31

263.

4	x	4	=	16
6	÷	6	=	1
2	-	2	=	0
13	+	13	=	26
				43

264.

2	x	2	=	4
9	÷	3	=	3
5	-	3	=	2
9	+	9	=	18
				27

265.

2	x	8	=	16
24	÷	4	=	6
26	-	12	=	14
10	+	18	=	28
				64

266.

5	x	9	=	45
21	÷	3	=	7
19	-	17	=	2
13	+	4	=	17
				71

267.

3	x	2	=	6
12	÷	3	=	4
14	-	3	=	11
3	+	9	=	12
				33

268.

2	x	8	=	16
16	÷	8	=	2
9	-	8	=	1
12	+	8	=	20
				39

269.

9	x	2	=	18
9	÷	9	=	1
9	-	1	=	8
9	+	9	=	18
				45

270.

2	x	1	=	2
6	÷	3	=	2
9	-	8	=	1
1	+	1	=	2
				7

271. The hidden words are highlighted.

D	P	S	E	I	N	A	T	O
E	O	A	D	T	S	I	P	N
I	N	T	A	O	P	S	D	E
A	D	P	N	S	I	E	O	T
T	E	I	O	A	D	P	N	S
N	S	O	T	P	E	D	A	I
P	A	N	S	E	T	O	I	D
O	T	E	I	D	A	N	S	P
S	I	D	P	N	O	T	E	A

272.

R	T	N	S	O	B	E	I	A
E	B	O	I	R	A	N	S	T
S	A	I	E	T	N	B	R	O
I	O	R	N	S	E	A	T	B
B	N	A	T	I	R	O	E	S
T	E	S	A	B	O	R	N	I
A	S	E	O	N	I	T	B	R
O	R	T	B	E	S	I	A	N
N	I	B	R	A	T	S	O	E

273.

I	T	N	B	R	Y	C	E	A
C	A	R	N	E	I	B	T	Y
B	Y	E	C	A	T	I	N	R
A	E	C	Y	B	R	N	I	T
R	N	I	A	T	E	Y	B	C
Y	B	T	I	N	C	A	R	E
N	R	Y	E	C	B	T	A	I
E	I	A	T	Y	N	R	C	B
T	C	B	R	I	A	E	Y	N

275.

O	I	E	T	U	A	F	C	S
T	S	C	O	F	I	A	E	U
A	U	F	S	E	C	T	O	I
C	O	I	U	A	S	E	T	F
S	E	T	C	O	F	I	U	A
F	A	U	I	T	E	C	S	O
E	C	A	F	S	O	U	I	T
U	F	S	E	I	T	O	A	C
I	T	O	A	C	U	S	F	E

274.

T	H	U	R	E	A	D	S	G
S	D	R	T	G	U	E	A	H
G	E	A	H	S	D	U	T	R
H	U	E	A	R	T	G	D	S
D	S	T	E	U	G	H	R	A
R	A	G	D	H	S	T	E	U
E	T	S	G	A	H	R	U	D
A	R	H	U	D	E	S	G	T
U	G	D	S	T	R	A	H	E

276.

F	G	E	H	O	B	S	I	L
S	B	L	E	I	F	O	G	H
I	O	H	G	L	S	F	E	B
E	S	F	I	B	H	L	O	G
L	H	O	S	G	E	B	F	I
B	I	G	O	F	L	E	H	S
O	L	B	F	H	G	I	S	E
G	F	S	L	E	I	H	B	O
H	E	I	B	S	O	G	L	F

277.

S	Y	E	H	T	R	I	L	A
T	R	L	A	I	Y	H	E	S
H	A	I	L	E	S	Y	T	R
I	S	R	T	A	H	E	Y	L
E	L	T	Y	R	I	A	S	H
A	H	Y	S	L	E	R	I	T
R	E	H	I	S	T	L	A	Y
L	I	S	R	Y	A	T	H	E
Y	T	A	E	H	L	S	R	I

279.

Y	H	A	R	C	I	P	E	F
F	I	R	P	A	E	Y	H	C
P	E	C	H	F	Y	I	A	R
E	C	P	F	I	H	R	Y	A
I	A	H	Y	P	R	F	C	E
R	F	Y	A	E	C	H	I	P
A	Y	I	E	R	F	C	P	H
C	P	F	I	H	A	E	R	Y
H	R	E	C	Y	P	A	F	I

278.

L	R	W	O	E	N	I	T	F
O	F	I	L	T	W	E	R	N
E	N	T	I	F	R	W	L	O
I	L	R	N	W	E	O	F	T
T	O	E	F	I	L	R	N	W
N	W	F	T	R	O	L	I	E
R	I	N	W	O	T	F	E	L
F	T	O	E	L	I	N	W	R
W	E	L	R	N	F	T	O	I

280.

G	W	T	S	H	A	C	D	O
A	C	S	O	T	D	G	H	W
D	H	O	G	C	W	A	T	S
H	D	W	C	A	G	O	S	T
O	T	C	H	W	S	D	A	G
S	A	G	D	O	T	H	W	C
W	S	D	A	G	O	T	C	H
T	G	H	W	D	C	S	O	A
C	O	A	T	S	H	W	G	D

281.

4	5	1
4	5	1
2	0	8

282.

2	4	6
4	6	2
6	2	4

283.

7	3	2
5	2	5
0	7	5

284.

3	8	2
3	2	8
7	3	3

285.

1	3	5	2
3	1	5	2
5	1	1	4
2	6	0	3

286. Note: This is the only solution that uses all the given numbers. You might get other solutions, but they do not use up all the given numbers.

9	8	1	0
5	6	3	4
4	2	9	3
0	2	5	11

287. Note: This is the only solution that uses all the given numbers. You might get other solutions, but they do not use up all the given numbers.

5	5	5	5
5	9	2	4
5	2	10	3
5	4	3	8

288. Note: This is the only solution that uses all the given numbers. You might get other solutions, but they do not use up all the given numbers.

1	0	8	1
5	1	0	4
4	1	0	5
0	8	2	0

289. Note: This is the only solution that uses all the given numbers. You might get other solutions, but they do not use up all the given numbers.

1	0	6	1	6
0	1	4	6	3
3	6	0	3	2
4	3	3	2	2
6	4	1	2	1

290. Note: This is the only solution that uses all the given numbers. You might get other solutions, but they do not use up all the given numbers.

7	8	2	3	1
3	7	3	7	1
8	3	1	1	8
2	2	7	1	9
1	1	8	9	2

291.

B	E	T
C	A	R
S	E	A

292.

D	O	E
M	A	N
Y	O	U

293.

E	R	A
P	I	E
D	E	N

294.

S	U	N
A	G	E
R	Y	E

295.

B	E	A	T
L	O	V	E
S	T	A	Y
H	E	R	E

296.

M	A	L	E
C	U	T	E
N	I	C	E
H	U	G	E

297.

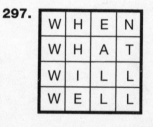

W	H	E	N
W	H	A	T
W	I	L	L
W	E	L	L

298.

F	O	O	D
M	O	O	D
G	O	O	D
F	E	E	L

299.

C	L	E	A	R
H	E	A	R	T
T	H	R	O	B
F	R	E	S	H
T	E	A	S	E

300.

M	U	S	I	C
M	A	K	E	R
M	A	G	I	C
P	I	A	N	O
V	O	I	C	E

301. Hope you didn't forget about Roman numerals. The three sticks can be used to produce the Roman numeral standing for nine as shown below.

302. The two sticks can be crossed to produce the Roman numeral standing for ten as shown below.

303. The fraction 1/1 = one, of course. Note that one of the sticks was used as a line in the fraction.

304. The sticks can be arranged to make a figure that looks like 7.

305. The sticks can be arranged to make the Roman numeral for 5.

306. The subtraction 1 – 1 = zero, of course. One of the sticks is used as the subtraction sign.

307. Note that three of the stick figures have been shaped into a square root sign. And, the square root of 1 is one.

308. Clearly, 11 – 1 = ten, doesn't it? The four sticks can be arranged to show this, with one of them standing for the subtraction sign.

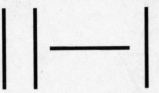

309. The three sticks can be arranged to form the number 17.

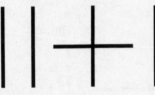

310. Of course, 11 + 1 = twelve. Note that two of the sticks were used to make the plus sign.

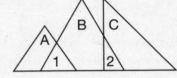

311. Nine. First, mark off only the segments that make up four-sided figures (squares and rectangles) with numbers as shown. For the sake of convenience, mark off the large squares or rectangles that include the smaller ones with letters. There are other ways to do this.

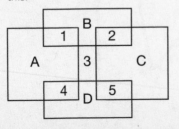

Here are the nine figures:
1. 1
2. 2
3. 3
4. 4
5. 5
6. A (which includes 1 and 4 as parts)
7. B (which includes 1 and 2 as parts)
8. C (which includes 2 and 5 as parts)
9. D (which includes 4 and 5 as parts)

312. Five

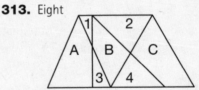

1. 1
2. 2
3. A (which includes 1 as a part)
4. B (which includes 1 and 2 as parts)
5. C (which includes 2 as a part)

313. Eight

1. 1
2. 2
3. 3
4. 4
5. A (which includes 3 as a part)
6. B (which includes 3 and 4 as parts)
7. B (which includes 1 and 2 as parts) (B is also part of a different triangle from 6. Look at the triangle "upside down")
8. C (which includes 4 as a part)

314. Eleven

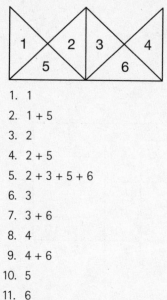

1. 1
2. 1 + 5
3. 2
4. 2 + 5
5. 2 + 3 + 5 + 6
6. 3
7. 3 + 6
8. 4
9. 4 + 6
10. 5
11. 6

315. Five. The circles are shown with different circumference weights (density of line).

316. Thirty-eight

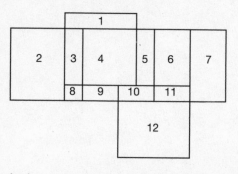

1. 1
2. 1 + 3 + 4

3. 2
4. 2 + 3 + 8
5. 2 + 3 + 4 + 5 + 6 + 8 + 9 + 10 + 11
6. 2 + 3 + 4 + 5 + 6 + 7 + 8 + 9 + 10 + 11
7. 3
8. 3 + 4
9. 3 + 8
10. 3 + 4 + 5
11. 3 + 4 + 5 + 6
12. 3 + 4 + 5 + 8 + 9 + 10
13. 3 + 4 + 5 + 6 + 8 + 9 + 10 + 11
14. 3 + 4 + 5 + 6 + 7 + 8 + 9 + 10 + 11
15. 4
16. 4 + 5
17. 4 + 5 + 6
18. 4 + 5 + 9 + 10
19. 4 + 5 + 6 + 9 + 10 + 11
20. 4 + 5 + 6 + 7 + 9 + 10 + 11
21. 5
22. 5 + 6
23. 6
24. 6 + 11
25. 6 + 7 + 11
26. 7
27. 8
28. 8 + 9
29. 8 + 9 + 10
30. 8 + 9 + 10 + 11
31. 9
32. 9 + 10
33. 9 + 10 + 11
34. 10
35. 10 + 11
36. 10 + 11 + 12
37. 11
38. 12

317. Thirty-one

```
+-----------------+-----------------------+
|        1        |          2            |
+--------+--------+-----------------+-----+
|        |   3    |       4         |     |
|   5    +--------+-----------------+  6  |
|        |   7    |       8         |     |
+--------+--------+-----------------+-----+
|        9        |         10            |
+-----------------+-----------------------+
```

1. 1
2. 1 + 2
3. 1 + 2 + 3 + 4 + 5 + 6 + 7 + 8
4. 1 + 3 + 5 + 7
5. 1 + 3 + 5 + 7 + 9
6. 1 + 2 + 3 + 4 + 5 + 6 + 7 + 8 + 9 + 10
    (the actual diagram itself)
7. 2
8. 2 + 4 + 6 + 8
9. 2 + 4 + 6 + 8 + 10
10. 3
11. 3 + 4
12. 3 + 4 + 7 + 8
13. 3 + 4 + 6 + 7 + 8
14. 3 + 7
15. 4
16. 4 + 8
17. 4 + 6 + 8
18. 4 + 6 + 8 + 10
19. 5
20. 5 + 3 + 7
21. 5 + 3 + 7 + 9
22. 5 + 3 + 4 + 7 + 8
23. 5 + 3 + 4 + 6 + 7 + 8
24. 5 + 3 + 4 + 6 + 7 + 8 + 9 + 10
25. 6
26. 7
27. 7 + 8

28. 8
29. 9
30. 9 + 10
31. 10

318. Thirty-two

```
+------------------+-----+---------------+
|        1         |     |      3        |
+------------------+  2  +-----+---------+
|        4         |     |             |
+--------+---------+-----+     5         |
|        |         |     +-----+--------+
|   6    |    7    |  8  |  9  |   10    |
|        +---------+-----+-----+--------+
|        |   11    | 12  |
+--------+---------+-----+
```

1. 1
2. 1 + 4
3. 1 + 2 + 4
4. 1 + 2 + 4 + 6 + 7 + 8
5. 1 + 4 + 6 + 7
6. 1 + 2 + 3 + 4 + 5 + 6 + 7 + 8 + 9 + 10
7. 2
8. 2 + 8
9. 2 + 8 + 12
10. 2 + 3 + 5 + 8 + 9 + 10
11. 3
12. 3 + 5
13. 3 + 5 + 9 + 10
14. 4
15. 4 + 6 + 7
16. 5
17. 5 + 9 + 10
18. 6
19. 6 + 7
20. 6 + 7 + 8
21. 7

304

22. 7 + 8

23. 7 + 11

24. 7 + 8 + 11 + 12

25. 8

26. 8 + 12

27. 9

28. 9 + 10

29. 10

30. 11

31. 11 + 12

32. 12

319. Thirty-seven

1. 1

2. 2

3. 3

4. 3 + 4

5. 3 + 4 + 5 + 6

6. 4

7. 4 + 5 + 6

8. 4 + 8

9. 4 + 5 + 6 + 8+ 9 + 10

10. 5

11. 5 + 6

12. 5 + 6 + 9

13. 5 + 6 + 9 + 10

14. 6

15. 6 + 7

16. 6 + 9

17. 6 + 9 + 10

18. 6 + 7 + 9 + 10 + 11

19. 7

20. 7 + 11

21. 8

22. 8 + 9 + 10

23. 8 + 9 + 10 + 11

24. 8 + 9 + 10 + 11 + 12

25. 8 + 9 + 10 + 11 + 12 + 13

26. 9

27. 9 + 10

28. 9 + 10 + 11

29. 9 + 10 + 11 + 12

30. 9 + 10 + 11 +12 + 13

31. 10

32. 11

33. 11 + 12

34. 11 + 12 + 13

35. 12

36. 12 + 13

37. 13

320. Seventy-two

1	2		3	4
5	6	7	8	9
10	11	12	13	14
			15	16

1. 1
2. 1 + 2
3. 1 + 2 + 3
4. 1 + 2 + 3 + 4
5. 1 + 5
6. 1 + 5 + 10
7. 1 + 2 + 5 + 6 + 7
8. 1 + 2 + 5 + 6 + 7 + 10 + 11 + 12
9. 1 + 2 + 3 + 4 + 5 + 6 + 7 + 8 + 9
10. 1 + 2 + 3 + 4 + 5 + 6 + 7 + 8 + 9 + 10 + 11 + 12 + 13 + 14 + 15 + 16 *(the actual diagram itself)*
11. 2
12. 2 + 3
13. 2 + 3 + 4
14. 2 + 6 + 7
15. 2 + 3 + 4 + 6 + 7 + 8 + 9
16. 2 + 6 + 7 + 11 + 12
17. 2 + 3 + 4 + 6 + 7 + 8 + 9 + 11 + 12 + 13 + 14 + 15 + 16
18. 3
19. 3 + 4
20. 3 + 4 + 8 + 9
21. 3 + 4 + 8 + 9 + 13 + 14
22. 3 + 4 + 8 + 9 + 13 + 14 + 15 + 16
23. 4
24. 5
25. 5 + 6
26. 5 + 6 + 7
27. 5 + 6 + 7 + 8
28. 5 + 6 + 7 + 8 + 9
29. 5 + 10
30. 5 + 6 + 7 + 10 + 11 + 12
31. 5 + 6 + 7 + 8 + 10 + 11 + 12 + 13 + 15
32. 5 + 6 + 7 + 8 + 9 + 10 + 11 + 12 + 13 + 14 + 15 + 16
33. 6
34. 6 + 7
35. 6 + 7 + 8
36. 6 + 7 + 8 + 9
37. 6 + 7 + 11 + 12
38. 6 + 7 + 8 + 11 + 12 + 13 + 15
39. 6 + 7 + 8 + 9 + 11 + 12 + 13 + 14 + 15 + 16
40. 7
41. 7 + 8
42. 7 + 8 + 9
43. 8
44. 8 + 9
45. 8 + 13
46. 8 + 9 + 13 + 14
47. 8 + 13 + 15
48. 8 + 9 + 13 + 14 + 15 + 16
49. 9
50. 9 + 14
51. 9 + 14 + 16
52. 10
53. 10 + 11
54. 10 + 11 + 12
55. 10 + 11 + 12 + 13 + 15
56. 10 + 11 + 12 + 13 + 14 + 15 + 16
57. 11
58. 11 + 12
59. 11 + 12 + 13 + 15
60. 11 + 12 + 13 + 14 + 15 + 16
61. 12

62. 12 + 13 + 15

63. 12 + 13 + 14 + 15 + 16

64. 13

65. 13 + 15

66. 13 + 14

67. 13 + 14 + 15 + 16

68. 14

69. 14 + 16

70. 15

71. 15 + 16

72. 16

321. There are several ways to do this. Here's one of them.

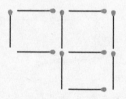

Here's another.

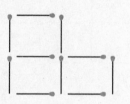

322. Remove the middle two upright sticks.

323. Note that the rectangle is on the left and stands up higher than the square, which is on the bottom right. There may be other ways to solve this puzzle.

324. There may be more than one way to do this. Here's one solution, achieved by removing the two mid-top upright sticks (as shown). Note that the two rectangles are on top and the square is on the bottom right.

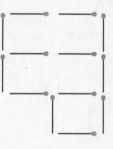

325. There may be more than one way to do this. Here's one:

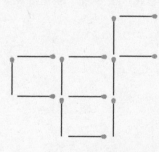

326. By removing the two upright matchsticks as shown, the result is two rectangles on top (staggered) and the square on the bottom of the diagram.

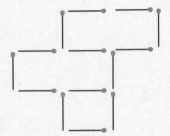

327. Note that the five squares form the outline of a cross.

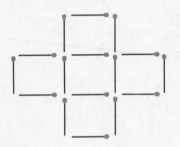

328. By removing the four upright sticks shown below you will get two rectangles on top and a square on the bottom of the diagram.

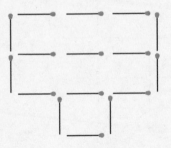

329. There may be more than one way to do this. Here's the solution I came up with.

330. Move 1 and 2 as shown. Note that 2 has to be reoriented into an upright position as well as moved.

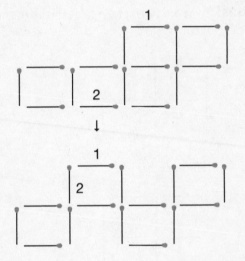

331. *Answer:* **c**. The reason is that **c** is a smooth figure; the others are straight-edged figures.

332. *Answer:* **b**. The internal line in **b** is the only one that is vertical (standing up); in the others it is horizontal.

333. *Answer:* **d**. As you can see, **d** is the only three-dimensional figure; the others are two-dimensional (flat).

334. *Answer:* **a**. As you can see, **a** is the only three-sided figure; the others are four-sided.

335. *Answer:* **a**. As you can see, **a** contains three dots inside the figure, which is an odd number; the other figures contain even numbers of dots (**b** = 2, **c** = 4, **d** = 6).

336. *Answer:* **d**. In **d** there are three lines inside the figure; in the others there are two.

337. *Answer:* **c**. As you can see, **c** is the only figure where the arrowhead is pointing vertically (up), not horizontally (to the left or to the right).

338. *Answer:* **b**. In all four figures, there is an internal line; only in **b** does the line go through the circumference of the circle; in the others the line just touches the circumference. Or, to put it another way, only in **b** does the internal line touch three arcs (going through one of them); in the others the internal touches two arcs.

339. *Answer:* **b**. Except for **b**, the dotted line is lying on the top surface (or face) of each three-dimensional figure. In **b**, it is below.

340. *Answer:* **c**. Except for **c**, the three internal lines intersect with each other; in **c** only two intersect.

341. Below is one way to do it. Other ways are variants of this with the lines at different slants. The equal triangles are shown with the same letters. Note the two larger ones are made up of **a** + **b**:

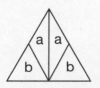

Here are the six triangles:

1. (left) a
2. (right) a
3. (left) b
4. (right) b
5. (left) a + b
6. (right) a + b

342. Note that the added line shown below produces three triangles, numbered **1**, **2**, **3**.

343. This can be done in several ways (that is with different slants of the line). But in all possible versions, the line (shown as dotted below) must go through the intersection point of the two given ones. Only in this way can the six slices be produced; otherwise seven will result.

344. This can be done in several ways (with different slants to the line). The underlying principle is that the new line must intersect both existing lines. Below is one solution.

345. By not making the new line intersect both lines as in the previous puzzle, you will get five slices as shown below. Again, there are other ways to get the same result.

346. The solution is shown below. There might be others as well.

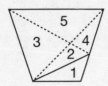

347. The solution is shown below. Again, there might be others as well.

The triangles are:
1. 1
2. 2
3. 2 + 4
4. 2 + 3
5. 3
6. 4
7. 4 + 5
8. 5

348. The solution is shown below. Others will have different slants to the lines.

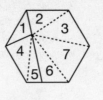

1. 1
2. 2
3. 3
4. 4
5. 5
6. 5 + 6
7. 6
8. 7

349. The solution is shown below.

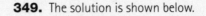

350. The solution is shown below. To help you identify the triangles, numbers are assigned to segments and below you will find a summary of the triangles.

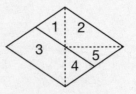

Summary of triangles
1. 1
2. 1 + 3
3. 2
4. 2 + 4 + 5
5. 4
6. 4 + 5
7. 5

351. *Answer:* Gillian (1st)—Fred (2nd)—Holly (3rd). Fred beat Holly. So, Holly is not the winner. It is either Fred or Gillian. He didn't beat Gillian, so she is the winner. They finished the race in this order: Gillian (1st), Fred (2nd), Holly (3rd).

352. *Answer:* Bettina (1st)—Mary (2nd)—Shamila (3rd)—Natasha (4th). We are told that Mary beat Shamila and that Shamila beat Natasha. The order of the three runners is, thus, Mary (1st of the three), Shamila (2nd), Natasha (3rd). Bettina beat Mary, so she came in front of Mary. Thus, the order of the four runners is Bettina (1st), Mary (2nd), Shamila (3rd), Natasha (4th). So, as you can see, Bettina finished first, Mary second, Shamila third, and Natasha fourth.

353. *Answer:* Anoush (1st)—Tom (2nd)—Lenny (3rd)—Joshua (4th). From now on you will be given only the answer without explanation, since the reasoning pattern is the same as in the previous puzzles, unless some tricky aspect requires commentary.

354. *Answer:* Chloe (1st)—Sally (2nd)—Dana (3rd)—Jasmine (4th).

355. *Answer:* Alexander (1st)—Sarah (2nd)—Danielle (3rd)—Ethan (4th)—Chris (5th).

356. *Answer:* Tyrell (1st)—Miriam (2nd)—Rick (3rd)—Jameel (4th)—Wes (5th).

357. *Answer:* Number 2 (1st)—Number 3 (2nd)—Number 4 (3rd)—Number 5 (4th)—Number 1 (5th). If 3 is not the overall winner, and since he could not place third, then he ended up second, followed by 4, who ended up third, and 5, who ended up fourth. This leaves the first and fifth slots open. Number 1 cannot end up first, so she ended up fifth, and thus 2 ended up the winner, by the process of elimination.

358. *Answer:* Number 2 (1st)—Number 1 (2nd)—Number 5 (3rd)—Number 3 (4th)—Number 4 (5th). Number 1 and Number 5 came in consecutively. Since Number 1 was not the winner, because he did not end up in the spot corresponding to his number, but he could have ended up 2nd, 3rd or 4th, followed right after by Number 5. Here are the three possibilities: (1) Number 1 (2nd)—Number 5 (3rd); (2) Number 1 (3rd)—Number 5 (4th); (3) Number 1 (4th)—Number 5 (5th). Since Number 5 did not end up fifth, we can discard possibility (3). Now, Number 3 came in right after 5. So, Numbers 1, 3 and 5 came in consecutively in one of two possible scenarios: (1) Number 1 (2nd)—Number 5 (3rd)—Number 3 (4th); (2) Number 1 (3rd)—Number 5 (4th)—Number 3 (5th). Number 4 did not win the race, nor did she end up second or fourth. This leaves only the fifth spot for Number 4. No other positioning would work for her, given the consecutive positioning of Numbers 1, 5 and 3. So, we discard scenario (2) since the fifth position in that one is occupied by someone else, not Number 4. This leaves Number 2 as the winner.

359. *Answer:* Everett (1st)—Corey (2nd)—Allan (3rd)—Betty (4th)—Dale (5th)—Frank (6th).

360. *Answer:* Jake (1st)—Buck (2nd)—Pam (3rd)—Sheila (4th)—Tyler (5th)—Lenny (6th).

361. *Answer:* Becky = 13, Frieda = 17, Tricia = 18. Clearly, if 13 is the lowest age and 18 the highest, then the only two ages that would work for Becky and Tricia are 13 and 18 respectively in this range, since we are told that Tricia is five years older than Becky and, of course, the difference between 13 and 18 is five. Now, Frieda is one year younger than Tricia, who is 18. So, Frieda is 17.

362. *Answer:* Brothers = 5 and 6; sisters = 10 and 11. The sum of the ages of the two brothers is 11 and they differ in age by one year. The only two ages that meet these requirements arithmetically are, therefore, 5 and 6 (5 + 6 = 11); no other number pairs differing by one and adding up to 11 exist. Since the overall sum of the ages is 32, this means that the sum of the ages of the two sisters is 32 – 11 = 21. Now, given that the sum of the ages of the two sisters is 21 and that they differ in age by one year, the only two ages that meet these requirements arithmetically are, therefore, 10 and 11 (10 + 11= 21). So, the two brothers are aged 5 and 6 and the two sisters 10 and 11.

363. *Answer:* 40, 20 and 10. A little trial and error will show that the oldest brother must be 40. Any other age will not work in accordance with the given arithmetical facts. The middle brother is half this age and is, thus, 20. The youngest brother is half this age and is, thus, 10 years old. If you subtract their ages you get, as told, 10 years: 40 – 20 – 10 = 10.

364. *Answer:* Sister = 12, brother = 21. The sister can be 11, 12, 13 or 14, since these are the only two-digit numbers that are possible, given the sister's age limit of 14. Any age below 11 does not produce digit reversals, of course. If the sister were 11, then the brother would also be 11. Adding these ages up produces 11 + 11 = 22, not 33, as told. If the sister were 14, then the brother would be 41. Adding these two up produces 55, not 33. If she were 13, then the brother would be 31. Adding these two up produces 44, not 33. So, the sister is 12 and the brother is 21. Adding these ages up produces 33.

365. *Answer:* 1, 2, 3, 9. Essentially, the puzzle reduces to the following question: What three numbers less than 10 are connected so that one is three times one of the three numbers and the other is three times the latter? The only three numbers that fit this pattern are 1, 3 and 9. As you can see, the second number is three times the first and the third is three times the second. So, the youngest brother is barely 1 year old. Another brother is three times as old, or 3 years old. A third brother is three times that age. So, he is 9. The fourth brother is twice the youngest, who is, as we now know, 1. So the fourth brother is 2 years old.

366. *Answer:* 14 and 41. Obviously, the ages are much less than 55, since this is what the two ages together add up to. Let's try a few reversals and see what they add up to, starting with the first lowest possible pairs, 11 and 11, 12 and 21, 13 and 31. Let's add these pairs up: 11 + 11 = 22; 12 + 21 = 33; 13 + 31 = 44. As you can see, we are getting close to the sum of 55. What's the next pair of digit reversals? It is 14 and 41. Let's add them up: 14 + 41 = 55. This means that the sisters are 14 and 41 years of age. There is another digit reversal that produces 55, namely 23 + 32 = 55, making the sisters 23 and 32 years of age. But we are told that neither sister is older than 20, so we need not worry about this possibility.

367. *Answer:* 5, 7, 11, 13. The prime numbers less than 36 are 2, 3, 5, 7, 11, 13, 17, 19, 23, 29, 31. The consecutive four that add up to 36 are 5, 7, 11, 13. Those are the ages of the brothers.

368. *Answer:* 8, 10, 12, 14. Let's do a little trial and error. Let's assume the first-born to be 12 years old, then the ages of the four would be 12, 14, 16, 18. Adding these up, we get 60, not 44. So, we conclude that the 12-year-old is not the youngest. Is she the oldest? If so, then the ages of the four would be 6, 8, 10, 12. These add up to 36, not 44. So, she is not the oldest. She might be the second- or third-oldest. Let's try second-oldest. The ages of the four would thus be 10, 12, 14, 16. Adding these up, we get 52, again not 44. Is she the third-oldest? This means that the ages of the sisters would be 8, 10, 12, 14. Adding these up, we get 44. So, the ages of the sisters are respectively 8, 10, 12, and 14 years of age. There is also a simpler math-based answer. Here it is: $44 \div 4 = 11$ (average age of sisters), $(12 + 10) \div 2 = 11$, $(8 + 14) \div 2 = 11$. Their ages are 8, 10, 12, 14.

369. *Answer:* Father = 50, mother = 48, son = 25, daughter = 24. Assume that the 24-year-old is the son. Thus, the father, who is twice as old, would be 48. The mother, being two years younger than the father, would be 46. The daughter, who is half the mother's age, would be 23. This is another way of saying that the mother is twice her daughter's age, and indeed 46 is twice 23. Let's add up the ages: 48 (father) + 46 (mother) + 24 (son) + 23 (daughter) =141. But we are told that the sum should be 147. So, we discard the original hypothesis, discovering by the process of elimination that the 24-year-old is the daughter (since we have just shown that it cannot be the son). So, the mother, who is twice that age, is 48. Now, the son could be 23 or 25 years of age, since there is a difference of one year between the two siblings. Let's assume that he is 23. His father, being twice as old, would be 46. But this means that the father would be younger than his wife, and we are told that she is the younger one. So, we discard 23 as the son's age. He is thus 25 and his father, being twice as old, is 50. The ages now add up to 147: 50 (father) + 48 (mother) + 25 (son) + 24 (daughter) = 147.

370. *Answer:* Roy = 10, Jake = 11, Gina = 13, Sophie = 26. The ages range from 10 (the youngest) to 26 (the oldest), adding up all told to 60. The third gamer is half 10 or 26; that is, the gamer is either 5 or 13. The third gamer cannot be 5 because we are told that 10 is the youngest. So, he or she is 13. So far we have discovered the ages of three gamers: 10, 13 and 26. The ages of all four should add up to 60. The ages of these three so far add up to 10 + 13 + 26 = 49. This means that the fourth gamer is 60 – 49 = 11. The age of this fourth gamer (11) is, as told, one year more than 10 in the set of ages. So far so good. Let's record the four ages in order from the youngest to the oldest: 10, 11, 13, 26. Now, let's match names to ages. Gina is not the youngest or the oldest. Nor is Jake. Thus, either Sophie or Roy is the youngest and the oldest in some order. We are told that Sophie is older than Roy, so she is the oldest and he the youngest. Sophie is thus 26 and Roy 10. Of the remaining two, we are told that Gina is older than Jake. So, she is the 13-year-old and he is the 11-year-old.

371. $(1 \div 1) + 1 = 2$; *or* $(1 \times 1) + 1 = 2$

Divide the first 1 by a second 1 and you get the value of 1; then add the third 1 to this and you get 2. Or multiply two 1's and you also get the value 1; adding a third 1 to this gives 2.

372. $(2 + 2 + 2) \div 2 = 3$; or $[(2 \times 2) + 2] \div 2 = 3$

Add three 2's and you get 6; divide 6 by the fourth 2 and you get 3. Or, multiply two of the 2's together and you get 4; add the third 2 to this, and you get 6; finally divide this by the fourth 2 and you get 3.

373. $(3 \times 3) - 3 = 6$

Multiply two threes together to get 9; subtract the third three from this result and you get 6.

374. $(4 + 4 + 4) \div 4 = 3$

Add three fours and you get 12; dividing this by the fourth 4, you get 3.

375. $(5 + 5 + 5) \div 5 = 3$

Add three fives to get 15; divide this by the fourth five to get 3.

376. $(6 + 6) - (6 \div 6) = 11$

Add two sixes to get 12; divide the other two sixes $(6 \div 6)$ to get 1; subtract the two results, 12 − 1, and you get 11.

377. $(7 + 7 + 7) - (7 + 7) = 7$

Add three sevens to get 21; add the two other sevens separately to get 14; subtract the two results, 21 − 14, and you get 7.

378. $(8 + 8 + 8 + 8 + 8) - (8 - 8) = 40$

Add five eights to get 40; subtract the two other eights separately $(8 - 8)$ to get 0; subtract the two results, 40 − 0, and you get 40.

379. $(3^3 \div 3) \div 3 = 3$

Three raised to the power of three (3^3) is equal to 27, using up two of the threes. Divide this by the third three and you get 9. Finally, divide this last result (9) by the fourth 3 and you get 3, as required.

   If exponent notation is not required then a possible solution is $(3 + 3 + 3) \div 3 = 3$—add three of the threes to get 9 and then divide this result by the fourth three to get 3.

380. $(2^2 + 2^2) \div 2^2 = 2$

Two raised to the power of two (2^2) is equal to four. Do this twice. Add up the result and you get $4 + 4 = 8$. In doing this you have used up

four twos in total. Raise two to the power of two again, to produce 4. This uses up the last of the twos. Now divide the previous result of 8 by the new one of 4 and you get 2.

   There are other ways to do this, but without exponents.

381. The seating arrangement is shown below. Note that in this arrangement Alex is diagonally across from Tina, whose seat is given to you, and that Bertha is seated to the immediate left of Alex. Fred is thus seated in the only remaining spot.

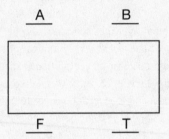

382. The seating arrangement is shown below. In the arrangement, Katharine is seated to the immediate left of Bianca, whose position is given to you. And in the diagram you can seen that Sara is seated to Katharine's immediate right. Since Vanessa did not sit on the same side as Katharine, then Cailin did. So, she sat where shown, leaving the final spot for Vanessa next to Sara (as shown).

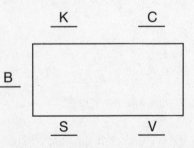

383. The seating arrangement is shown below. As you can see, Peter is seated to Sid's immediate right. His partner, Larry, thus faces him on the opposite side. The rest of the puzzle is easy, since you are given the positions of Sid and Tom. As you can see, Tom's partner, Andrew, faces him on the other side. Sid and Rick, being partners, sit opposite each other at the two heads.

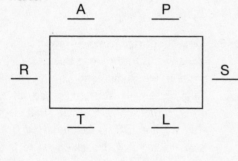

384.

 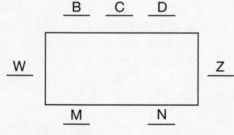

The seating arrangement is shown below. We are told that Beth sat to Caitlin's immediate right. So, the only possibility for her seat is shown on the diagram as being to Caitlin's right. Beth did not face Dina. So, she faced either Mark or Ned, since Wes and Zooey were at one of the two heads of the table. There are no others left. In order for Ned to sit to the immediate left of anyone, he must be at the opposite end of the table on the other side of Beth and Caitlin; otherwise he would be sitting to the right of someone. This leaves Mark as the one facing Beth. Ned thus fills the other spot on Mark's side and Dina fills the remaining spot on Caitlin's side. Now, since Ned sat to the left of Zooey, this implies that Zooey sat at the head of the table near Ned, leaving Wes to fill the other head table seat.

385. The seating arrangement is shown below. If Sarah did not sit next to Chris, then the only seat she could have occupied was the one opposite Chris, given that there are only four seats. Alex sat to Sarah's immediate left, so he sat where shown below, which is to the left of Sarah. This leaves Danielle to fill the seat facing Alex.

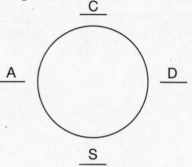

386. The seating arrangement is shown below. Sophia sat to the immediate right of the pianist. So, Sophia is clearly not the pianist. Since the pianist is neither Vanessa nor Bianca, it is Marcel. So, Sophia is seated as shown on the diagram. Bianca sat right across from the pianist, Marcel, leaving Vanessa as sitting across from Sophia (the only spot left for her).

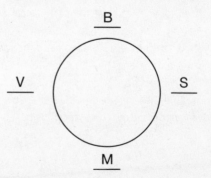

387. The seating arrangement is shown below. No one sat across from Matt, so he was the one who occupied the seat next to Alex (actually to Alex's right). William sat to Matt's immediate right, so he sat on the same side and right next to Matt as shown. Since Inez and Edward sat right next to each other on the same side of the table, they sat on the other side from Matt, since there is only one seat left on Matt's side to occupy, not two. Edward is thus on the other side facing Terry since we are told that Edward and Terry sat directly across from each other. So, Terry is the one occupying the third seat on Matt's side, as shown, leaving Inez to occupy the seat to the right of Edward. So, by the process of elimination, Rita sat opposite Alex.

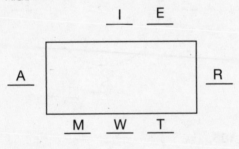

388. The seating arrangement is shown below. Louise and Yvonne sat across from Ariana. So they occupied the two corner seats on the other side in some order. Louise sat to Shirley's immediate right. So, given Shirley's position at head table, she sat at the corner near Shirley, leaving Yvonne to sit at the other corner as shown in the diagram. Dina sat directly across from Yvonne and, thus to Ariana's left, leaving Cynthia to sit on Ariana's other side, since we are told that she sat on Dina's side. This leaves Martha to occupy the seat opposite Ariana.

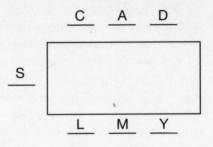

389. The seating arrangement is shown below. Since Mariana sat on the same side as Jack (whose position we know) and to the immediate right of someone else, then she sat at the other corner on Jack's side. That someone else, we are told, is Quentina. So Quentina is at the head of the table next to Mariana. Peter occupies the last seat next to Mariana on Jack's side. We are told that Vanessa sat to Frank's immediate right. So, Frank occupies the other head table seat near Vanessa. And we are told that Vanessa sat to Helen's immediate left, leaving Omar to occupy the final seat to Helen's immediate right.

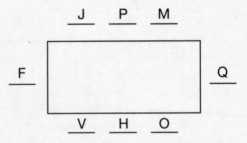

390. The seating arrangement is shown below. Since Asha sat to Rona's immediate left, she occupied the corner seat on the side shown in the diagram. Asha sat directly across from Trinity. So, we put T there (as shown). Asha, Kevin and Pat sat on the same side of the table, and Trinity, Misha and Lucy sat on the other side. Pat sat to the immediate right of Sabrina, meaning that he occupied the other corner seat on Asha's side and, thus, that Sabrina occupied the other head table seat. Kevin occupied the remaining seat on Asha's side. Pat sat directly across from Lucy. So Lucy sat facing Pat as shown on the diagram, leaving Misha to sit in the remaining seat facing Kevin.

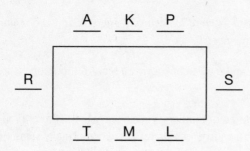

391. "Joy to the World"

392. It's raining cats and dogs

393. Beauty is in the eye of the beholder

394. No one knows what the future will bring

395. The best things in life are free

396. You should always hope for the best

397. *You Only Live Twice*

398. You always hurt the one you love

399. *Some Like It Hot*

400. A picture is worth a thousand words

CHAPTER 9

401. If the coin in the hand is not a nickel, then it is a dime. The nickel is obviously in the other hand.

402. The farmer has four children—three daughters and one son, who is, of course, a brother to all three.

403. If a man leaves a widow it means he is dead. So Frank was dead when his wife remarried.

404. Still 400 pounds. If you don't see this, just weigh yourself on a scale with one foot lifted up and see what happens.

405. A dozen is a dozen, so it takes 12 bills of any denomination to make a dozen of them.

406. One hour and twenty minutes is equivalent to 80 minutes. So there is nothing to explain. The puzzle says the same thing in two ways.

407. The last tomato was left in the box, after the other six were handed out. The box and the remaining tomato were then handed out to one other family member.

408. The son comes from a previous marriage by Frank, and may be unknown to Mary, although he is legally her stepson.

409. They are daughters of the same father but of two different mothers, since obviously the father produced one daughter from one marriage, and the other from another marriage. The two are legally stepsisters.

410. He deflated the tires, which lowered the height of the truck, then drove it through and filled the tires with air and continued on his way.

411. 6. The numbers opposite each other form this pattern: one is double the other: 2–4, 5–10, and thus 3–6.

412. ⇨

The arrowheads are alternating, pointing right, then left, in both a clockwise and counterclockwise direction.

413. AAAAAA6. The digit tells us how many *A*'s are in the expression. So, A1 means that there is one *A*; AA2 that there are two *A*'s and so on. This pattern goes in clockwise order. So, the next one after five *A*'s is six *A*'s, which translates in terms of the logic wheel as AAAAAA6. Another possibility might be A0, as a starting point: A0, A1, AA2, etc. But then this would mean that there would be no A (since A0 = "zero *A*'s") to show in the wheel and thus would not fit into the wheel.

414. Right. The words directly across from each other are opposites. So the opposite of left is right.

415. 32. Starting at 1 and moving in a clockwise direction, each subsequent number is twice the one before it.

416. F. The letters across from each other are consecutive letters in the alphabet: *A–B, C–D,* thus, *E–F.*

417. K. Starting with *A* and moving in a clockwise direction, every letter is the second one after the previous one in the alphabet: *A (B) C (D) E (F) G (H) I (J) K*

418. Mood. Two immediate words in a clockwise direction are reversals of each other; that is, they can be read as words from left-to-right and from right-to-left: *Live–Evil, Pest–Step,* and thus *Doom–Mood.*

419. There. The words opposite each other refer to opposite orientations, locations or directions: *Up–Down, Left–Right,* thus *Here–There.*

420. D. Starting at *ABCDEF* and moving clockwise, one letter is dropped in an alternate pattern as follows: *ABCDEF*–drop first letter in the sequence (*result: BCDEF*)–drop the last letter (*result: BCDE*)–drop the first letter (*result: CDE*)–drop the last letter (*result: CD*)–drop the first letter (*result: D*).

421. A = 5¢, B = 25¢, C = 25¢. Box A = 5¢, which is discovered when it is opened up. So, it is one of the two boxes labeled incorrectly. The other one is, clearly, Box C which is labeled as having 5¢, but which, as we have discovered, is not the case. So, by the process of elimination, Box C = 25¢. Box B = 25¢ is the box that contains the amount indicated by its label.

422. Box A = 15¢, Box B = 5¢, Box C = 10¢. If Box A = 15¢, then the other two boxes contain 5¢ and 10¢. Since they are labeled incorrectly, this means that Box C = 10¢ (not the 5¢ indicated by the label) and, by elimination, Box B = 5¢.

423. Box C = 7¢. The number on the label of Box C is a divisor of the number on Box A, of course. So, it is the one labeled incorrectly. The sum of coins in the other two boxes is 28¢ + 15¢ = 43¢. We know that there is 50¢ in total. So, the amount in Box C is in reality 7¢.

424. A = 10¢, B = 10¢, C = 30¢. C = 30¢ is labeled correctly. This leaves 50¢ - 30¢ = 20¢ to be distributed in A and B. We are told that they hold equal amounts of money, so they both contain 10¢.

425. A = 0¢, B = 50¢, C = 40¢. Since the amounts in the boxes are 0¢, 40¢ and 50¢, it is obvious that the amount in C is 40¢. Why? Because the only possible sum of two numbers that produces 40¢ in this case is 40¢ + 0¢. It does not contain 0¢, because that is what its erroneous label says. So by elimination it contains the 40¢. Now, since A is labeled incorrectly, it does not contain the 50¢. That leaves 0¢ as the only possibility for A. Thus the remaining 50¢ is in B.

426. A = 5¢, B = 20¢, C = 15¢. The only given numbers that can be subtracted to produce a difference of 5¢ are 20¢ - 15¢. Thus these are the amounts in boxes B and C. Since these boxes are labeled incorrectly, this means that B contains the 20¢ and C the 15¢, given that B contains more than C. By elimination A contains the 5¢.

427. A = 5¢, B = 20¢, C = 15¢. Since the total amount in the three boxes is 40¢, then the missing amount is 20¢, given that 20¢ + 15¢ + 5¢ = 40¢. The 20¢ is not in A, since we are told that the actual amount it contains is the one shown on the label of either B of C—that is, either 15¢ or 5¢. So, the 20¢ is either in B or C. Now, we are told that B does not contain the lowest amount, namely 5¢. It does not contain the 15¢ either, because that is what its erroneous label shows. So, it contains the 20¢. C does not contain the 5¢ shown by its label, so it contains 15¢. And A is thus the one with 5¢ in it.

428. A = 25¢, B = 25¢, C = 0¢. Box C is empty, so it contains 0¢. C's label of 25¢ thus applies to the contents of one of the other two, A or B. This means that 25¢ is actually in both these boxes, otherwise the total would not be 50¢. Thus, both A and B have 25¢ in them.

429. Box A = 3¢, Box B = 9¢ and Box C = 27¢. The only three numbers that fit the statement are 3, 9, 27: 9 is three times 3, and 27 is three times 9. If you add the three up you get 39. So, Box A = 3¢, Box B = 9¢ and Box C = 27¢, since the amounts are distributed in alphabetical order, that is, *A—B—C*.

430. A = 5¢, B = 25¢, C = 5¢. If the amount of money in B were 5¢ more, then it would contain 35¢, and leave nothing for the other two boxes, since the total amount in the three boxes would add up to 35¢ (0¢ + 35¢ + 0¢ = 35¢). So, it contains 25¢, 5¢ less than shown. This means that A and B together contain 10¢, since 25¢ + 10¢ = 35¢. We are told that they contain the same amount, so each box contains 5¢.

431. 6F. Each pair consists of a digit and alphabet character in order. Thus, the first pair shows the first digit and the first alphabet letter (1A), the second shows the second digit and the second alphabet letter (2B), and so on.

432. KK. Each letter is the second one after the previous one in the normal alphabet sequence; moreover, each letter is doubled. AA (BB) CC (DD) EE (FF) GG (HH) II (JJ) KK.

433. MAD. Each pair of words are reversals of each other (that is, they are legitimate words if read either left-to-right or right-to-left).

434. X24. The number indicates what position in the alphabet sequence the letter holds. A is the first letter (= A1), D is the fourth letter (= D4), and so on.

435. 9. The third digit in each triplet is the sum of the previous two.

436. 1. The third digit in each triplet is the difference that results from subtracting the previous two.

437. 27. The last two digits in each quadruplet is the product that results from multiplying the first two.

438. 2. The number indicates how many vowels are in the word.

439. 6. The number indicates how many letters are in the word.

440. 28. The digit results from adding the numerical positions of the alphabet characters together: A = 1 and B = 2, so 1 + 2 = 3, hence AB3; C = 3 and F = 6, so 3 + 6 = 9, hence CF9; and so forth. So, B = 2 and Z = 26, hence BZ28.

441. *LOVE.* TRUE LOVE—LOVE AFFAIR

442. *WORLD.* NEW WORLD—WORLD WAR

443. *OFF.* LIFT OFF—OFF BASE

444. *CARD.* WILD CARD—CARD SHARK

445. *CARPET.* RED CARPET—CARPET BEETLE

446. *MOON.* BLUE MOON—MOON PHASE

447. *PADDLE.* DOG PADDLE—PADDLE BOAT

448. *SPOT.* SUN SPOT—SPOT CHECK

449. *ESTATE.* REAL ESTATE—ESTATE TAX

450. *RUN.* TRIAL RUN—RUN AROUND

CHAPTER 10

451. *Answer:* (b). All the words end with two *L*'s.

452. *Answer:* (b). The words describe periods of the day in sequence. So after *evening* comes *night*.

453. *Answer:* (a). The four sports mentioned are played with a ball, as is basketball, Hockey is played with a puck.

454. *Answer:* (a). The letters in the number words increase by one: *one* (= three letters), *four* (= four letters), *seven* (= five letters), *eleven* (= six letters), *fifteen* (= seven letters).

455. *Answer:* (b). The four vehicles mentioned all have four wheels, as does a skateboard. A bicycle has only two.

456. *Answer:* (a). The four words have one vowel each in the usual sequence—*a, e, i, o, (u).* The vowel, *u,* in the word *sun* completes the sequence.

457. *Answer:* (a). The first four words start with letters that are in alphabetical order—*a, b, c, d.* Thus, the next word must start with *e.*

458. *Answer:* (b). The four words refer to things found in nature. A pebble is also a naturally occurring thing.

459. *Answer:* (a). The four words have the two vowels *ea,* as does *retreat.*

460. *Answer:* (a). The four words begin with two consonants, as does *try.*

461. *Answer:* (a). The numbers in the sequence increase by three.

462. *Answer:* (b). The numbers in the sequence decrease by four.

463. *Answer:* (b). The numbers increase by 1, 2, 3, 4, 5 and so on. Thus, 3 (= 2 + 1), 5 (= 3 + 2), 8 (= 5 + 3) and so forth.

464. *Answer:* (b). The numbers in the sequence are, actually, the numbers in their usual order, only paired off: 12, 34, 56, 78, 910, 1112 = 1, 2, 3, 4, 5, 6, 7, 8, 9, 10, 11, 12. Thus, the next number pair is 13, 14 or, following the same "pair style" of the puzzle, 1314.

465. *Answer:* (a). The pattern is hidden in consecutive triplets of the sequence. The first two numbers in the triplet are added together to produce the third: for example 1, 1, 2 (= first triplet), 1 + 1 = 2; 3, 5, 8 (= second triplet) and 3 + 5 = 8. So, the last triplet (6, 3, ___) is completed by 9, since 6 + 3 = 9.

466. *Answer:* (b). Did you notice that this puzzle is the exact opposite of the previous one, arithmetically speaking? The first two numbers in the triplet are subtracted (instead of added) to produce the third: 2, 1, 1 (= first triplet); 2 – 1 = 1; 8, 5, 3 (= second triplet): 8 – 5 = 3; and so on. So, the last triplet (9, 3, __) is completed by 6, since 9 – 3 = 6.

467. *Answer:* (b). This is another triplet puzzle. The first two numbers in the triplet are multiplied together to produce the third: 1, 2, 2 (= first triplet); 1 × 2 = 2; 3, 2, 6 (= second triplet); 3 × 2 = 6; and so on. So, the last triplet (5, 5, __) is completed by 25, since 5 × 5 = 25.

468. *Answer:* (b). Here's yet one more triplet puzzle. You must have caught on by now! The second number in the triplet is divided into the first to produce the third: 8, 4, 2 (= first triplet), 8 ÷ 4 = 2; 12, 6, 2 (= second triplet) and 12 ÷ 6 = 2. So, the last triplet (32, 8, ___) is completed by 4, since 32 ÷ 8 = 4.

469. *Answer:* (a). The triplets are made up of three consecutive numbers and each triplet starts with a number in order. So, the first triplet starts with 1 (= 123), the second with 2 (= 234), the third with 3 (= 345) and so on.

470. *Answer:* (a). The first two identical digits are multiplied together and the result is shown by the next digit or digits: 224 = 2 × 2 = 4; 339 = 3 × 3 = 9; 4416 = 4 × 4 = 16; 5525 = 5 × 5 = 25; and so on.

471. *Answer:* (a). The two lines, vertical (|) and horizontal (—), are simply alternating in the sequence: vertical (|), horizontal (—), vertical (|), horizontal (—), etc.

472. *Answer:* (a). The direction of the arrowheads is rotating in a clockwise fashion: leftward (←), upward (↑), rightward (→), downward (↓), etc.

473. *Answer:* (b). This time the direction of the arrowheads is rotating in a counterclockwise fashion: leftward (←), downward (↓), rightward (→), upward (↑), etc.

474. *Answer:* (a). The number of sides of consecutive figures increases by one: the first one has two; the second one has three; and so on.

475. *Answer:* (b). The figures make up consecutive pairs showing opposite orientations of identical form.

476. *Answer:* (b). The first four dark figures are paired off with the next four corresponding white figures: dark circle + white circle; dark square + white square; dark triangle with white triangle. So the dark diamond is paired with the white diamond.

477. *Answer:* (a). Consecutive pairs face in opposite directions. So, since the last figure faces up it will thus be followed by an identical figure facing down.

478. *Answer:* (b). The number tells you how many symbols there are in the term. So, 1@ = one @; 2## = two ##'s; and so forth. The number of symbols, as you can see, increases in numerical order. So, the next number of symbols in the sequence is six.

479. Answer: (b). The letters are the first letters of the numbers written out in order: One, Two, Three, Four, Five. The next number is, of course, Six (= S).

480. *Answer:* (a). Each letter is the first letter in the word describing the figure that follows it in the sequence: *T* = triangle, *S* = square, *D* = diamond. So, *C* = circle.

481. *Answer:* Hexagon. Each word describes a figure that increases in number of sides by one in a sequential way: angle = two-sided figure; triangle = three-sided figure; and so on. A hexagon is a six-sided figure.

482. *Answer:* Snap. Each word in the sequence is followed by its reversal: stop—pots, spin—nips, pans—snap.

483. *Answer:* 76. This time, each number in the sequence is followed by its reversal: 23—32; 45—54; 67—76.

484. *Answer:* 54. Did you miss this simple one? Each number is a factor of 9 in order: 9 (= 1 × 9), 18 (= 2 × 9), 27 (= 3 × 9) and so on.

485. *Answer:* ⇑ Did you miss this simple one too? The arrowheads are rotating in a clockwise direction.

486. ∩ Each figure points (or is oriented) in the opposite direction of the one preceding it.

487. There. The words in the sequence form consecutive pairs of opposites: clean—dirty, near—far, here—there.

488. S. The letters are the first letters of the words for the days of the week in order (starting on Monday): Monday (M), Tuesday (T), Wednesday (W), Thursday (T), Friday (F), Saturday (S) and, of course, Sunday (S).

489. EV. The letter pairs consist of the first letter of the alphabet paired with the last one (= AZ), the second letter of the alphabet paired with the second last one (= BY), the third letter of the alphabet paired with the third last one (CX), the fourth letter of the alphabet paired with the fourth last one (DW), and thus the fifth letter of the alphabet paired with the fifth last one (EV).

490. G. Subtract the two digits and you get a number indicating the position of the given alphabet letter in order: (1) 43=A = 4 – 3 = 1 = first letter of the alphabet, A; (2) 51=D = 5 – 1 = 4 = fourth letter of the alphabet, D; (3) 63=C = 6 – 3 = 3 = third letter of the alphabet, C; (4) 71=F = 7 – 1 = 6 = sixth letter of the alphabet, F; so (5) 9 – 2 = 7 = seventh letter of the alphabet, G (G=92).

491. Down. The proportion consists of opposites.

492. Four. The proportion indicates the number of sides in each figure: a triangle has three sides and a rectangle four.

493. Hand. A hat is put on the head and a glove on a hand.

494. Hands and Knees. Walking involves legwork, while crawling is done on one's hands and knees of course.

495. Drink or Sip. Meat has to be chewed, while water has to be drunk or sipped.

496. Odd. Eight is an even number and nine an odd number.

497. Tree or Plant. A page is part of a book and a leaf is part of a tree or some other plant.

498. Liquid. Daisy is a type of flower and water a type of liquid.

499. Now or Present. Ate describes an action that happened in the past or before the present time, while eating describes a present action or one that is happening now or in the present.

500. Body. This needs no explanation.